Arab Voices

Comparative Studies on Muslim Societies
General Editor, Barbara D. Metcalf

Arab Voices

The human rights debate in the Middle East

Kevin Dwyer

University of California Press
Berkeley   Los Angeles   London

Published in 1991
by the University of California Press
Berkeley   Los Angeles   London

First published 1991
by Routledge
11 New Fetter Lane, London EC4P 4EE

© 1991 Kevin Dwyer

Typeset from author's disks by
NWL Editorial Services, Langport, Somerset, England

Printed in the United States

Library of Congress Cataloging-in-Publication Data
has been applied for

LC 91–050123
ISBN 0–520–07490–3 cloth
      0–520–07491–2 paper

2   3   4   5   6   7   8   9   10

Contents

Acknowledgements

Many individuals generously gave me their time and I would like to thank them here. The list below would be even longer but some people expressed a wish not to be named. For those whose words found their way into this book, I hope they find their thoughts reasonably faithfully set down.

In Tunisia: Rachid Bellaluna, Abdelmajid Bettaieb, Khemais Chamari, Muhammad Charfi, Khadija Cherif, Frej Fennich, ᶜazza Ghanmi, Rachid Ghannouchi, Hayat Griba, Jalila Hafsiya, Nadia Hakimi, Bouchera al-Hajj Hmida, Salah ed-Din Jorshi, Sahnoun Jouhri, Hediya Jrad, Hedi Khelil, Abdelaziz Krichen, Ziyad Krichen, Tahar Labib, 'Amal ben ᶜaba, Hmida Naifer, Gilbert Nakkache, Emna bel-Hajj Yahya, Khalil Zamiti, Abdelqadr Zghal.

In Morocco: Jacques Alessandra, Muhammad Guessous, Abderrahim Jamai, Jocelyne Laabi, Abdellatif Laabi, Ahmed Khamlishi, Fatima Mernissi, Muhammad Mekki Naciri, Fathallah Oualalou, Ali Oumlil, Muhammad al-Qebab, Moulay Rachid, Jamil Salmi, Jamal Zyadi.

In Egypt: Muhammad ᶜamara, Muhammad Sid Ahmed, ᶜadel Amin, Galal Amin, Elizabeth Taylor Awni, Judy Barsalou, Nadia Ramses Farah, Nur Farhat, Cherif Hetata, Enid Hill, Barbara Ibrahim, Saad ed-Din Ibrahim, Nabil al-Hilali, Fahmi Howaidy, ᶜadel Hussein, Walid Kazziha, Hind Khattab, Ann Lesch, Hoda Lutfi, Kamal Abu al-Magd, Hassan Nafaᶜa, Mona Makram Obeid, Alain Roussillon, Nawal Saadawi, Muhammad Sayed Saᶜid, Hania Sholkami, Mona Abu Sinna, Mourad Wahba, Sayed Yassin, Latifa Zayyat.

In London: Ramsey Jamil, Phi-van Lam, Kathy Leclerc, Hanny Megally, Ewa Turlo.

My special thanks go to the Ford Foundation for its financial support to enable me to carry out this work, and to the European Human Rights foundation for additional financial aid.

Note on transcription

In transcribing Arabic into the Latin alphabet I have kept in mind the general reader rather than the specialist.

Accordingly:

- Most common Arabic names are written here in their usual Anglicized manner, for example Muhammad, Oman, Hussein; where individuals are widely known by names taking another form I have adopted that form.
- The Arabic definite article, used in many names, is transcribed here as al- (some transcriptions elsewhere use el-). In certain cases, the article's l changes, doubling its following consonant, but I have consistently retained the article's l for simplicity's sake (except in some well-known names where I have sometimes also been obliged to use el-, for example Saad el-Din).
- The following transcriptions have been used for various Arabic letters:

    c for ع , the Arabic ᶜain, pronounced as a strong, voiced, guttural consonant;
    gh for غ , the ghain, pronounced as the guttural French 'r' in 'gris';
    ' for ء , the hamza, an unvoiced glottal stop;
    h for ح , the ha', a strong breathy English 'h';
    [kh] for خ , the [kh]', as the 'ch' in Scottish 'loch';
    sh for ش , the shin, as the 'sh' in the English 'shut';
    dh for ذ , the dhal, as the 'th' in the English 'the';
    [dh] for ظ , the [dh]ad, as an emphatic 'th' in the English 'the';
    q for ق , the qaf, as a strong guttural English 'k'.

I have not distinguished between other non-emphatic and emphatic consonants or between long and short vowels.

Preface

VALUES

In a world where human communities in their great variety believe many different things and where people, when they do not actually try to dominate one another, still often show little tolerance for ways of behaving other than their own, there are many people who struggle against this and who seek a solid bedrock of values upon which to build a vision of a common humanity, a set of values around which all people, whatever their origins and beliefs, might come together and work in concert.

'Human rights', '*les droits de l'homme*', '*ḥuquq al-insan*' – the very existence of these and comparable terms in many world languages may point to where such a bedrock might lie, and may indicate that the vision is already being put together. However, while it is arguable that in the contemporary world these terms have an undeniable power to connote something good and desirable, it is also undeniable that beneath the superficial similarity of the terms there is much disagreement over their meaning and often a suspicion and mistrust of them.

To those who argue that attaining full human rights is a universal human aspiration, others may respond that the notion of human rights is simply a product of one particular civilization's history. To those who say it is above politics, others answer that it bears the implicit (or even explicit) imprint of one political ideology. Is human rights a clearly defined and well-understood concept (perhaps as enshrined in international agreements), or is it subject to many varied and sometimes contradictory interpretations? Is it an authentic reflection of moral conscience, or a tool manipulated by opportunistic local, national, and international political forces? Is it a need deeply felt by masses of people, or the plaything of an intellectual elite? Is it a sign of human progress towards a life of greater dignity and quality, or does it betray a parochial view that disregards life's deeper needs (such as environmental protection, peace, disarmament, assured food supplies)?

Nowhere do these and related questions arise more sharply than in the Middle East, and nowhere are they discussed with greater urgency. Many factors contribute to this. Human rights are frequently and sometimes systematically violated by assertive state authorities that, emerging from colonial tutelage, attempt to dominate remarkably diverse ethnic, linguistic, religious, ideological, and economic constituencies, and try to weld them into unified nations of obedient citizens. Predictably, representatives of state power will often argue that at critical moments in the nation's history (and such moments appear in their rhetoric only too frequently) human rights may be of only secondary importance.

But many Middle Easterners have ideas about human rights that are more nuanced and less self-serving than that, ideas that must be understood in the context of the sustained contact between the Middle East and the West going back at least to the time of Muslim penetration into Spain and Europe in the eighth century, through the Crusades of the eleventh century and beyond, and into the more recent colonial and post-colonial periods. This contact has forged complex, many-tiered, starkly ambivalent, and often actively hostile attitudes in many Middle Easterners towards Western traditions, Western forces, and Westerners themselves. The idea of 'human rights', closely associated with the West over the last few decades, is prey to this same complexity. And so it happens that even as human rights are flagrantly violated, the notion of 'human rights' may itself be contested in good faith.

The debate over human rights is made more resonant by the fact that Middle Easterners, living in widely varied geographical and cultural settings spanning the area from Morocco in the west to the Gulf states in the east, have at their disposal an Arabic language that in its many forms – classical, modern standard, local and national dialects – makes communication possible (although not perfect) over this vast area; and they have access, as well, to a broad, common cultural frame of reference reaching back at least to the birth and spread of Islam over the last fourteen centuries, that provides a shared repertoire of deeply affecting words, ideas, and symbols to inform and structure people's perceptions and to motivate them to action.

That there is now a sentiment widely shared throughout the region that the nations of the Middle East face a severe crisis at once economic, social, cultural, and political, only makes the discussion of human rights more acute, since many Middle Easterners believe that hard thinking about basic social options is now imperative and that the very nature of their societies hangs in the balance. These people naturally have serious disagreements about how to proceed and upon what basis to act.

These disagreements and differences of values animate the many voices that will be speaking out in the pages that follow. Although these voices will not provide definitive answers to the fundamental questions they are raising (there surely are no such answers), they do convey something of the complexity inherent in the notion of human rights, and demonstrate the need to set this notion in the context of the local, national, and regional history and culture.

CONFRONTATION

A few years ago, I went to the distant outskirts of Cairo to interview a well-known and widely respected Muslim religious scholar. He greeted me politely, motioned for me to sit down on a long couch opposite him, asked whether I would prefer tea or coffee, and, fixing me with a hard but not unsympathetic look, posed what seemed at first to be a fairly perfunctory question.

What is it, exactly, that you want to know?

I had barely finished the equally perfunctory and deliberately open-ended answer that I often gave when opening conversations – I was interested in discussing what he thought were the most significant problems his society was facing – when he confronted me with what would turn out to be a long series of questions.

On whose behalf are you doing this research?
Where does the money for this research come from?
Tell me more about the organization that is giving you money: where is it based and why would it support your research?
What is your political position behind this research?
When you're not carrying out this research, whom do you work for?
For whom did you work before this?
Why did you leave that work?
Tell me more about why you were dissatisfied with your previous work?
That answer is too general: could you give me a specific example?
You said that before you moved to England you taught in American universities. In which universities did you teach?
You have published a book on Morocco? What is it about? Who is its publisher? Where is the publisher based?

It was only after I had answered his final question that he then returned to the first, 'What is it, exactly, that you want to know?' in a manner that showed he was willing to talk to me.

The religious scholar hadn't posed his questions in a hostile manner, but neither was he trying to ingratiate himself with me. Through his questions he (and others who were to ask me similar questions throughout my research) was trying to situate me and prepare himself for the discussion that might follow. To some extent this was only natural – we all need to do this, in one way or another, when we meet people for the first time. But the thoroughness and precision of his questions showed that he wanted to define me more sharply, for I was not simply a researcher but an outsider, a Westerner. Even more problematic, I was a citizen of the United States, a nation whose actions constituted, to most Middle Easterners I met, a direct challenge to some of their most deeply held political and ethical beliefs.

To many Westerners, of course, throughout much of the 1980s the Middle East was continually in the headlines of newspapers and the leading feature on nightly television news programs, with highly charged and often pejorative epithets like 'terrorist', 'barbaric', 'fundamentalist', 'xenophobic', 'anti-Western' being applied to the people and political movements of the region. People living in the West were sometimes directly affected: a death sentence was pronounced on the novelist Salman Rushdie by Ayatollah Khomeini and forced the writer into hiding; a London-based journalist was imprisoned in Iraq and executed by the Iraqi authorities. Also, a number of Western journalists and other Europeans were seized as hostages in the Middle East. These events raised the fears of many Westerners that they and their way of life were under attack.

However, Middle Easterners had their own grounds for fear as their headlines and television news programs often told stories of Western – and most particularly US – attacks on Middle Easterners and interventions in Middle Eastern affairs.

Some of the problems arose in Europe. In France, people of North African origin living in France were frequently attacked and sometimes killed, either by police actions (grotesquely labeled as 'unfortunate mistakes' by police officials) or in racist attacks; places of Islamic worship were damaged and desecrated. And in both France and Great Britain Muslim girls found it difficult, or impossible, to attend school in what they saw as 'Islamic' dress.

But the most serious problems occurred in the Middle East itself. The civil war in Lebanon – the US had given tacit approval, at the very least, to the Israeli invasion of Lebanon in June 1982 and to the periodic bombings and continued occupation by Israel of parts of that country from 1982 on. The revolution in Iran and the war between Iran and Iraq that followed – the US had strongly supported the Shah's repressive regime up until the very end, appeared implacably hostile to the new Iranian government, and openly sided with Iraq although it was clearly the aggressor in the war with Iran. In July 1988 the US mistakenly shot down an Iranian Airbus, killing 290 civilians.

Also, hadn't the US provided some intelligence and perhaps even logistic support for Israel's bombing of an Iraqi nuclear power installation in 1981? And hadn't the US done the same to assist Israel's bombing of the PLO headquarters in Tunisia in October 1985? And hadn't the US failed its subsequent promises to protect Tunisia by allowing Israeli agents to assassinate Abu Jihad, the second-highest PLO official, on Tunisian soil in 1988? And hadn't the US transgressed even more dramatically by sending its own planes from bases in Great Britain to bomb Libya in April 1986, threatening to do so again as 1988 ended, and shooting down two Libyan jets in January 1989.

If this wasn't enough, Middle Easterners had every reason to see all these US actions against the background or even as a logical extension of continuing US support for Israel and its policy of denying national rights to Palestinians. This support has crippled the credibility of US policy throughout the Middle East, for Palestinian rights is one fundamental issue on which Middle Eastern opinion is, to all intents and purposes, unanimous.

Given these highly charged events and their contentious historical context, and the misunderstandings and intolerance that seemed their inevitable consequences, I found it much less surprising to be asked the kinds of questions the religious scholar posed, than to find that most of the people I met (but not all) were willing to spare me some of their time and were willing to take most (but not all) of my answers to their questions at face value.

ANSWERS AND QUESTIONS

What, in fact, were my purposes in the work I was carrying out in the Middle East? How did I situate myself with respect to the societies I was born and grew up in, and those that I was studying? What, exactly, was it that I wanted to learn, and why should anyone be willing to help me?

I have spent much of the past twenty years working on and studying the Middle East, first as an anthropologist, later as a human rights researcher. Anthropologists try to understand how other people behave and why they behave as they do by going to live among them for extended periods, learning their language, and entering into their daily lives. Beginning in the late 1960s, I had spent several years living in and studying Moroccan villages, made occasional visits to Algeria, Tunisia, and Egypt, and taught anthropology courses on the Middle East in American universities. In 1978, I went to London to work for the human rights organization

Amnesty International, directing their Middle East research department for the next six years. There, I was concerned with day-to-day violations of human rights throughout the area from Morocco through Iran.

Whatever other problems arose in the course of my work as an anthropologist and as a human rights researcher, one set was common to both: how can we understand and act sensibly in a world where people hold different beliefs, behave differently, often cling to these differences tenaciously, and sometimes even challenge the right of other people to follow their own way? By what right does any individual or group intrude upon others, or attempt to persuade, convince, or even impose beliefs?

These questions arise in a somewhat softened form in anthropology, for conventional anthropologists believe they are simply 'observing' or 'interpreting' the world; but the questions become sharper in the work of Amnesty International, which actively seeks to change the world we live in.

Amnesty International, founded in 1961 and based in London, has more than 700,000 members, subscribers and supporters in over 150 countries and territories, and it is fully funded by its members and supporters from the general public. The organization's purpose is to investigate and document specific human rights violations, and to improve the human rights situation worldwide by discussions with government authorities, moral persuasion, publicity, and mobilizing international opinion. It bases its activity on the United Nations Universal Declaration of Human Rights and other international instruments but limits its own activity to certain rights related to prisoners: no one should be imprisoned for their beliefs, color, sex, ethnic origin, language or religion, provided they have not used or advocated violence; all political prisoners should have fair and prompt trials; no prisoner should be executed or subject to torture or other cruel, inhuman, or degrading treatment or punishment.

Amnesty International not infrequently faces the criticism that, founded and based in the West and with a large portion of its membership in the West, it pursues a 'mission' that is neo-colonialist and a subtle form of cultural imperialism, seeking to impose Western values on societies whose values may be very different.

With special regard to the Middle East, Amnesty International's critics charge that the organization's mandate is inspired mainly by the West's Christian tradition, that it does not do justice to the precepts of Islamic civilization, and derives from views of state institutions, civil society, and the individual, that are rooted in the Western experience. More broadly, critics claim that the organization as a whole shows little understanding and takes little account of the kinds of political, social, economic, and cultural problems that face the Third World in general and the Arab world in particular.

In specific instances it may well be that Amnesty International's approach can be improved and made more effective in particular local, national and regional contexts. But whatever merits these criticisms may have for specific situations in the Middle East they certainly raise other related and very significant questions that could be posed for any region of the world: are notions of human rights different in different localities? Can there be a universally applicable notion of human rights? Is there any evidence that a human rights consensus is gaining ground? Does an emphasis on 'universal' human rights ignore the variety of human beliefs and hide what may be substantially different notions of human rights held by different peoples? Might not a universalist approach weaken rather than strengthen forces seeking to improve the human rights situation in various parts of the world?

During my years at Amnesty International, I mulled over these questions more or less continuously, wondering how I might go about raising and exploring them with regard to the Middle East. When I left Amnesty International in 1984 I obtained financial support for research into these issues from the Ford Foundation's office in Cairo and from the then newly established European Human Rights Foundation. I carried out the research and writing over the rest of the decade.

RESEARCH

If my main aim was to understand Middle Eastern notions of human rights, in what countries would I do this, what kinds of information would I seek, whom would I talk to, and what kinds of questions would I ask?

First of all, I needed countries where the discussion of human rights was relatively open and where many currents of opinion would be represented. I also needed countries where I, an American living in London, would be reasonably free to travel and do the research. These considerations narrowed my choices to Morocco, Tunisia, Egypt, Jordan, and Kuwait.[1]

But I knew I would not be able to cover five countries adequately (in fact, aware of the complexity of the individual countries, I had very strong doubts that one researcher could cover even one of these countries thoroughly). Yet, I wanted to include at least three so that the research might have broad relevance and enable me to explore the similarities and differences between various national situations.

Egypt, by any criterion, would certainly have to be included. Morocco also demanded inclusion: it ranked (with Algeria) as the second most populous Arab country (after Egypt), was becoming an important Arab cultural and intellectual center, had its own fledgling human rights movement, and was also the country of the region I knew best. I chose Tunisia largely because it had, in the Tunisian Human Rights League, the best developed and most articulate human rights organization in the entire Middle East.

A critic might argue that, with each of these three countries having relatively strong ties to the West, this selection was not fully representative of the Middle East.[2] True as this is, this criticism did not seem to me to be a telling one, at least as far as my aims were concerned.

In the first place, with each Middle Eastern country having unique characteristics, any choice of countries is bound to reflect these singularities and in this way be unrepresentative of the region as a whole. At the same time, since any real understanding of the human rights discussion requires setting it in its local cultural context, I was sure that the risk of an unrepresentative selection was more than balanced by the potential gain in specificity and concreteness.

In addition, one is able to encounter in each country most and perhaps all of the major currents of opinion expressed in other countries, because ideas circulate easily throughout the region: books are widely diffused, literacy has been expanding, and writers, journalists, academics, and other intellectuals travel frequently, as do the vast number of migrant workers. Although of course the various viewpoints do not have the same social power and numbers of supporters in each country, they are voiced everywhere by their proponents with equal fervor. At least in Morocco, Tunisia, and Egypt these viewpoints could be somewhat more freely expressed than elsewhere and there was every likelihood, as well, that this (relative) freedom of expression would lead to a dialectic of ideas and a richness of discussion that would not be in evidence elsewhere. Richness in this domain would be consonant with the fact that Egypt, Morocco, and Tunisia today constitute the most significant cultural and intellectual centers in the Arab world.

What kinds of information was I most interested in, and who would be most able and likely to provide it? No one working on the Middle East over the last ten to fifteen years could fail to notice that the notion 'human rights' already has substantial mobilizing force throughout the region and that the Arabic term that translates 'human rights' *(huquq al-insan)* has wide currency. Even where Middle Easterners wish to challenge 'human rights', most have to place their challenge within the framework and utilize the common vocabulary of what has become the dominant 'human rights' terminology.

The people explicitly using (or criticizing) the notion of 'human rights', articulating it, working with it (or against it), are almost always 'intellectuals': journalists, writers, political and religious figures, academics, students, lawyers, certain kinds of militants and activists, and so on. Although many are engaged in organized political activity, their main work is in the cultural arena, articulating ideas and concepts and spreading their views through writings, speeches, discussion, argumentation. Their social task, in general, is to make some sense of the turbulence around them, to give it a convincing and consistent order, and to persuade others of the fairness, accuracy, and coherence of their insights.

Intellectuals, then, were to be my primary interlocutors. Although their numbers are not large, they have a growing influence on other people's views as a result of the expansion of print and electronic media, the importance of higher education, and the increasing general literacy of the population. Also, intellectuals in the Arab world (and perhaps more generally in the Third World) are likely to have backgrounds more similar to those of people in positions of power, and to have greater influence on people in power, than is the case in the West. As well, intellectuals travel widely, visit other countries of the Middle East, discuss the current situation with their counterparts, and so naturally contribute to the spreading of ideas throughout the region.

Working with intellectuals had other implications too. Many intellectuals in the Arab world (and in the Third World generally) occupy somewhat ambivalent, conflicted positions. Frequently educated in Western universities (or in their own country's Western-styled universities) and occupying professional positions that are often far removed from those of the mass of their compatriots, such intellectuals can easily face the accusation, not always well meant, that they have been 'corrupted' by their Western experience, that they do not have the 'authentic' values of the people at heart, that they have become a 'fifth column' for the West. (There are, of course, many intellectuals who have not had Western training, and some of these appear in this book; they face corresponding accusations, also not always well meant, that they are too insular, inward looking, 'traditional'.)

These accusations may become more wounding when the intellectual becomes active in the domain of human rights. Although ideas related to human rights are certainly not the exclusive property of any one civilization or tradition, the notion of human rights as it is being promoted today is seen by most Middle Easterners to be inextricably linked to the actions of the West. Not only are the immediate historical antecedents of 'human rights' usually attributed to the Enlightenment and the French and American revolutions, but also since the end of World War II and the elaboration of the United Nations Universal Declaration of Human

Rights, most human rights initiatives are seen to have come from the West, either from international state organizations such as the UN that for a long period were dominated by Western nations, or through the political utilization of human rights by Western governments (most notably by the US), or from non-governmental organizations based in the West such as Amnesty International, the International Commission of Jurists, and the Anti-Slavery Society.

Intellectuals thus sometimes stand accused of conflicting loyalties and both they and their views of human rights are accessible targets for the complex feelings towards the West that have been generated by colonial and post-colonial history. I hoped, then, that as well as exploring human rights issues, I might also cast some light on the role of the intellectual in Arab society.[3]

How would I address these intellectuals? Since I was interested in how *they* approached human rights issues, what were the problems as *they* saw them, what was the cultural context of this discussion as *they* saw it, I would usually direct my conversation towards what I knew of their interests rather than try to impose my own. I made a conscious effort to allow their thoughts to carry them where they wanted, but I felt it necessary occasionally to push discussion in a direction that more narrowly satisfied my needs. Inevitably what resulted was a blending of our concerns.

Many of the people I was meeting write extensively, but for a number of reasons I decided to concentrate on the words they spoke to me.[4] There is a vitality to the spoken word, and a currency, that is often lost in writing; also, I was less interested in what might be called the 'academic' or 'learned' discussion of human rights than I was in its more everyday, common use. The spoken word would also have a responsiveness to my questions that the written word could never achieve.[5]

Some of the people I met I had known for a number of years, either from my work as an anthropologist or from my time at Amnesty International. Many others were either introduced to me by these friends or colleagues, or were simply mentioned by them for me to contact on my own. I approached a number of people with no introduction simply because I had heard about them, or read something they had written, or because of the position they occupied. Meetings unfailingly led to the mention of more names, and many of these I was unable to talk to for lack of time. I make no claim to have talked to all, or even almost all, of the people with interesting ideas about human rights, but I do hope that I am conveying to the reader something of the interest that those I did talk to conveyed to me.

WRITING

Three countries – Morocco, Tunisia, Egypt; many individual speakers, each having a well-articulated position and together reflecting many varied points in the intellectual compass and many distinct political, ethical, and religious perspectives; a central subject matter – human rights – for which there is no agreed definition but which is an object of great contention and debate; all in play within a cultural environment that has been built over centuries and channeled the aspirations of millions of people: each of these aspects made it very difficult for me to imagine, to say nothing of write, a text reasonably faithful to the research.

As I thought about what such a text might look like, I wanted also to take into account (although not necessarily adopt) the views of many of the Middle Easterners I was talking to. They were for the most part long-time and intense students of their own societies, and some of them thought that my work might be moderately useful to them in bringing together points of view different from their own.

But they were perhaps more interested in the contribution my research might make towards dispelling what they felt were unfair and inaccurate Western attitudes towards Arabs.[6] These attitudes, they felt, had been formed not only by the popular Western media but also by much of Western scholarship and so-called 'serious' study of the Middle East.[7] Why the Western public appeared to be so strongly anti-Arab, and how its views might be changed, was a topic people raised with me again and again and on which I became something of an informant myself.

As we discussed how Western scholarship had contributed to these attitudes, we focused on what might be called 'orientalist' fallacies: presuming the West to possess a rationality superior to that of other civilizations; distilling a supposedly general 'underlying world view' (be it Arab, Middle Eastern, or Islamic), and so inevitably oversimplifying the diversity of forces and opinions that constitute any living society; interpreting what people mean as systematically different from what they say, and so claiming to have a deeper, truer insight into people than they have into themselves; artificially segmenting life into separate analytic domains (such as 'the economic', 'the political', and so on), thus losing a view of the whole; assuming that one researcher is capable of surveying, objectively and comprehensively, the full extent of a very complex society, of establishing a representative sample of all opinion and giving each of them their due.

We also seemed to agree that, given the subject of the research and the tense relationship between the West and the Middle East, it made more sense for me to try to write for a general, literate audience than for a narrowly academic and professional one, and made more sense to seek a focus that was situated somewhere between the day-to-day events that journalism attends to and the deeper but often esoteric matters that scholars study.

I am in fundamental sympathy with most of these ideas. In fact, it is useless for me now to ask whether these are my informants' ideas or mine, since they emerged mainly in conversations in which, on these subjects at least, we were all seeking answers to common questions.

Taking these ideas and some others into account, I rejected a straightforward chronological retelling – that would be too confusing and disorderly. At the other extreme, a rigorously analytic presentation, summarizing, reworking, and putting into my own words what had been said to me would negate the very purpose of the research, which was to hear how Middle Easterners themselves thought about and worked with notions of human rights.

One solution might be to limit each chapter to a discussion of one country. But this had serious drawbacks: it would mistakenly isolate each country and insulate the intellectuals in one country from those in the others, despite the fact that socially, economically, and culturally, deep and significant ties exist between these countries and between their intellectuals.

In addition, throughout the Middle East the issue of Arab unity – the desire and potential for joint action and even union in one form or another – has been a recurring theme since the birth of Islam and the subsequent growth of an Arab Islamic empire. In the contemporary period it has been at or near the top of the political agenda at least since the time of Nasser. Whether reflected in various regional associations like the Arab League or the Arab Lawyers Union, or in the recent formation of the Arab Maghreb Union and the Arab Cooperation Council, these aspirations are deeply felt by many of the region's inhabitants (although they do not all agree on the form which this joint activity should take).[8] It was therefore important that my writing reflect the impulse towards regional integration and avoid the simplifications of a narrowly national approach.

Another solution might be to structure the book thematically, perhaps along the fault lines of various international conventions: treating, for example, civil and political rights in one section and economic, social and cultural rights in another. But this would tend to abstract discussions from their national cultural contexts and would have the added disadvantage of forcing the ideas of Middle Easterners into a framework they had little role in constructing.

Yet, if I wanted to stay close to the actual words spoken to me, how would I avoid a book that might be crippled by phrases such as 'in Morocco Muhammad said this, but in Tunisia Ahmed said that; on the other hand, Gamal in Egypt disagreed with both of them; but back in Morocco, Abdelkabir had taken another approach entirely'.

As I wrestled with this problem, I recalled the somewhat cryptic words spoken at the very outset of the research, in February 1985, by Muhammad Guessous, a long-time friend and sociologist who, among his many other activities, teaches at the University of Rabat, in Morocco. Muhammad had said,

Whatever problems may appear to be most acute on the surface here and in the Middle East, the fundamental problem is that there are three great areas of unexamined, even forbidden territory in our society, in our culture, in our psyche. These three great areas – they are so vast that I call them continents – are the continents of power, of religion, and of sex. And it is practically taboo for us to really explore them.[9]

I turned over Muhammad's formulation in my mind many times after that, played with it, revised it, and in the end transformed it entirely, but it assisted me in developing the approach in this book.

The continent of 'religion' came to look more like a broad territory of key concepts a community uses to articulate a notion of itself – that is, what is the substance of the 'we' whose rights are in question? Religion is certainly a part of this, but so too are ideas about 'identity', 'history', 'continuity and rupture', 'the nation'. These and related topics came to dominate my discussions in Egypt.

The continent of 'sex' began to look more like a domain where the private and the personal reign, and where the key issues are ideas about the 'individual' and the role of liberty. These issues were the focus of many of my talks in Morocco.

Finally, 'power' came to look more like the terrain where individuals come together in groups and seek to engage in public activity and influence public life. In Tunisia, many of my discussions turned on the problems and difficulties that associations and organizations faced – in particular the Tunisian Human Rights League and the women's movement.

Although in each country my discussions developed a particular emphasis, all subjects came up in a significant way in all three countries. So I decided that, as well as having each chapter focus on one country and on the dominant themes that had emerged during my discussions in that country, I would introduce that theme early in each chapter by bringing in speakers from the other two countries to comment on it. In that way, I hoped each chapter would reflect the particular problems and provide a deeper discussion of one country, but would also allow this discussion to be set in its regional context.

This would have at least two other potential advantages: it would enable the reader to hear some points of view juxtaposed with others, to hear a person's ideas as part of a conversation with his or her peers (to whom many of the arguments are implicitly addressed, in any case). Also, speakers would appear again and again throughout the book, and readers might begin to feel at home with some of the voices.

The particular issues in each country emerged gradually, as different speakers gave different emphases to the problems and developments in their societies. Other researchers would probably have encountered other individuals with quite different points of view; even had they met the same people, they most likely would have encouraged different emphases to come out in their discussions.

There are certainly many different ways to approach the issue of human rights and I don't offer the steps I have taken as a recipe. But, idiosyncratic as they may be, they are not arbitrary. The themes that are highlighted in what follows – the role of religion and identity in society, notions of the individual and personal liberty and freedom, the problems of organizing activity and associations to achieve social goals (particularly with regard to promoting human rights and improving the situation of women) – speak directly to central aspects of the 'traditional' discussion of human rights as it has developed internationally. But at the same time, in the ways in which these ideas are formulated and put into action, much is also said about the particular Middle Eastern contexts in which they have arisen, about the particular individuals who here give them voice, and also perhaps about what it means for a Westerner, an American, to explore these issues in today's Middle East.

Most of the people I talked to placed their discussion in the context of the profound crisis their societies faced, a crisis they were sure their compatriots felt too. Because of this endemic sense of crisis, because of its role as the frame to most of our discussions, I thought it best to introduce these discussions as they were often introduced to me, with the notion of 'crisis' setting the tone.

1 Introduction: 'Azmatology'

There is so much talk in the Arab world of crisis, al-'azma, *that I now refer to it as 'azmatology'. As for myself, I try not to use the word too much anymore.*

(Muhammad Guessous, Morocco)[1]

CRISIS

The debate over human rights in Morocco, Tunisia, and Egypt takes place within the context of an intense discussion about basic societal options and directions, a discussion called forth by the gravity of each country's situation. Although not among the poorest Third World nations, Morocco, Tunisia, and Egypt confront grave economic problems – negative trade balances, high budget deficits, high unemployment, food production insufficient to meet the needs of populations growing at an annual rate of close to 3 percent, and high per capita foreign debt.[2] Income distribution is very uneven and the large poorer sectors of the population bear a major share of this burden; but the middle classes, too, are under strong economic pressure. Social unrest is never far beneath the surface and occasionally erupts explosively.

Although the governmental structures in each of these countries have remained relatively stable over the last two decades, this stability does not mean the absence of threats to the government's legitimacy. As well, the basic cultural orientations – Western or Eastern, religious or secular, 'democratic' or 'authoritarian', bureaucratic or charismatic, pluralist or monolithic (to name just a few) – are subject not only to serious discussion, but constitute stakes over which important social groups and forces contend.

Egypt, with a population of more than 50 million, contains about one-third of the Arab world's population. Its size, its central regional location, its uniquely long history as a unified state, all encourage Egyptians to see themselves as the center of the Arab world and also, in many ways, as special within it.

Against the background of this rather solid heritage, Egypt's recent history has been marked by a series of abrupt ruptures: the July 1952 revolution that led into the Nasser era, the Suez crisis in 1956, the June 1967 war with Israel, Nasser's death in 1970 and the subsequent reversal of many of his policies by Sadat, the October 1973 war with Israel, the assassination of Sadat in October 1981.

The convulsive nature of Egyptian political life may now seem somewhat muted since Hosni Mubarak took over the presidency after Sadat's death. But, with very serious economic problems afflicting Egyptian society and with occasional eruptions of social unrest, with a resurgence of Islamist religious movements and moments of increased tension between Muslims and Christian Copts, many Egyptians tend to see this relative lull as a momentary respite rather than as a new-found equilibrium.

Morocco, with a population close to 25 million, is (along with Algeria) the second most populous Arab country; Tunisia, much smaller, has a population of about 8 million. Both countries underwent significant periods of French colonial rule (seventy-five years in Tunisia's case, forty-four in Morocco's) and both gained independence from the colonial power in 1956.

In the more than three decades since independence, strong influence from France and, more broadly, from the West, has continued: Tunisian and Moroccan elites are largely educated and trained in the universities and institutions of the former colonial power, the main political options adopted in both countries have been avowedly pro-Western, and the economic systems show a strong 'liberal' cast with a modern private sector struggling to establish itself. Both countries have strong authoritarian state structures: Tunisia's (from independence until 1987 under President Habib Bourguiba) has been largely secular, often paternal (with a heavy-handed repressive manner), and always striving for monolithic control; Morocco's (under King Hassan II, who succeeded his father in 1961), dynastic with a taste of divine right (a kind of modern caliphate), iron-fisted, and ubiquitous.

Hassan's rule met dramatic threats in the early 1970s when two nearly successful coup attempts almost dethroned him, but since the mid-1970s the king has built upon Morocco's claim to the Western Sahara to forge a broad national consensus, successfully expanding and strengthening his administrative control over the country as a whole. Tunisia, suffering since at least the mid-1970s from the arbitrary and stagnant nature of Bourguiba's rule, and witnessing a sapping of governmental legitimacy because of the deteriorating economic situation and a growing challenge from Islamist forces, seemed to breathe a collective sigh of relief when, in November 1987, the newly appointed prime minister General Zine al-Abidine Ben Ali constitutionally deposed President Bourguiba. As president since then, Ben Ali initiated a number of long-awaited measures – new laws on press freedom and on the formation of political parties, for example, but these are only partial steps and have been subject to much criticism. The underlying economic and social problems inherited from the Bourguiba period still remain.[3]

'YOU DON'T EXPECT THE BARBER TO SLIT YOUR THROAT' (MOROCCO)

When I began this research in early 1985, I wanted at first some insight into the general atmosphere, the political mood, the 'state of play', so to speak, in each of the countries. Yet, in whatever way I approached these early conversations, they were inevitably dominated by one motif, a motif that continued to be significant in the years that followed: the sense of crisis – a crisis that, according to the people I spoke to, pervaded Morocco, Tunisia, and Egypt, and pervaded the Arab world as a whole.

I went first to Morocco, a country I had been studying and visiting for more than fifteen years. Naturally I began by renewing contact with some old Moroccan friends and acquaintances who were likely to speak freely about the general situation. A lawyer friend said,

This is a very difficult time: everything here seems more or less blocked, everyone is in a state of suspension. Why? Well, first of all, because there is a general consensus on the question of the war in the Sahara, anyone against it is afraid to speak out; and because a lot of people are afraid of what the Islamist movements or the army might do. There just seems to be no real alternative to those who control power right now, although many people would like to see some kind of change. But nobody wants to try anything, and in any case, nobody knows what to try.

A woman I knew who taught in a public high school said,

The government seems to be becoming more repressive, but the students are unable to mobilize themselves, unlike a few years ago. Now, the only people who demonstrate are a few students full of nostalgia. But nobody takes them seriously, everybody thinks they are just going through the motions.

More ominous, she went on to say, was the growing role the state was playing in cultural matters, a domain that had always been an outpost of the opposition and that the state had ignored until recently. Towards the end of 1983 King Hassan II had delivered an important speech in

Casablanca, encouraging the government to become increasingly active in the cultural arena. After serious public unrest broke out in January 1984 to protest price increases imposed on basic foodstuffs, the government began to close down some of the old local cultural centers, place new personnel in others, and take an active role in animating them. This was to signal what became a deliberate government policy throughout the 1980s – an effort to control the cultural domain through the traditional means of censorship and harassment, but also more subtly by promoting meetings, conferences, celebrations, and so on.

Early in my first trip to Morocco I went to see Muhammad Guessous, a professor of sociology at Muhammad V University in Rabat, a staunch activist and official of the major leftist opposition party, the Socialist Union of Popular Forces (USFP – l'Union socialiste des forces populaires). Muhammad, then in his late forties, had earned a doctorate in sociology from Princeton University and is widely known in Morocco, in the Arab world, and in the West as one of the keenest analysts of contemporary Arab society.

Guessous, true to his sociological vocation, began by pointing to the two main demographic trends underlying much of what was occurring in Moroccan society: the transformation from a predominantly rural society to one where the number of city dwellers had reached almost 50 percent of the total population; and the increasing youthfulness of the population – 80 percent of Morocco's population had been born after independence in 1956 and had had no direct experience of colonial rule.

In themselves, these figures may not have much significance, but Muhammad went on to trace some of their consequences. He did this in an English that was fluent, spiced with expressions he had picked up while doing his undergraduate and graduate studies in Canada and the United States, and some that he concocted idiosyncratically.

> When I discuss our current problems, I like to start from some common daily events we observe and about which we read more and more every day. I'll pick four: the new craze of break-dancing, the recent death in Cairo of a young Moroccan woman, the spate of corruption trials we've been experiencing lately, and finally what is happening in the schools.

He then went into detail on each of these.

> Break-dancing – you know, this peculiar dance where people imitate robots or act as if they were robots – well, a couple of weeks ago there was a break-dancing festival not far from my house. Six hours before it started there were 1,000 kids waiting to get in; a few hours later there were about 2,000. You could tell they were from some of the poorest sections of town. And I ask myself, where in the hell do these kids get 26 dirhams

(about $4.00 US) to spend on this? Do their families even spend 26 dirhams a day on their own needs?

The second example is the case of Samira Mirieni, a young Moroccan woman, married with two children, who was found dead in Cairo, naked, absolutely naked – she had been thrown to the street from the second-floor apartment of one of the greatest musical composers in Egypt. The inquiry showed that she had been brought to a drinking party by a rich Saudi who had also brought along an Algerian woman poet. It seems the man had killed her during some sort of fight, probably caused by a fit of jealousy on her part because another woman was getting into the picture. Well, a Moroccan woman, with her two children and husband still in Casablanca – for anyone who knows anything about Moroccan mores, how can you conceive of a 23-year-old Moroccan girl, a mother and a wife, being found absolutely naked in a god-forsaken place like Cairo? I mean, what the hell is going on here?

Thirdly, look at these corruption trials. There are lots of them. What strikes me is that the amounts of money involved are enormous and, in each case, the people brought before the court and the case itself are described as though this was the most ordinary, normal thing in the world. And we're talking about officials at many different levels, including school principals taking money from parents.

And finally, what is going on in the schools, both among teachers and students? For example, it is so much harder now to get teachers interested in public affairs, even to mobilize them to defend their own bread and butter, despite the fact that their standard of living has declined radically. Some estimates say that the standard of living of university teachers has declined by 60 percent, both in gross terms and relatively, in the last six years. So it's not surprising that teachers are now encouraging a new craze in private lessons – these are becoming a kind of racket: teachers seem almost to terrorize the kids, or to somehow convince the parents that if their kids don't take private lessons, they'll never pass an exam.

At the same time, in the schools, there is another new phenomenon: some parents are withdrawing their kids from the schools saying, 'What good does it do us if school degrees of whatever kind, even university degrees, cannot guarantee us even an ordinary job? What's the point? I might as well send them to learn some profession, some skill – that way they will be a lot more useful to me.'

Muhammad was by now well launched on his theme – he could in fact speak uninterruptedly for very long periods, for hours even (he was often a featured speaker at USFP public rallies, and he could hold a crowd spellbound). But now he stepped back, figuratively, and resumed a more sociological tone.

These kinds of events are all so shocking – shocking when compared to what is most likely, most probable in our society, when compared with our norms and models of behavior. But now it is the unlikely that we are seeing more and more.

When a system begins to produce things that don't belong to the realm of the conceivable, and when so many of these things begin to occur at the same time, one is bound to wonder what is happening altogether. Because we all know that life would be impossible and men would go nuts if we were operating in a world where nothing could be predicted. What makes life possible, what makes rational behavior possible, what makes it possible for us to cope with events, to suffer and endure them, to accomplish certain purposes no matter how modest they are, is the fact that you are normally used to dealing with somewhat determinate situations. You go to a barber, you see him holding a knife; but you don't expect the barber to slit your throat just like that.

Now the whole set of possibilities seems to be changing. Hence my hypothesis: could it be that suddenly we are dealing with a society that is going berserk? Could it be that the realm of the possible, the probable, the likely and the unthinkable is suddenly changing in a very drastic way?

The opposing hypothesis would be that these changes are only superficial, that they are only variations on the same theme. Musically, you can sing the same song in a hundred different ways; every artist wants to sing it differently and what makes him different is the way he sings it. But you recognize it is the same musical structure.

Muhammad went on, talking about this and other more specific issues. But for me he had already posed a fundamental question: how general was this notion of crisis, and how would such notions color the discussions I hoped to have on the specific issues of my research? In my subsequent visits to Tunisia and Egypt, the notion of crisis cropped up again and again, although in different ways.

'FREEING THE MIND' (TUNISIA)

Several weeks later I was in Tunisia. This being still early in 1985, much of the general conversation revolved around the health and stubbornness of President Bourguiba, and the problems of succession created by his unwillingness to share power or to prepare for handing it over. Many people seemed to both wish for and fear his sudden death or incapacity. Although most people felt he had overstayed his usefulness to the country, people were also afraid that any change in the *status quo* might precipitate a political crisis with serious consequences. As a result, much time was spent wondering who was up and who was down in the president's favor and speculating over the meaning of the latest palace anecdotes. Perhaps most importantly, Tunisians' sense of themselves during that time was very low, as they faced the thought that they might indeed deserve the ruler they had.

Among the first conversations I had in Tunisia was with Hedi Khelil, a university teacher specializing in the post-colonial French literature of the former French colonies. Hedi was in his early thirties and just beginning his career as a university teacher. He had given much thought to getting the best out of his students and he described his pedagogical technique as one that proceeded by provocation. As part of his effort to push his students to confront their own identity as Tunisians, Hedi was currently discussing with them a novel, *Muhammad Cohen*, written by a Tunisian Jew. Passionately in love with the cinema and with writing – a book of his on the cinema was about to be published in Canada[4] – Hedi tended to be silent and somewhat distant in my early meetings with him but, as a mutual friend of ours aptly remarked, 'He's somewhat mysterious, that's part of his charm.'

Hedi was scathing in his criticism of the general attitude of the students he taught.

> *What disappoints me about teaching, what disappoints me more and more, is my impression that everything is in the process of becoming standardized. That is, there is no longer the possibility of communicating words that are alive. It's as though the students have become deaf to all words that aim at communication, at real communication. To have real communication you have to be willing to confront things, to struggle, even to enter into conflict – you can't have it in this sort of total conformism that is all around us.*

And he went on,

> *You know, it isn't a question of making the students feel that they live in a crisis. They know they do. It's a question of making them see that the crisis isn't as bad as all that, that it's not the end of the world. The crisis is not an evil. The essential question is, 'What to make from this crisis?' Are we going to think about it and create something out of it, or are we going to be satisfied with living it as a shame, as a kind of dead-end, as a curse? Well, sometimes they live it in a triumphal manner, which is ridiculous: you know, of the sort, 'Arabic is our language, it always will be, and it always must be.' But most of the time, they live it as a curse.*
>
> *So I tell them, 'Look, if you have something inside you to express, write it. If you have texts you want to write, testimonies that are somewhat distinct from the routine, write them and I promise to find a way to publish anything that is good.' You know, exams, papers, that's all fine within the context of the schools. But if they have texts that they've created, I would even sell myself to get them published.*

Hedi was hoping, clearly, that some spark of originality, of creativity, might help move Tunisia out of what many agreed was a depressing predicament. But he was also discouraged, finding that no matter what he did – and this might involve cajoling his students or even deliberately angering them – he could not seem to light those sparks.

What accounted for what many Tunisians felt was a lack of creativity? A somewhat different perspective on this same problem was offered by Abdelaziz Krichen, an agronomist about 40 years old who during his younger days had been very active in the leftist student movement. He was now trying to produce the fourth issue of *Mensuel*, a new bilingual journal (in Arabic and French) he had founded. The journal was in serious financial difficulty.

We had started by discussing ideas about identity and authenticity, taking as our starting point a long article entitled, 'Tunisiens, notre identité', that he had written for *Mensuel*'s inaugural issue. Among other points, he argued that the notion of identity was intimately tied to the basic problem of national development.

> For me, the notion of 'identity' itself may have little importance, but behind it there is a real, all-encompassing societal phenomenon that is very important. Let me give you a very simple example. We've got a big problem here with our deficit in milk production. In order to increase production, we have to have more milk from our cows. What would be done in any country of the world to solve that? Well, you would try to increase the national herd and you would try to improve the production of each cow. So, the aims would be both quantitative and qualitative.
>
> But in Tunisia, and in a lot of developing countries, what do we do? We try to find the breed of cows abroad that produces the most milk. The world average is about 2,000 liters per cow per year but, in some small corner of northern Ireland, or in Holland – it doesn't matter where – there are cows which produce 6,000 or 8,000. So, we'll import the cows, and we'll pay a lot of money for them. And what do we find? After five or six months, these imported cows are giving 300, 400, 500 liters per year, if they manage to survive that long.
>
> To this example I could add examples from all branches of the economy, from all sectors of social life. It is always the same reasoning: 'If there's a problem, then the solution exists outside.' We go outside, looking for the solution. We try to apply that solution here, and it's a disaster. So you say to yourself, perhaps that wasn't the right solution. And again you go looking outside for another solution, and again it's a failure.
>
> Behind this, then, there is an attitude that you find in all politicians and in all the intelligentsia – an all-embracing, global attitude. And when I talk of politicians, I'm talking even of those who are strongly nationalistic, even those who took up arms against the colonizer. The point of reference is

always the West.

So the problem is, to put it simply, one of decolonizing the elites, decolonizing their psychology. It seems to me that this is a very important notion. There have been thousands of texts up till now on the Third World, or from the Third World, on the problem of economic independence and political independence. But this problem of psychological independence, of freeing the mind – well, a lot of people have alluded to it, but it hasn't been tackled as the real problem that it is.

So, the real problem behind this is to say, 'Ok, we have problems of all sorts. We've got to think these problems through and find solutions starting from our own particularities, starting from our own specificity, from what we are.' Now this doesn't in any sense mean rejecting all that is not us, not at all. That would be ridiculous. But it is a question of taking ourselves into account, and taking the other into account also. This is obvious. We can't solve problems here by parachuting down methods and production systems that are completely unsuited to our current situation.

This is why the question of identity, of authenticity, is now at the forefront – even if part of the reason for that is just that these words are in fashion today.

Krichen was by temperament an active personality and he had shown a good deal of optimism in launching *Mensuel* in spite of Tunisia's difficult economic situation. But his view of Tunisia's future prospects was anything but optimistic.

All of Tunisia's political and intellectual elite – even people who fought in a radical way against colonialism – all of them carried the model that to have a successful Tunisia we had to reproduce here what had succeeded elsewhere. What is interesting today, what explains the renewed interest in discussing identity today, is that now we realize that we are failing.

This model of development, this culture in fact – everybody has to admit that today it's a failure. So now everything is being called into question. The religious movements are pulling things in one direction. The monetarists – the Chicago boys, Milton Friedman, etc. – are pulling in another direction, proposing solutions here similar to those proposed in Latin America, Chile, Argentina. They argue that our dead-end isn't a result of our having imitated the West, but follows from the fact that we haven't imitated them totally.

So, starting from this all-embracing perception of failure, there are all kinds of interests pulling and pushing in different directions. And to put things clearly, those today who put forward a perspective such as the one we are trying to put forward in Mensuel – respect for and taking into account our own particularities, but in a spirit of respect and without complexes toward what is happening outside – well, this is still the position of a very small minority.

'THE MAFIAS, THE NEW RICH, THE MILLIONAIRES, AND ALL THE POVERTY' (EGYPT)

One of the many striking things about Egypt is the intensity of its intellectual life. This is particularly true of Cairo, which holds about one-fifth of the country's population and certainly a much higher proportion of its intellectuals. Whether at its major universities – Cairo University (alone having more than 100,000 students), Ain Shams, the American University of Cairo – in its newspaper offices, at various research centers and institutes, thousands of well-informed Egyptians study and analyze Egypt and the world situation, forming highly developed interpretations of what is happening around them. (That they often do so in crowded and noisy offices, with salaries that are normally so inadequate that they must hold other jobs as well, makes their efforts even more striking.)

Then, in their teachings, or in newspapers, or in their independently published articles and books, they diffuse their ideas to a public of very avid readers, supplied with the latest books, pamphlets, and leaflets by the numerous Cairo street stalls.

Among the first people I saw in Egypt was a journalist in his mid-thirties whom I shall call Gamal. Gamal worked for the Al-Ahram Institute, a research organization associated with Al-Ahram publications (a publishing house that produces the daily newspaper of the same name and a weekly *Economic Al-Ahram*). Gamal had returned to Egypt in the early 1980s from the United States, where he had earned a doctorate in economics.

Gamal first spoke in general terms, stressing that the problems in Egypt were of a fundamental sort and that the basic rights of most Egyptians were violated daily: essential needs – safety, housing, clean air, play areas for children, protection from traffic – were all neglected. There was perhaps some anxiety among the masses about the lack of democracy in Egyptian political life but Gamal was sure that for them, this took a back seat to other more pressing problems.

Gamal pointed out, also, that the educational system was deteriorating rapidly. Public education, one of the great achievements of the Nasser period, had worsened noticeably over the last six or seven years: middle-class families would now no longer send their children to the public schools, and there was now a clear division between public and private education. Gamal noted that many Egyptians saw this as evidence that Egypt was becoming two countries, a country of the privileged and a country of the poor. But, as yet, there was no consensus about a solution.

And then Gamal deplored the economic prospects for recent university graduates and referred to his own circumstances as well.

The situation has degenerated, too, at the university level, where it now appears that higher education is not tied to greater monetary rewards after graduation. Of course, here in Egypt, at least university graduates are guaranteed employment, because the state is the employer of last resort. But wages are so low – graduates in the human sciences or letters would make forty-five Egyptian pounds a month (then about $65 at the official rate of exchange, but substantially less on the black market), engineers or technicians about sixty – so low that everyone simply has to take a second job. I myself only earn 180 Egyptian pounds a month at my job here, and even that is not enough to live on.

Shortly after seeing Gamal I went to talk to Sayed Yassin, director of the Al-Ahram Institute and by training a sociologist. When we started to talk about contemporary Egypt he began, as many Egyptians do, by summarizing recent Egyptian history.

For me, the Egypt of the post-war period can be summarized by saying that Nasser was the thesis, Sadat the antithesis, and Mubarak the synthesis. Sadat was the antithesis to Nasser, both economically and politically. Economically he initiated the open-door policy, infitah, which in effect means capitalism. And politically he adopted pluralism, political pluralism. The whole logic of this process, reinstituting capitalism in Egypt with both its political and economic sides, was the antithesis of Nasser.

What Mubarak is now trying to do is what he calls the 'productive open-door policy' (infitah intagi), instead of the 'exploitative open-door policy' (infitah istighlali). In other words, he is trying to arrest the negative aspects of capitalism by imposing some limitations, such as trying to control the import of goods, trying to increase productivity, trying to arrive at a certain policy for social justice. Well, of course he hasn't succeeded in all this, but he is trying to move in this direction.

And, of course, he faces a lot of problems. It is a matter of the rigidity of the new regime in Egypt. By 'new regime' I mean the new social class that benefited from the open-door policy and the power that it wields. This new social class is an alliance between politicians and businessmen and some media people. And these three groups have organic interests in common, and are resisting any radical change in the system that might be called for by Mubarak.

But there is one area where there has been real movement, the movement towards democratization. There are strong pressures from different groups for more of this, and I don't think this movement will be easy to stop. Unless of course the regime has to face a serious crisis – then, perhaps, it will reverse this progress.

A number of these issues came up in a conversation I had around the same time with Muhammad Sid Ahmed, a well-known Egyptian journalist, editor of *Ahali*, the newspaper of the leftist National Progressive Unionist Party.

When I met him at his home in Zamalek (an island section of Cairo, situated in the Nile) he was obviously tired, having been awake most of the previous night helping his son prepare for his baccalaureate exams in mathematics. But his answers were nonetheless clear and to the point. After some historical background, Muhammad Sid Ahmed began to discuss Egypt under Sadat and under Mubarak.

> By 1973 Sadat was moving pretty clearly towards the West. So with him we had a reversal of policies, from a policy that had been socialist oriented, to its opposite, especially after 1973. But when Sadat began to introduce pluralism it was not genuine pluralism – it was really only window dressing to show that he was moving from the eastern orbit to the western one. He was saying, you know, 'I am no longer following the eastern system but the western system.'
>
> And also, Sadat could not run a police state as openly as Nasser did, because Nasser had an ideological justification for this, whereas Sadat had none. So Sadat turned to more political techniques, and his brand of pluralism served these purposes: he would have a party on the right to test how far he could go without provoking a backlash, and a party on the left that would be made to carry the responsibility for whatever disorder arose. But then Camp David happened, and Sadat's trip to Jerusalem, and here he antagonized a lot of forces.
>
> Sadat lived a dilemma and a contradiction, because he projected an unreal image of society. This was true in all fields, in economics as well as in human rights. In economics he had an institutional framework that was fine for a socialist-oriented policy, but not for a capitalist one. This created freakish phenomena, aberrations, and monstrosities: for example, the mafias, the new rich, the millionaires, and all the poverty that is all around us. And all this developed because there were no checks and balances that are necessary if the game of capitalism is going to work: you can't have capitalism with a one-party system, or even with a multi-party system that is controlled from the top.
>
> This all showed what a manipulative idea both human rights and democracy could be. They were a product of Sadat's desire to project the image of a system more or less respectful of these values, but that in real terms remained basically totalitarian. And he proved this: the day he saw that pluralism threatened his control, he put everyone in prison. And he was killed because of that. That was the drama of the whole situation, that was its inner conflict.

I asked him how this situation had developed under Mubarak.

> The main problem for Mubarak is that he is a Sadat nominee, he is not a man with a vision, he is not a man with a policy of his own. So up until now he is a man who has inherited power and has not yet had the guts or the ability to seize power. Mubarak has been following a policy of survival –

change is introduced only enough to avoid the backlash that killed Sadat.
It has not yet been proven that he wishes to go beyond this.

We are now living a respite, a period of armistice, a temporary social
armistice due to fatigue, social fatigue. Thirty years of convulsions. There
is fatigue, and there is also the apprehension of a terrible situation getting
out of hand. And both these are working together to get a wide range of
forces from the left to the right to accept the principle that everybody should
have a say in order to prevent any one party from having the only say.

Now, under Mubarak, there is a sort of consensus, a kind of pause, and
pluralism is the expression of that pause. Today, at this critical moment
when things have to be rethought and looked at anew, the right of the others
to express themselves becomes more important than my own right to
assert myself at the expense of others. At the same time, I win from the
others their protection of my right to talk. This is an important guarantee
for me, more important than if I tried to gain my right to express myself by
joining the attempt to repress others, or if I stood for the repression of others.

Now this idea has a widespread consensus, but I think it is temporary,
I don't think it can go on indefinitely, because there is not enough cake to
go around. And that is the problem of the developing countries: in the last
analysis, this pluralism cannot become genuine, authentic, because
there is not enough cake to distribute.

And then Muhammad Sid Ahmed put this in the context of the wider
Arab world:

The system is threatened here, and in Arab countries all over; we are living
in a period when many regimes are falling to pieces. We have Lebanon
as an obvious case, we have what happened in the Sudan, we might have
it eventually within a decade in Iraq, in Saudi Arabia or in the Gulf. In fact,
it may be that these countries are staying whole only because of the Gulf
war [between Iraq and Iran], a war, you know, that is both accelerating
disintegration and retarding it: accelerating because it disaggregates the
society, retarding because it encourages national unity.

'WHAT TO MAKE FROM THIS CRISIS?'

Frequently full of insight, often inconclusive, at times contradictory, the
varied testimony of the people I spoke to was always voiced with
apparently sincere conviction and definite rhetorical power. The notions
and sentiments of crisis they implied or explicitly expressed testified to a
societal complexity (and to a complexity in their own thinking) that
confounded simple analysis, disturbed ready-made understandings, and
was often profoundly disorienting to all of us involved in exploring the
problem.

The issues they addressed were at times political – the legitimacy of rulers and their vision (or lack of it), the difficult choice between radically different political ideologies and styles (capitalism, socialism, pluralism, one-party rule, democracy, authoritarianism, and so on); or economic – the gulf between rich and poor, the lack of national wealth, the monetary pressures facing most social classes (including intellectuals); or socio-cultural – crumbling educational systems (and the demoralization of teachers, students, parents), diminished possibilities for social mobilization, entrenched and reactionary interest groups, censorship and the domination by the state of cultural affairs; or international – the dependency of Third World countries on more powerful economic centers, the crisis in the wider Arab world; or even personal – a strong pressure for conformity, a broadly felt sentiment of failure, a 'colonized' psychology, an absence of originality, an erosion of moral values. Often the issues were all-embracing: ideas about identity and authenticity, comments about what one person later referred to as a 'civilizational crisis'.

In the face of the complexity of this crisis and its vivid immediacy in Morocco, Tunisia, and Egypt, some people may feel the need for a more 'objective' view, may want to observe it from a distance and wonder why the notion of 'crisis' has become such a central theme in the last quarter of the twentieth century.

In this vein, some analysts may suggest that there is something about the character and rapidity of change in today's world, together with our seeming incapacity to assimilate such change, that makes the feeling of crisis so widespread. Or, looking at other parts of the world, some might argue, fairly, that the feeling of crisis is not unique or peculiar to the Arab world, but reflects the attitudes of many Third World people, particularly in Africa and Latin America.[5]

Or there may be something about intellectual activity itself that fosters notions and feelings of crisis. Perhaps intellectuals see crises because of their frustration, their belief that they have better ways to solve problems but are usually too distant from positions of power to exert any influence. Perhaps intellectuals see crises because they are trained to penetrate social problems, to perceive how deep and intractable they are, how impossible to solve.[6] It may even be that the social function of intellectuals is not to solve problems at all but instead to *produce* 'crises', to propose new ways of looking at and doing things, ways that necessarily challenge older, better internalized practices and attitudes.[7]

Or perhaps intellectuals may be moved by much more mundane considerations: facing declining living standards and increasing competition for jobs, they may, in a kind of pathetic fallacy, project onto the world their own personal dilemmas, leading them to views that are bleak or even apocalyptic.

As interesting as these suggestions may be – and some of them certainly have something to recommend them – they all treat the problem of crisis as a problem of thinking about rather than living in the world. None of these suggestions would provide much assistance to people I spoke to, to Moroccans, Tunisians, and Egyptians attempting to cope with pressing problems not only in their daily lives, but with problems that also exist on the level of local, regional, national, and international activity.[8] The 'objective', distanced, decontextualized perspective would seem, simply, to turn away from rather than face the immensely difficult, complicated situations that people confront in Morocco, Tunisia, and Egypt; and to turn away from the kind of question Hedi Khelil asked, 'What to make from this crisis?'

What could be made from this crisis, what was being made from it by people within it? Were people becoming, as Muhammad Guessous in Morocco suggested at one point,

> *more individualistic, more egotistic, more opportunistic, dealing with social rules not as compelling, not as obligations, not as integral parts of their own identity, but only as tools? You use religious norms when it suits you; you use some moral rules when they suit you and break them when it suits you; you call upon family solidarity, tribal solidarity, neighborhood solidarity, when it suits you and break them when it suits you.*

Or, was it as Muhammad Sid Ahmed in Egypt suggested, that under the pressure of crisis,

> *There are still those who are for an exclusive ideology, be it leftist, or Islamic, or whatever, and this is incompatible with human rights. But many of us, on the contrary, think that the situation is too threatening to have one ideological trend take over – we have all had enough experiences of one ideology taking over at the expense of others to know what this means. So, the elites are becoming aware that a certain opening up of the system is indispensable, and these elites are beginning to promote human rights.*

These two views far from exhausted the possibilities, of course. But they reflected crucial questions being posed in the Middle East and North Africa about the relationships between individuals, social groups, and society as a whole, about the future course society might or should take. These were questions that I was going to pursue over the next several years, exploring, confronting, and collecting the views of a wide variety of Moroccan, Tunisian, and Egyptian thinkers and activists. But before one could reach any conclusions on these questions one had to hear these people speaking for themselves.

Part I

Egypt: identity, religion and visions of society

2   Universal visions, local visions

VISIONS IN PLAY

For a period of several weeks in June 1986, streets in the major cities of
Morocco were alternately deserted and packed with people. The Moroccan national soccer team, victorious in the preliminary rounds of the
World Cup, was participating in Mexico in the final round against the
world's premier teams. Moroccans, at times glued to television sets in
their homes or in local cafés, at times jubilant in the streets after another
in a series of unexpectedly strong Moroccan performances, were in a state
of exhilaration, a mood one old Rabat resident said he hadn't seen since
the independence celebrations in 1956.

The exhilaration permeated not only Morocco's cities but also the
kingdom's remote rural areas where, barely fifteen years before, many
youngsters had not even known how to play football. Now, however, with
active government support, many villages had their own teams and participated in local leagues and regional tournaments. During the World Cup
competition, young men in the villages would congregate around the few
available television sets and cheer on the Moroccan team even while,
perhaps in the same room, their fathers would perform the evening prayer
and ignore the latest Moroccan shot on goal or the agile defense of their
goaltender Zaki.[1]

In the cities, the World Cup competition was not simply a source of fun
and excitement; long discussions were reported to be taking place within
the Ministry of Interior where officials feared that mass demonstrations
might turn into outbursts against the government, of the sort Morocco
had experienced in 1981 and 1984 when people protesting against a
worsening economic situation had taken to the streets and engaged in
violent clashes with the police. To prevent such outbursts, street barriers
and other crowd control measures were put into place on the eve of the

crucial match against the West German team, a match that would determine whether Morocco would avoid elimination.

As it turned out, the Moroccan team narrowly lost to the West Germans in a closely fought match and the popular demonstrations did not materialize. But throughout the period of the World Cup competition many people in Morocco – in the press and on television, in personal conversation and friendly banter – were led to reflect not only on the importance of football in Morocco (and in the Arab world and the Third World as well), but also on the nature of Moroccan society itself.

Among the many remarks I heard were:

You know, what the French captain said was terrible, that 'the weakest team in the whole tournament is Morocco'. The authorities were so afraid of a popular reaction to this remark that they didn't allow it to be published until after our victory over Portugal.

After our match against England, the Moroccan players went to shake hands with the English players. But in fact, the English players should have come over to us because we had played the better game.

The psychology of the Moroccan team is a greater variable than for the West Germans. The West Germans have in their favor a highly rationalized and systematic game, and also great physical force, so the psychological problems that may be on the inside don't appear on the outside. The Moroccan team lacks these qualities of rationality and physical force. Also, because of our feelings of inferiority, the psychological problems appear only too readily.

The attitude of the officials in our game against the West Germans was horrendous – they saw it as a game between West German humans and Moroccan animals, and their role was to protect the humans. And both officials were from countries with great cultural attachment to Germany – from Austria and Hungary. Why wasn't there an official from the Third World?

The opposition is trying to use football as a weapon against the government, arguing that all we need to do, in football as in other things, is to devote sufficient resources and we can then come up with victory. Victory is a question of will – once the will is there results will follow. You can have victory only when you have made the decision to win.

There was another more general argument regarding football that I heard not only in Morocco but in Tunisia and Egypt as well. A Tunisian phrased it most clearly,

You know, football is a major stake in the political game – you can see this from the coverage it is given in the national press and on television. But

*for us – people who want to construct a truly Islamic society – football is
really the 'opium of the people', it is a distraction that keeps the people
from addressing the real problems of society. Unfortunately we can't
come out and openly attack football because it is just too important for the
people right now.*

Attacking football as an intoxicating distraction was done not just by
religious militants; similar remarks were made to me by secularists, leftists, and once by a Moroccan villager.

Football, of course, is only one stimulus for reflection about the nature
of society: offering a widely shared set of public events, it can be easily
used by people to communicate the complex views they hold about the
nature of their own community and the place of that community in the
wider world.

For example, among other things the previous comments suggest that
some Moroccans believe: there is competition between nations and this
competition is unfairly weighted against Third World competitors; their
own community in some respects is, and is seen by others as, inferior to
other communities; their community is frequently unjustly insulted and
slighted, particularly by the dominant Western European powers; their
community lags behind others but there may be techniques to narrow and
perhaps even eliminate this lag; that Moroccans have a pride in good
performance, a desire to succeed and gain world recognition; an essential
ingredient in securing better performance is the proper political will and
representation. And, also, some people reject this competition *in toto*,
reject the field on which it is played, the rules that govern it, and argue
instead for another vision of society altogether.

Behind these comments and to some degree cutting across them lie
two very different models of society: one that sees society as 'transparent',
another that sees it as 'opaque'. Both models portray the hope that a
better future is possible for societies now experiencing profound crises,
and both convey dissatisfaction that one's own present-day society has not
reached the standards one would wish it to attain.

But here the similarities end. The 'opaque' model joins the view that
one's own community is a disappointment to the belief that current
problems are extremely complex, that no one has yet found definitive
solutions to them, and that to solve such questions requires building
societies where free debate can take place and where the various social
groups and instances can each express their voice. Those who support this
model usually (although not always) point to Western societies as having
already made considerable progress in embodying these traits; as a result,
other societies that have attempted to suppress criticism and dissent and

to speak with one voice have fallen behind, and have laid themselves open to Western domination.

For some who suscribe to the 'opaque' model, lag and external domination may be only temporary and might be eliminated if the right pragmatic, piecemeal steps are taken – after all, hadn't the newly independent nations already gained substantial freedom of action in the post-colonial world? For others, dependence and backwardness may be structural and require a radical, even revolutionary, transformation – how else could one shed the metropolitan domination that was continuing even after the West's formal political domination had ended?

The 'transparent' model carries with it a very different configuration of beliefs, and in particular argues that solutions to today's problems are already known, and the task is simply to apply them. Most of the supporters of this view (but not all) take as exemplary Islamic society in an earlier historical period, when it was under the direct guidance of the Prophet Muhammad and his immediate successors, and point to the lessons contained in Islam's revealed Truth.[2] In this vision today's society has strayed from the true way – because of evil rulers, or the persistence of heterodox beliefs, or lack of proper education and family structure, or domination by the West (or any combination of these) – and fallen into a degenerate state that can be transformed only through renewed attention to the fundamental sources of Islam, primarily the Qur'an and the life of the Prophet.[3]

It would be a mistake, however, to correlate rigidly the 'transparent' model with religious thinkers and the 'opaque' model with secularists: as we shall soon see, many speakers whose frameworks are religious in fact suscribe to the 'opaque' model, and some secularists tend towards the 'transparent'.

Much of today's debate in the Middle East about the ills of society, the ways to correct them, and how to construct a better future, and therefore much of the debate over the key terms in this book – 'human rights', 'democracy', 'freedom', 'identity', 'history', 'secularism', 'religion' – is framed with these models in the background.

But any individual's views may represent a complex mixing of these models and the key terms themselves are so intimately related to one another that it is impossible to ask people to treat them one by one and to focus on each of them in turn. In this part I have not asked people to do this, but have simply tried to elicit and listen to the arguments they make that invoke these core issues.

We shall first hear speakers from Morocco and Tunisia: a university professor, an establishment religious scholar, the leader of a sometimes persecuted, sometimes legal Islamist group, and several self-styled 'progressive' Muslims.[4] Then, after a short outline of contemporary Egypt, we shall hear from Egyptians: two men who address the relationship between human rights, identity, and religion; two women who focus on questions of identity and secularism; and finally, several so-called 'new traditionalist' Islamic thinkers who discuss central aspects of their religious visions.

'ISLAMIC HUMAN RIGHTS ... DON'T MEAN THAT EVERYTHING IS PERMISSIBLE' (MOROCCO)

A Moroccan university professor was describing to me one day how his students' attitudes had changed.

> *Over most of the last two decades a kind of secular, leftist ideology dominated the universities. But now there is an alternative in the form of Islamic ideology. A few years ago I had many, many students working with me, working with what I would call my basically rationalist approach. Now I have only two students and many of the others are in effect saying to me, although in a very nice way, 'Leave me alone, we don't want an approach that raises problems, we want one that has answers.'*

And he went on,

> *I now realize that one of the biggest mistakes our generation committed was to have ignored religion altogether, to have thought it had become totally outdated. It was as though we were still thinking in the old evolutionary pattern, as though religion was a kind of dinosaur: perhaps a few relics still existed, but we knew they would soon be extinct.*
>
> *So, we ignored religion, even though it was one of the only real centers of legitimacy in our societies. And what happened? Because we abandoned it, it became a tool in the hands of the rulers; or it was used by underdeveloped charlatans who transformed it into a merchandise like they had done before. Perhaps the only encouraging sign in this is that some people, behind a religious or metaphysical language, are really using a political language expressing political and social protest.*

In the mouth of an avowed secularist these words are perhaps not surprising, and we need not agree with the details of his categorization to recognize the essential argument behind it: that, in the Arab Middle East in the last quarter of the twentieth century, the language of religion has come to dominate discourse about the nature of society, much as leftist vocabulary dominated the immediate post-independence years.

This does not mean that religious sentiments dominate all actors on the

Middle East scene, nor that all actors carry the same vision of Islam, but simply that the arguments that seem to resonate most powerfully in the public arena are those that utilize religious symbols and vocabulary, and that set themselves within a religious framework. This is true even when the focus of discussion is not in itself religious – as in the case, say, of human rights.

A member of Morocco's Council of Religious Scholars, Muhammad Mekki Naciri, opened a discussion with me by saying,

Human rights may be something new for the West, but we in Islam have had it since the beginning. We have no differences between whites, blacks, Jews, Muslims – everyone is free. We never persecuted the Jews here the way they did in France and England. In England and in the US you fight against the blacks – why just the other day there were news items about fighting between the police and blacks in London.

Muhammad Naciri had made, in a short statement, a summary of many of the points that occur again and again when some Muslims discuss human rights with a Westerner: that although many Westerners may claim human rights as a major achievement of Western civilization, Muslims may argue just as sincerely that human rights is central to Islam, and may argue as well that the West's rhetorical emphasis on human rights cannot hide the fact that within Western society basic human rights are violated every day.

Muhammad Naciri went on,

You know, the United States talks about human rights a lot but look at the violations it supports, such as in South Africa. England, too, argues against sanctions for South Africa. And Israel is allowed to slaughter and to kill – the US will not even condemn Israel in the UN for bombing the PLO headquarters in Tunis. And look, I have been to New York, and I've seen how people live in the slums there, forced to live among garbage. And look at Ireland – England was the colonial power there and now look at the problems they have. And the English talk about their 'exemplary democracy'!

I had no difficulty conceding that this critique of the West was largely justified, if a little self-satisfied; it was also finely aimed at an American who had been living in England for ten years. But how, I asked, was the issue of human rights posed within Islamic society?

Naciri answered,

Well, human rights as such is not a separate domain in Islam, but part of the very essence of our beliefs. More specifically, we know what these rights are from our jurisprudence, from the accumulated experience of our learned men who have been called upon to decide cases and disputes.

From this we know that there are five essential principles: the protection of life, the protection of property, the protection of the family and our family line, the protection of religion, and the protection of human intelligence. These five elements are the logical foundations of Islamic law. Therefore, for example, anything harming human intelligence is against Islamic law.

He went on,

But you can see that Islamic human rights, Islamic freedoms, don't mean that everything is permissible, although this is the view you tend to take in the West. For example, you know that Saudi Arabia didn't subscribe to the Universal Declaration of Human Rights. Why? Because the Universal Declaration of Human Rights specifically permitted the acceptance of atheism, and that would allow propaganda against our religion. It would also allow a group, such as the Baha'i, which isn't even a religion but is just a sect, to try to impose itself as a religion.[5] These kinds of groups can't be allowed to insult the established religion.

And also, the Universal Declaration of Human Rights was for complete equality between men and women. For us, women are equal to men in law, but they are not the same as men, and they can't be allowed to wander around freely in the streets like some kind of animal.

Was there a need, I asked, for organizations to promote and protect human rights in Middle Eastern countries, organizations such as those that had recently been formed in Morocco, Tunisia, and Egypt?

Well, these countries do not have a completely liberal political system, or they have a single-party state. So the opposition needs some protection, and these organizations are primarily there to protect the opposition's political rights. As such, they aren't necessarily a bad thing. But, of course, the problem arises when they begin to get support from abroad, and external forces start to use the organizations to fight other battles.

In this short discussion, many key points were suggested and touched upon that were going to appear again and again in the course of my discussions with intellectuals in Morocco, Tunisia, and Egypt: the relationship between the Islamic world and the West; the notion of rights and freedoms and the particular issues of freedom of religion, the equality of men and women, and the relations between Muslims and non-Muslims; the relationship between political rights and other rights; the role of religion in society; the importance and effectiveness of human rights organizations; the question of the vulnerability of national institutions to foreign domination. These were among the most contentious issues in current debate as individuals sought to articulate their views of human rights while retaining a notion of their own identity, of themselves as bearers of a particular cultural and civilizational heritage.

'HOW CAN WE DEVELOP A VISION . . . WITHOUT OUR OWN HISTORY?' (TUNISIA)

Muhammad Mekki Naciri is an establishment religious figure in Morocco; Rachid Ghannouchi, on the other hand, is the leader of a religious movement in Tunisia, the Islamic Tendency Movement (MTI – Mouvement de la tendance islamique) that, ever since its beginnings in the early 1970s, has had a stormy relationship with the government, at times being illegal and clandestine with many of its members in prison or under the threat of imprisonment, at other times tolerated and allowed to operate more or less openly. In 1987, in the waning months of the Bourguiba period, many of its members were arrested or went underground but, in the somewhat more tolerant atmosphere of Bourguiba's successor, Ben Ali, MTI candidates were permitted to stand as independents in national elections in the spring of 1989. Even so, the attempts by the MTI beginning in 1989 to gain full legal recognition as a political party, termed *An-Nahda* (Rebirth), have been repeatedly turned down by the government.

When I met Rachid Ghannouchi in late 1985, he had been released from prison only a little more than a year earlier after having served three years of a ten-year sentence. He spoke to me from a small office in central Tunis in a room stacked with back issues of the MTI's journal *Maʿrifa*, a publication that had been able to appear only sporadically because of government prohibitions.

When I asked him what importance he and his movement gave to human rights, he answered,

> The concept of human rights is not new to the Islamic movement because the concept of a human being is not new to Islam. If human rights are being violated by Muslims today or have been in the past it is because of their ignorance of Islam and this leads to their decline.
>
> Human rights is a concept that has developed with the development of civilization, and that sees the human being as an entity that, regardless of race, color, or creed, has rights. This is a stage, a good stage, a progressive stage in the development of the idea of the human being. It emerges from a period when rights were given only to specific categories of people: to monarchs, feudal lords, capitalists, to Westerners or to Easterners. Islam pushes this development even farther: Islam is here to take man from existing merely as an economic or political or nationalist being, or as a sexual being – that is, as a man or woman – and make a human being in the full meaning of the word.

Rachid Ghannouchi was accepting that human rights was central to Islam, but I wondered how he distinguished between an Islamic view of human rights and the international view, which did not have religious foundations.

This has to do with the source of human rights. Are these rights that man gives to himself, or are they natural? Until now, there is no agreement between intellectuals as to what these rights are – does it mean the right to form a political party, the freedom of the press, the freedom to travel, to trade, to express opinions? If the rights were natural rights there would be no disagreements. Since there is no agreement, this kind of discussion between intellectuals does not give a good basis for discovering what human rights are. What one man sees as a right another does not.

Human rights must have a sound basis, a good source, and we believe God is this source. God gives man rights that no one can take away. What parliament decides by a majority of 51 percent today is a right; tomorrow it might not be. Human rights is not a toy to be played with, it needs a warranty and we believe that warranty is God. We differ from others, Muslims and others, because we believe man has rights that do not come from the discussions of intellectuals or parliamentarians, but come from God.

How had he come to his own vision of human rights, on what sources did he lean, and how did he come to be sure that his vision had validity in the face of other visions?

Rachid Ghannouchi began his answer by comparing his own personal itinerary with that of the Islamic community (*'umma*) as a whole. He had begun his studies in the Zitouna, the Tunisian university that specializes in Islamic and classical studies, then had studied philosophy and graduated from university in Damascus, Syria, where he had been active in the Arab nationalist movement.[6] After graduation he went to France and studied for one year at the Sorbonne, then returned to Tunis to teach philosophy in the secondary schools.

In my opinion the journey I have made is similar to the journey of the Islamic 'umma. The 'umma is being liberated bit by bit from a period of historical decline and a period of direct and indirect imperialism – intellectual, cultural, economic, and political imperialism.

I was brought up in a religious family but this was a personal religion, a private religion, and did not represent an ideology or a certain outlook on life. When I studied philosophy and contemporary ideas, I left religion because I found this purely private religious outlook couldn't stand up to Western ideas. This led me to Arab nationalism – which grew out of Western ideas of nationalism. But the repeated failures of the Western experience, the failure of nationalism, the failure to solve the Palestinian problem, the failure of liberalism and socialism in dealing with questions of progress and growth – all these failures made my generation and today's generation question the Western experience and question the idea of imitating the West, a path that had led the 'umma to fragmentation and increasing decline. From that position we moved to return to Islam.

What did this 'return to Islam' mean for relationships between the Islamic *'umma* and the non-Muslim world?

Our return to Islam does not mean that we isolate ourselves from the world around us or from people who do not believe as we do. To the contrary: Islam calls for people to live together, to cooperate and to have a dialogue in order to strengthen and support a set of values such as freedom, democracy, and justice. These are human values, not just Muslim values. And since the 1970s, to support these values, we have had relations with non-Muslims, such as Marxists and liberals and so on.

This is because the Islamic vision of man and existence is a worldwide one and not a national one. Islam is a message to man and not simply to Arabs, or to the Chinese, the French and so on. And that message is that God is one; that human beings, male and female, are all from one source, God; that the means of livelihood were created for all peoples by God; that the greater their love of God and the nearer they are to Him, the greater will be their reward. According to the Islamic vision, the world is a table of plenty and people take from it in accordance with their needs and their efforts. God created people to gain knowledge and not to war against each other. Relations between the Islamic 'umma and the human 'umma are relations of peace, dialogue, cooperation – not war. War is hated in Islam except for defence of liberty and values. It is not for gaining control, for booty, or for invasions.

It was difficult to see at this point whether Ghannouchi was talking of an ideal Islamic society as he would like one to be, or whether he was attempting to present a vision of the actual Islamic world but neglecting the incontrovertible realities of glaring social divisions, inequalities, and disparities. To just take one concrete example, I asked Ghannouchi how he saw the relationship, within an Islamic society, between Muslims and non-Muslims.

'The key notion here', he answered, 'is cooperation':

The foreigner in our country, living within the Islamic 'umma, is not persecuted – Christians and Jews, and members of different races, are not oppressed. The Islamic 'umma is formed from many races. No one has ever been persecuted in the Islamic 'umma because of his color or his belief. The Christian minorities persecuted in Europe under the Catholics found refuge within the 'umma, the Jews persecuted in Europe under the Catholics found refuge within the 'umma. Under the 'umma, all peoples and all religions are allowed to exist.

While much of what Ghannouchi had just said was true, the term 'cooperation' that he used disguised the fact that Christian and Jewish minorities in Islamic societies had had a 'protected' status which, while certainly ensuring many rights, was in no way tantamount to equality. But sensing that this was a delicate issue, I decided to postpone discussion on it for the moment and return to it later in our talk.[7]

For the moment, I chose another tack, asking Ghannouchi what he thought of international efforts to define human rights. He answered,

Take for example the Universal Declaration of Human Rights – we have some reservations regarding its wording. In general we support it as a stage of development for the human being but we feel it is not universal. It incorporates the perspective of one specific culture and is deeply influenced by Western and secular concepts. Now, you know the Tunisian Human Rights League has been attempting to elaborate its own charter by basing it on the Universal Declaration of Human Rights. We support the idea of such a charter, but I am cautious about the philosophical bases of the Universal Declaration and I do not think the League's charter should be based on it.[8] I think a universal concept of human rights must come from the philosophical vision of all peoples.

I asked Rachid Ghannouchi whether he had reservations about the Universal Declaration's view that men and women were fully equal. He answered,

Well, if you really want to look at this matter carefully, you have to look at the Tunisian Personal Status Code and its effects.[9] We have asked for a reexamination of the situation of the Tunisian family and a study of the effects of this law upon the family. We need to know whether the effect has been positive or negative. We all know that there has been a great increase in divorce in recent years. Has the Tunisian family become more harmonious as a result of this law or not? If there was a full reexamination of the situation of women and of the family we would then be in a position to make specific proposals for changes.

Rachid Ghannouchi had begun to speak more concretely and, hoping he would continue in this vein, I now returned to the contentious subject of the place of non-Muslim minorities within an Islamic society – what would be their civic and religious rights, what positions would they be able to occupy in government? After all, such communities are quite numerous in certain areas of the Middle East: 10 percent of Egypt's population, for example, were Christian Copts, Palestine had an important Christian minority, and Tunisia itself still had a small Jewish community.[10]

Ghannouchi answered,

The right to live in an Islamic society, to be a national in it and to have rights, is given to everyone whether or not the person is a Muslim, even if the person has no religion. Nationalism is for everyone and each national

has equal rights and duties. If there are differences between rights of Muslims and non-Muslims these are minor and deal with the faith of the individuals and the fact that the society is based on an Islamic faith. As far as national citizens' rights are concerned, all citizens would have equal rights. All rights are equal except perhaps that some crucial posts would require a Muslim.

For example the head of state must be a Muslim because if the state is to be run on Islamic lines the head of state must defend the religion and imprint the society with the stamp of Islam. Ministers on the other hand might be non-Muslims or even without religion – for example, the minister of agriculture, of health, of art. But the minister of education, no – this must be held by a Muslim. Posts dealing with instruction, with values and morals must be held by Muslims. Other ministers can be non-Muslims. And those below the ministers can be non-Muslims. But the minister, the one responsible in these areas, must be a Muslim.

Both Naciri and Ghannouchi, each in his own way and in very general terms, had touched upon notions of identity, history, relations between the Islamic and non-Islamic worlds, and human rights, all placed within the context of a universal Islamic religious tradition the fundamental unit of which, the *'umma*, knew no national boundaries.

Yet another perspective, also phrased within a religious framework, was offered by some Tunisians who had grown disillusioned with the MTI in the late 1970s and who soon formed a loosely knit unit calling itself 'progressive Muslims'. They founded a journal at the beginning of the 1980s, called *15–21*, referring to the next century in both the Muslim and the Christian calendars.

The thinking of the 'progressive Muslims' had moved through several stages. A man who had been close to them during the first few years but had since become an independent journalist told me,

Their main starting-point was that it was necessary to distinguish between Islamic thought on the one hand and religion on the other, because Islamic thought was a human creation and therefore subject to error. This was a crucial step, because up until then the view that dominated was that this patrimony, all of it, was unquestionable.

He continued,

But as we began to study the earlier Islamic thinkers we began to see how much of what we had taken for given had in fact been subject to much discussion throughout Islamic history, and how these discussions were often not resolved satisfactorily, or were resolved just through force. For example, there were many Islamic thinkers who argued that the general interest (meslaha) took precedence over specific textual injunctions, and that the fundamental aims (maqasid) of the religion took precedence over specific textual prescriptions. For example, some said that the aim of securing justice might take precedence over cutting off a thief's hand.

Shortly after this discussion I went to talk with Hmida Naifer; he had been the second in command in the MTI before the split in 1980. At the time I spoke to him he was the editor of *15–21* and a professor in the Faculty of Theology at the University of Tunis.

Naifer began to explain how the *15–21* group's approach differed from that of the MTI.

The first differences between ourselves and the MTI emerged when we began to use the term 'Tunisian Islam'. We first said it without thinking much about it, but it took on more and more importance as time went on.

In traditional Islamic thinking, there is only one Islam. Even in our own society, today, this way of thinking – that there must be only one Islam – is seductive for that part of the population that feels it has no future. This kind of thinking leads easily to fanaticism.

But how can we develop a vision without our own history, even if this special history has only 300 to 400 years? So our big problem was how to talk about Islam while taking into consideration our particular Tunisian historical situation.

For example, look at Tunisian history: we have always had to face an external threat, whether it was from the Ottomans, the Egyptians, the West, or even now, from Libya and Algeria. Because we are a small country, because we don't want to be dominated either by the East or by the West, and because we are largely urban, our usual response to this, which is specifically Tunisian, is to see cultural change as taking precedence over the political struggle. And because another essentially Tunisian characteristic is the spirit of dialogue, and also to live in good understanding with our minorities – with the Jews and with the Christians – pluralism is a real possibility here.

Naifer had described characteristics that he thought might distinguish Tunisian Islam within a universal Islam – cultural innovation and a spirit of dialogue.

He then took this one step further.

For me what is most important in all human life is to be able to change traditions. And one of the fundamental aims of Islam, in addition to those usually cited of justice, the dignity of man, the protection of life, property, intelligence, and so on, is the aim of encouraging the creative, progressive side of man. You can see this logically if you take the Qur'anic verse that says that God creates continually, and juxtapose this with the verse about man being God's representative on earth.

Naifer's argument, strongly distinct from Naciri's and distinct, too, although to a lesser extent, from Ghannouchi's, sought to accommodate a universal religious belief system and particular national characteristics by elaborating a national Islam – thus opening the way for a new approach to the identity question. It sought, too, to reconcile the demands of a unitary system and the needs of individual creativity. As such, it was seen by some as very fertile – people in Morocco and in Egypt would on occasion point to the *15–21* group as leading the way in this area; others, even some who were in sympathy with their aims, found their approach disorienting and accused the 'progressive Muslims' of incorporating too many Western elements and questioning what was basic to Islam.

Within this general framework of discussions much intense debate was taking place, nowhere more so than in Egypt. But in order to understand these discussions in their particular setting, we must first look more closely at today's Egypt.

3 Egypt since the July revolution

TWO DEATHS

Nasser and Sadat both died in the full exercise of their leadership, but the circumstances of their deaths had little else in common. Nasser (b. 1918), his youth spent in the anti-colonial struggle against the British who had dominated Egyptian political life since the 1880s, had led his country for eighteen years when he died from a heart attack at the end of an Arab summit meeting in Cairo in September 1970. He was, at that moment, completing negotiations aimed at reconciling Yasir Arafat of the PLO and King Hussein of Jordan, whose forces had been engaged in vicious 'Black September' fighting when the King sought to evict the PLO from Jordan.

At Nasser's death, the Egyptian people expressed an intense national grief, with millions filling the streets of Cairo as the funeral procession made its way to the Rais' final resting place in the Gamal Abd al-Nasser Mosque in Heliopolis, on the outskirts of Cairo.

Anwar Sadat, born in the same year as Nasser and his early associate from the time of their first military postings in the late 1930s, was with Nasser a member of the Free Officers group that seized power in July 1952. He became president upon Nasser's death, less than a year after he had been named vice-president, and he led Egypt for eleven years until his own death in 1981. On 6 October 1981, while reviewing a military procession honoring the eighth anniversary of the Suez canal crossing that opened the October 1973 war with Israel, Sadat was killed when soldiers – members of an extremist Islamist group called *Jihad* – turned on him with grenades and machine-guns as they passed in front of the reviewing stand. Sadat and seven others were killed in the attack.

There was little public mourning at Sadat's passing, no mass demonstrations, no conspicuous outpourings of personal grief. His funeral was attended almost exclusively by foreign dignitaries and official personalities.

To understand why Egyptians responded so differently to the deaths of these two men, each of whom had marked post-colonial Egypt with a highly personal stamp, would require a sustained examination of Egyptian society over the last four decades – at least back until the Free Officers' revolution in July 1952 – and somewhat farther back as well.

But perhaps it may be more briefly encapsulated in the words of two Egyptians I met. The first, a man who had been no more than 20 years old when Nasser died and who was against much of what Nasser had done, said to me in some bewilderment,

> *For us, Nasser represented something that we could have been, although it didn't work out. But Nasser had something that we were, something that we could be, and now that he's gone we're missing it. There is something lacking, I don't know exactly what, but without him we are just not what we could be.*

And an Egyptian woman said to me, 'Sadat performed a *coup d'état* on our Egyptian identity and personality, on everything we had come to believe we were.'

Perhaps the different responses to the deaths of Nasser and Sadat were also related to the fact that in their last years, each faced serious internal threats and each met these threats in a distinctive way. After Egypt's defeat by Israel in the June 1967 war, Nasser tendered his resignation but was called back to office by popular demand. He responded by encouraging criticism and initiating a reexamination of the policies that had led to failure. Sadat, attacked from almost all quarters for his signing of the Camp David accords, for the continuing poor performance of the economy, and for unfulfilled and withdrawn promises of political liberalization, responded by tightening control and increasing repression. In early September 1981 he had more than 1,500 people of every possible political persuasion arrested, and took a number of other measures to stifle free expression; barely a month later he was assassinated.

NASSER'S EGYPT

When the Free Officers seized power in July 1952, they were responding to the defects of a system marked by decades of intrusive colonial rule, political party opportunism, and royal arbitrariness. Constantly at odds with one another, these forces, separately or in combination, had been unable to provide sustained solutions to the most pressing Egyptian problems.

The Free Officers assumed power in July 1952 with hardly a shot fired, forcing the abdication of King Farouk. Colonel Gamal Abd al-Nasser emerged as the dominant figure and when he assumed overt control as president of the country in February 1954, a long period in Egyptian history began when its political fortunes were tied largely to the policies and decisions of one man. Over the eighteen years of his rule, his name became inextricably associated with very substantial Egyptian economic and political initiatives, both nationally and internationally, and the special bond that he established with the Egyptian people is today recalled with some nostalgia, even by many who disagreed with his policies.

The new regime faced threats on many fronts already during the first year of its rule: serious labor unrest, denunciation as a military dictatorship from sections of the Communist Party, opposition from the political parties and from the Muslim Brothers, and difficulties with the Regency Council acting for the infant crown prince.[1] An Agrarian Reform Law decreed in September 1952 limited the size of landholdings and attempted to weaken the rural landowning class that had dominated Egyptian politics, but the opposition continued its attacks. The regime responded more strongly in January 1953 by banning all political parties and declaring a three-year period of transition during which the military leadership, now constituted as the Revolution Command Council (RCC), would lead the country. In June 1953 the monarchy was abolished and Egypt was declared a republic.

During the transition years, as Nasser became the undisputed leader of the RCC, serious plots and threats from the Muslim Brothers and other political groupings were uncovered, and the repressive apparatus of the state expanded its role, with many arrests during the period of Muslim Brothers, leftists, and communists.

In January 1956 a new constitution was promulgated, transforming Egypt's parliamentary system into a presidential one and making explicit that Egypt was an 'Arab nation' and that the state was dedicated to promoting social cooperation among citizens through economic planning and social welfare. Other legislation provided for universal male suffrage and for the creation of a regionally organized National Union, in which all Egyptians were to be members and which was designed to mobilize and channel popular support for the regime. The National Union was to screen and select nominees for election to the National Assembly. In June 1956 Nasser was elected president.

This began what one Egyptian commentator called the 'populist' phase of Nasser's rule, a period from 1956 to 1962 of 'national construction and economic development, out of which would evolve a new socialist, democratic and cooperative society' (Dessouki 1983: 10). Yet during this period a number of developments on the national and international level were to direct Egyptian attention away from internal problems.

During late 1955 and early 1956 Egypt was seeking massive loans from the World Bank to finance construction of the Aswan Dam, a project that had come to symbolize the Egyptian government's efforts to develop economically and 'modernize'. The US and Great Britain had promised to provide substantial supplementary financial support. However, in mid-July, after Egypt had displayed increasing independence in international affairs – participating in the Bandung Conference of Afro-Asian states in 1955, securing arms agreements with Czechoslovakia, and recognizing the People's Republic of China in May 1956 – both the US and Britain withdrew their offers, and the World Bank did the same shortly thereafter. To make matters worse, the offer was withdrawn while Nasser was attending a conference with leaders of the non-aligned states.

On 26 July 1956 Nasser responded by nationalizing the Suez Canal. The Israelis, encouraged by Great Britain and France, moved into the Egyptian Sinai in late October, the British and French landed forces at Port Said, and Egyptian territory was bombarded. With both the US and the Soviet Union encouraging a cease-fire, hostilities ceased in early November, and British and French forces withdrew towards the end of December, with the Canal indisputably in Egyptian control.

Egypt's victory in the Suez affair added to Nasser's already growing international stature and assured him the status of a preeminent world leader. Among his other significant international initiatives was the formation in 1958 of the United Arab Republic, a union between Egypt, Syria, and Yemen, by which Nasser gave concrete effect to the regional longing to transcend the limits of the narrow nation-state. From then on Nasser was closely identified in the public mind with pan-Arab aspirations.[2]

The dominant economic priorities during the first years of Nasser's rule consisted of major infrastructural and large-scale industrial development. But by the early 1960s neither the economic projects nor the National Union had fulfilled hopes of increasing national wealth or building and mobilizing national spirit, respectively. In his early years Nasser had not discouraged private sector and foreign capital involvement in the development of the economy but by the early 1960s the private sector had not satisfied expectations and Nasser had come to believe that his economic goals and those of big capital were incompatible. 'Socialist' laws were enacted, including those that guaranteed civil service or public sector employment to all graduates of universities and technical institutes, and a number of nationalizations took place. Through these measures much of the economy – with the exception of private cultivators, small retail and service firms, and manufacturing firms of fewer than ten persons – came under state control. To encourage more active popular participation in national life, the Arab Socialist Union (ASU) replaced the National Union, and was designed to combine a vanguard with a mass base, melt class differences, mobilize the dispossessed against reactionary enemies, act as a counterweight to the armed forces, and carry Egypt's social experiment to other Arab countries.[3]

These measures provided no immediate relief from Egypt's problems and by the mid-1960s Egypt's predicament had become acute. Opposition movements, particularly the Muslim Brothers, were also posing serious threats to the stability of the regime and Nasser responded, in some cases preemptively, by arresting many of its members and executing one of its leading figures, Sayyid Qutb, in 1966.

These internal problems were at first dwarfed and then magnified by Egypt's defeat in the June 1967 war with Israel in which, among other losses, the Sinai fell into Israeli hands, thus depriving Egypt of one-half of its oil production.

On 9 June, immediately following this defeat, Nasser resigned from the presidency. Egyptians took to the streets to demand his return but even after he did so, discontent over conditions in Egypt and demonstrations continued during the next few years. In March 1968 he issued a manifesto, 'Mandate for Change', that proclaimed his intention to rid the regime of corruption, liberalize the political system, rebuild the country's defenses, and revitalize the Arab Socialist Union. The last years of Nasser's rule were marked by much soul-searching among Egyptian intellectuals, a questioning of long-cherished assumptions about Arab unity, socialism, and other large ideological systems all encouraged by Nasser himself.

Nasser also began to widen his search for financial support: he began to show a more accommodating face to the Arab leaders of the more conservative states of Saudi Arabia, Kuwait, and the Gulf states and, although still heavily dependent on Soviet military aid, Nasser had already begun to make some tentative overtures to the West before his death.

However one may evaluate Nasser's other achievements, he was certainly the figure most responsible for carrying Egypt out of a colonial period during which its notions of itself had become confused and chaotic, into an era strongly marked by clear leadership, will, direction, and meaning. Egypt during his rule was transformed from a country in which wealth was very unequally distributed to one that had become, by Third World standards, relatively egalitarian. The cost of this was inefficiency in public sector production, the stimulation of consumption rather than production, and the growth of a highly repressive security apparatus. But, judging from the popular response to Nasser during his time and the longing that many Egyptians express today for a leader of

Nasser's stature, this was a price most Egyptians were then willing to pay and that some would still be willing to pay now.

EGYPT UNDER SADAT

In his first years as president Sadat gave frequent lip service to Nasser's qualities as a leader, but he none the less moved relatively quickly to distinguish himself from Nasser, beginning early on to replace Nasser's personnel, arrest opponents, and redirect policy as part of the 'revolution of rectification' he announced in May 1971.

Sadat moved on several fronts to dismantle Nasser's legacy and establish his own stamp on Egyptian public life. Soviet experts were expelled in the summer of 1972 (although a major arms deal was concluded with them in early 1973); by the early 1970s Sadat also began to move closer to an alliance with Saudi Arabia and the other wealthy states of the Gulf. These measures prepared the way for Sadat's surprise attack on Israel when the Egyptian army crossed the Suez Canal to open the October 1973 war. Although not an unqualified military success, Egypt succeeded in puncturing the image of invulnerability that Israel had gained over the years. The war initiated the diplomatic maneuvering that eventually led to Sadat's visit to Jerusalem in November 1977, the signing of the Camp David accords in March 1979, and Egypt's recovery of the Sinai.

On the economic front, Sadat began to remove many of the restrictions on the private sector and on foreign capital investment that had been imposed during Nasser's rule. Sadat's 'open-door' policy *(infitah)* aimed to encourage a free market economy, attract foreign capital, revitalize the public sector by promoting keen competition from an enlarged private sector, and stimulate a rapid transfer of technology.[4]

From 1975 to early 1977 (particularly the second half of 1976) Sadat experimented with significant liberalization of the political system. Various tendencies had always existed within the ASU and after the 1973 war these tendencies began to push for a pluralistic system. In March 1976 these were allowed to emerge as distinct 'platforms': Rightists, Leftists, Nasserists, and Centrists. After the parliamentary elections of October 1976 in which the Centrists, clearly aligned with the president, won 280 of 352 seats, Sadat decided in early January 1977 to allow the establishment of true political parties.

However, Egypt's economic problems during this period remained acute and, requiring major foreign capital assistance, Egypt had to agree to a number of austerity measures recommended by the international lending community. Among these measures, the removal of subsidies on basic foodstuffs was postponed until after the elections of October 1976. On 18 January 1977 the Prime Minister announced to parliament price increases on a number of consumer goods, including sugar, flour, macaroni, rice, and butagaz.

The next day, rioting broke out up and down the Nile Valley, especially in Cairo and Alexandria – shops were looted, police precincts attacked, officials harassed. Police and army response was violent: according to official figures, seventy-seven people were killed in Cairo alone and many arrests were made, particularly among the left.

This signalled the end of Sadat's liberalization policy. Although political parties were shortly thereafter legalized for the first time since 1953, the 1977 law enabling this was very restrictive, and new political formations faced official harassment and obstructions on many levels. Sadat formed his own political party, the National Democratic Party (NDP) in July 1978 (with which the ASU was merged), and encouraged formation of an official opposition party, the Socialist Labor Party. How.. .., Sadat's rule took on an increasingly authoritarian cast, manipulating multipoint referenda, a docile parliament, and the state-controlled mass media and local civil servants to secure predictable voting support.[5]

As the 1970s came to an end, the social, economic, and political situation continued to worsen. The signing of the Camp David accords in March 1979, the accusations from within Egypt and from the rest of the Arab world that these accords abandoned Palestinian national rights, the breaking of relations with Egypt by most Arab states and the resultant exclusion of Egypt from the Arab League, all gave a broad-based opposition to Sadat a clear and emotive focus for its hostility.

In addition to attacks from the Socialist Labor Party, which had refused to fill the role of docile opposition for which Sadat had cast it, and from seventy prominent Egyptian intellectuals representing a broad spectrum of opinion who, in May and June 1980, signed a declaration condemning Sadat's rule by referendum and the peace treaty with Israel, Sadat also faced growing opposition from Islamic groups.

This was something of an irony, for throughout much of the 1970s, Sadat had given substantial support to these groups in his struggles with the left, and had also sought to enhance his stature among the wider population by strongly publicizing his piety and deep religious belief. But this was to little avail as radical Islamist groups gained in power and stepped up their attacks, both verbal and physical, on the regime. By late 1979 and early 1980 many arrests of members of such groups had been made following a number of bombings in which they were suspected to have had a hand. Sectarian violence had also broken out between Copts and Muslims on several occasions, most notably at Zawiyat al-Hamra, outside Cairo, and Sadat was coming to believe that there was an extensive religious conspiracy against him.

Although in 1980 Sadat attempted to blunt religious opposition by introducing a consultative council *(shura)* – a concept that has deep roots in Islamic history and doctrine – and he introduced at about the same time a 'Law of Shame' that made criticism of divine teaching or of the regime a crime to be judged by a special 'Court of Values', these measures were unsuccessful and succeeded only in attracting and sharpening criticism.[6]

When Sadat finally moved against his opponents, he appeared to have lost the power to discriminate between real and symbolic threats to his power. On 5 September 1981 he arrested more than 1,500 people of all political persuasions and then closed down a number of political publications, withdrew recognition of the Coptic Pope, and banned the activities of a number of Muslim and Coptic associations. Ten days later he expelled the Soviet ambassador and more than 1,000 Soviet technicians. Less than a month later he was killed, and few people in Egypt mourned him.

EGYPT AND MUBARAK

Hosni Mubarak succeeded to the presidency, as did Sadat, from the position of vice-president, to which Sadat had appointed him in 1975 at the age of 47. Unlike Sadat, he was not a member of the Free Officers but was a professional soldier nonetheless, trained in the air force (with advanced training in the USSR) and highly praised for his role as chief of staff of the air force during the 1973 war with Israel. Although little known to the public at large at the time of his accession, he had carried out many important tasks during his vice-presidency: delicate diplomatic missions to other Arab states, to Africa, Europe, and the US; supervision of the day-to-day affairs of the presidency and the cabinet; heading the NDP and the Supreme National Security Council.

In less than a decade of rule, Mubarak has so far achieved a number of important milestones in a style much less flamboyant than his predecessors. While never renouncing the Camp David accords, he has been sufficiently cool in supporting them to have won Egypt's reentry to most Arab institutions, culminating in 1989 in Egypt's formal reinstatement in the Arab League which, in early 1990, agreed to return its headquarters to Cairo from Tunis. Relations with Syria were reestablished at the end of 1989 after a hiatus of twelve years following Sadat's visit to Jerusalem, and in early 1990 Mubarak made the first visit by an Egyptian president to Syria since 1977. Although relations have not yet been reestablished between Egypt and Libya, Qadhdhafi and Mubarak began a series of summit meetings in May 1989 that have led to a number of substantive accords. Mubarak's increased international profile was also evident when Egypt secured the presidency of the Organization of African Unity in 1989 and when, in the second half of 1989, Mubarak began to assume a more active role in attempting to break the Israeli–Palestinian deadlock.

Internally the parliamentary elections of both 1984 and 1987 were perhaps the most democratic in recent Egyptian history with non-governmental parties obtaining 139 of 448 seats (of these seats an alliance between the tolerated but still illegal Muslim Brothers (36) and a coalition of the Socialist Labor and Liberal parties (56) gained 92 seats, and the Wafd gained 35).[7] The advances made by the Muslim Brothers, who increased their total substantially from the eight seats they had won in the 1984 elections, was indicative of the continuing, even growing, power of religious sentiment as a political force, and Mubarak's period of rule has been marked by continued agitation in this sector, along with many arrests and accusations of torture.

The most serious social unrest during Mubarak's rule was the mutiny in Cairo in early 1986 of some 20,000 conscripts of the Central Security Forces – whose tasks include guarding many official buildings and other significant landmarks – during which they rampaged through sections of Cairo and its outskirts, attacking luxury hotels and other symbols of wealth and prestige. Although certainly fueled by Islamist sentiment, another root cause was the continuing failure of the Egyptian government to find even temporary, to say nothing of lasting, solutions to Egypt's economic problems. Strikes in the industrial sector, often met by strong police and army responses, have also been a hallmark of Mubarak's rule, and in 1988 state of emergency regulations (in effect almost continuously since 1967 and uninterruptedly since the assassination of Sadat) were renewed for another three years.

As Mubarak's rule nears the end of its first decade, Egypt's fundamental economic problems remain. The rate of population growth has been, if anything, increasing: from 33 million in 1976, Egypt's population had reached 54 million by 1988 (with the population of greater Cairo having grown in the same period from 7 million to more than 13 million), and it was estimated that it would pass beyond 75 million by the end of the century. Agricultural production continues to lag behind population growth, and although wheat production has recently been improving, Egypt continues to be dependent on imports for 60–70 percent of its wheat needs.

Receipts from tourism have recently been rising, but oil income has remained roughly constant and foreign remittances are down. These factors, and the inability of Egypt to reduce its balance of payments deficit means that Egypt continues to be heavily dependent on foreign loans. As a result, Egypt finds itself perennially in a debt repayment crisis and precariously balanced between the demands being made by lending agencies and the need to avoid a serious social crisis and a repeat of a popular explosion of the sort that occurred in January 1977.

4   Egyptian voices

'HUMAN RIGHTS IS JUST A BY-PRODUCT'

One of the people I met early in my visits to Egypt who outlined the human rights issues for me from a historical perspective was the sociologist Sayed Yassin, director of the al-Ahram Institute.

Yassin began by asking me a number of questions about the state of American social science. He followed closely what he called 'radical social science' and he wanted to know whether I noticed any new trends in this field. He had just written an article that promoted the idea of a social science with an Arab identity and he gave me a copy, asking for my comments.[1]

When I asked Yassin about the role of human rights in Egypt, he wanted to talk first about what he saw as capitalism's fundamental contradiction and, perhaps for my benefit, he placed this in the context of European history.

> *Bismarck, you know, was the first in Europe to see that you had to give the working class a bit of the cake. You know, at that time, he was faced with a very active communist movement. When he issued his well-known social laws giving some rights to the workers, he succeeded in breaking the workers' movement into two halves, one that wanted to back the laws and one that felt Bismarck was sabotaging the coming revolution. So this was the first time a European politician perceived the basic problem of European capitalism: you cannot keep the wealth in the hands of the few and give the mass of workers nothing but some words about political freedom. This attempt to balance economic rights and political rights was the result of the development of European capitalism, and eventually led to the idea of the welfare state, which of course is not without its own problems. But the start was made by Bismarck.*
>
> *Now for us in Egypt, in the period from 1945 to 1952, what we may call the* ancien régime *faced the same problem, what we call the social question – the immense gap between the rich and the poor. The* ancien

régime failed to bridge this gap, showing the failure of the bourgeois classes in Egypt to see the importance of balancing democracy, politically speaking, with the economic and social rights of citizens – a balance Europe has more or less succeeded in achieving.

After the army and then Nasser came to power, the new government responded by trying to satisfy the basic needs of the people, by giving the people basic economic and social rights. And in order to express the various interests of the population and not simply to reflect the political face of capitalism, Nasser adopted the concept of 'social democracy' – meaning economic and social rights, and political freedom practiced through the unique party.

So you can see that the notion of rights began to be debated in a specific context, a revolutionary context, and there was not so much respect for traditional political rights – there was more emphasis during this period on economic and social rights. But I think you have to be fair here: the revolution was indeed faced with a lot of resistance from opposing groups – the Communists on the one hand and the Muslim Brothers on the other. It is very normal for revolutionary governments not to obey the traditional rules of human rights when dealing with opponents. Speaking politically, I can well understand a revolution arresting its opponents – if there is a threatened coup d'état prepared to overthrow the new regime, what else can you do as a political authority? But torturing them is another matter altogether, that is something different and must be condemned.

How did Nasser articulate the notion of human rights, of democracy?

Nasser called his concept of democracy 'social democracy' and its key element was the idea of the unique party. The unique party was to unite all the active categories of the population – soldiers, intellectuals, workers, and peasants. Nasser refused the idea of political pluralism – he said this was related to the capitalistic system – and he was right. Of course, nowadays the people here do not understand clearly the relationship between political pluralism and capitalism.

I asked him if he could spell out this relationship.

It is well known historically that pluralism – what is called 'western democracy' or simply 'democracy' – is the political face of capitalism, pure and simple. This is an historical fact, not an explanation – by that I mean that Western democracy does not explain capitalism, because it is capitalism that emerged first. Economic liberalism began in Europe much before political liberalism. It was only much after economic liberalism was in place that the idea of 'one man, one vote' took hold, and this was only as a result of the struggle of the workers. But even when it took hold, it really only gave the masses the illusion, the feeling of participating in the whole process. Of course, real decision-making power is not a *prerogative of the masses at all in that system, but is much more directly related to economic power. And that is why here, in Egypt, we see the idea of 'democracy' as related to this European or Western context, and we see it as the other face of economic liberalism.*

I wondered what he thought were the main ideological trends in Egypt, and how these were related to human rights.

Well, you can speak about three visions of the world, three world outlooks: you have the liberal outlook, the radical outlook, the conservative outlook. Each outlook has its ideological and organizational reflection in our social system. The Wafd and the Nationalist parties adopt a liberal outlook, the Muslim groups adopt a conservative outlook, and one political party – the National Progressive Unionist party – adopts a radical outlook.

Each of these currents of thought will focus upon a certain aspect of human rights: the liberal will focus on political rights, not on economic and social rights; the radical will focus on both at this moment, but more emphatically on economic and social rights; the conservative will focus on political freedom because they need to be recognized as a legitimate political force in this country, but they will address economic and social rights only in a very vague way. This is a basic ideological struggle here now.

But this is not simply an ideological struggle because many of the superficial differences between groups in fact grow out of a more profound difference – a different idea of our identity as Egyptians. If I can borrow an idea from Michel Foucault, the French philosopher, you have to use an 'archeological' approach and ask: what are the ideas, the concepts, that these struggles are built upon? Underneath the superficial aspects of the struggle you will find certain models of society in the minds of these people. For example, the Islamic group will say, 'Well, we are a Muslim society, and as Muslims we have our own concept of human rights, a concept that bypasses the Western concept. So, why should we adopt the Western concept?'

So you see, there is a basic conflict of ideas in the country, between secularists and the call for modernization and modernity on the one hand, and the Muslim Brothers and Islamic groups and the call for authenticity on the other. As this conflict goes on, a lot of Egyptian intellectuals are revising their own initial ideas.

In addition to his brief historical outline, Sayed Yassin had raised other important issues: the relationship to Egyptian (and some might say broader Middle Eastern) realities of notions developed primarily in the Western European context, and whether one of those concepts, 'democracy', was likely to grow deep roots in Egyptian society. Both of these issues also touched upon the notion of Egypt's 'identity'.

I later raised some of these subjects with Muhammad Sid Ahmed, a well-known Egyptian journalist and a leading figure of the leftist National Progressive Unionist party. Our discussion moved quickly from democracy to another notion tainted by association with the West, that of 'human rights'. Muhammad Sid Ahmed placed his observations in the context of the history of Egypt since the 1952 revolution.

> *You know, Nasser made a distinction that was to become quite famous, between social liberation or emancipation (al-ḥurriya al-igtimaᶜiyya) on the one hand, and individual social and political freedoms (al-ḥurriya al-siyassiyya) on the other. What he really meant by this was that the rights of individuals as such were illusory in countries like ours, because in real terms these were only the rights of the elites, of certain privileged classes. This means a kind of Athenian or Spartan democracy of the few, the very few, while the masses of people have none of these benefits.*
>
> *So the July revolution was seen as a great step forward, as an effort to widen the range of people who would enjoy human rights. But this idea meant improving the human rights of the community, even if the individual's rights had to suffer as a result. This had many positive aspects in so far as it promoted social welfare, social emancipation. But one of the problems was that the argument of social progress could be used to justify anything, and in particular to justify the repression of all opposition. There is a growing awareness throughout the Arab world, and particularly in Egypt, that this was a main defect of the liberation movement, this neglect of human rights.*

How had the situation changed after the death of Nasser?

> *After Nasser's death in 1970, Sadat came to power and very quickly began to use the negative aspects of Nasser's legacy – the repressive techniques he had built up – in order to unseat the Nasserite group. It was only then that he began to bring up the issue of human rights and democracy, and then only to neutralize forces that normally would have been in opposition to him.*
>
> *Since Sadat's assassination, Mubarak has succeeded in reducing some of the tension that marked the Sadat years. But, in the area of human rights, you have the same problems. What Mubarak has done is to remove some of the heat, but his game has been to neutralize the various constituencies by what I call 'reciprocal neutralization': he has given some freedom to the opposition in order to hit at the Sadat establishment, but yet the ultras of the Sadat period are still allowed to keep some positions of state power so they can act to neutralize the opposition.*
>
> *So here you see that again, human rights is not part of the basic government program; human rights is just a by-product of the game of reciprocal neutralization.*

Were there any major differences between Sadat's approach to human rights and democracy and Mubarak's?

In some ways the game played by Mubarak has gone farther than the game played by Sadat. Sadat's game was basically, 'I want political parties so that they will contain the opposition forces, not so they will unleash them. My brand of pluralism aims to orchestrate, manipulate, contain, and is not to go beyond that. I will only accept parties as long as the pluralism benefits me and is not detrimental to me.' This was Sadat's game.

Mubarak is more tolerant in this area, because it has been proved that playing the game Sadat's way was counterproductive and brought about his assassination. So Mubarak allows more leeway: he has permitted the build-up of recognized, legitimate parties and even some non-recognized, more or less tolerated parties.

Of course, with the Communists, the threat of arrests and trials is held over them like the sword of Damocles. But the only people who are very harshly treated and tortured – and with more torture than took place in the days of Nasser, and much worse than under Sadat, because under Sadat torture had decreased – are those who carry arms. And this applies both to people on the extreme left accused of carrying arms, as well as those on the fanatic religious right. So the boundaries have been shifted: there is tolerance of legitimate parties and even of unlegalized parties – but of course with some strings attached to their operations.

It is the same with human rights: there is improvement and deterioration simultaneously. There is improvement insofar as there is a more liberal approach to opposition, as long as you do not resort to bearing arms against the regime. But if you do, then there is deterioration – there are many cases of torture of members of extreme leftist groups, of Muslim Brothers, of Islamic fundamentalists.

What Muhammad Sid Ahmed seemed to be saying was that issues like human rights and democracy were not fundamental building blocks upon which the Egyptian political system was being constructed, but were instead secondary effects of the interplay of social and political forces. When I suggested this, Muhammad Sid Ahmed answered,

Yes, that's true. But there is another dimension to the human rights question beyond the idea of what these freedoms are and how they are expressed: there is the problem of identity. Human rights is an expression of identity, of self, and here there is a great crisis.

First of all, identity has gone through so many upheavals in so short a time: are we socialist or capitalist? Are we pan-Arab or Egyptian? Are we pro-Israeli or pro-Arab? Are we part of the Islamic circle or the African circle or the Arab circle? All these problems are not settled. So there is an identity crisis. No one knows who he is, and the more you don't know this, the more the identity issue becomes overwhelming.

And this colors the human rights problem. There is frustration, and a feeling that the West has taken over this issue. This is felt about the peace movement too, because the peace process is identified with Sadat's turn toward the West. And the extreme reaction in the other direction is to go back to your roots, to your Islamic roots, leading to the upsurge of radical Islam.

So the identity problem is crucial for human rights. Because first of all, when you start to look for a definition of human rights, you are seeking to identify your identity. But which identity? Is it a liberal, modern identity? Then you'll have one definition of human rights. Is it a socialist modern identity? That gives you another set of values for human rights. Is it an Islamic identity? That has totally different implications for human rights.

With all the discussion about human rights and all the organizational activity on this and related issues that had been taking place over the last few years, I wondered whether Muhammad Sid Ahmed thought this was a passing fashion or an aspect that would remain central to Egypt for the foreseeable future.

The human rights question is now the subject of very strong debate and I think it will become more and more so in the future – I see it as becoming a central problem, because human rights is very much linked to the question of whether we will have an even, steady transition or a cataclysmic one. Everybody feels that change is indispensable, everybody feels that things around us are disintegrating. The question is how change is going to occur and in what direction.

The protection of human rights would provide a basic and indispensable ingredient in the face of a disintegrating system, here and elsewhere in the Arab world. One way to avoid the disintegration becoming too chaotic and too threatening is to get some consensus. For consensus to come about it is important to guarantee some freedom of expression, some human rights. And this consensus has to include an agreement that there will be some kind of pluralism, some tolerance for others with whom you do not agree.

Did he think, I wondered, that the forces promoting such a consensus on human rights, on pluralism, were strong enough to ensure a relatively peaceful transition? 'No', he answered,

I do not think the transition will be quiet. I do not think that the forces able to keep it quiet have the upper hand. I think that the forces that might erupt on the scene in an uncontrolled manner are more likely to take over than those that would keep the change under control. Here the religious right has to be kept in mind.

You have to bear in mind that the Islamic groups are setting up other values for human rights, values that are in opposition to those brought up

with liberal political and secular ideas. Secularism is a key issue – secularism is opposed by the Islamic groups who see it as a violation of their right to community. This has put secular people on the defensive. And because the political parties have the problem of trying to gain the support of the Islamic groups, they deemphasize issues that would anger the Islamic groups. Even a left politician has to be careful about what he says and how far he can go.

I had heard the left frequently criticized by committed secularists for its lack of principle in trying to gain the support of religious groups, and it was likely that Muhammad Sid Ahmed, as an articulate spokesman on the left, had his own predicament in mind. I asked Muhammad Sid Ahmed how he now saw the relative strength of what he had termed 'the religious right' and secular forces?

What is happening right now is that there has been a very violent verbal and symbolic offensive by the Islamic groups. They imagine that everything is conspiratorial. There is nothing more damaging for human rights than a conspiratorial attitude, an attitude that reached its summum in the terror of the French Revolution. You look upon everything that is not in line with your own thinking as a conspiracy against you and you end up attributing objective social phenomena to a subjective conspiracy.

Now, there has been a strong reaction to this offensive on the part of many people including not only committed secularists but also strong and devout Muslims who have not wanted to swallow what the Islamic groups are trying to make people swallow. Of course, just because there is a strong reaction doesn't mean that the offensive is no longer there.

Between them, Sayed Yassin and Muhammad Sid Ahmed had talked at length about the problems of the contemporary Egyptian political system, and the strains in the notions of democracy and human rights. They had also alluded to other issues that seemed inextricably linked to these: the question of identity and a people's sense of its own history and, related to this, religion and the secular nature of the state.

'ENEMIES BECAME FRIENDS, FRIENDS ENEMIES', AND 'EVERYBODY BEGAN TO TALK ISLAM'

In many of my talks with people over the next few years, I sought to get a better perspective on these issues. The theme of identity came up again and again, once quite explicitly by Latifa Zayyat, a woman who had been imprisoned during the Sadat period but who, since her release, had come to head a 'Committee for the Defense of Egyptian Identity'. Latifa Zayyat seemed to be her mid- to late fifties. She was somewhat hesitant at the outset but soon warmed to her subject.

She began by saying that in thinking about the question of Egyptian identity we had to begin by recognizing the upheaval brought about by Camp David and Sadat's trip to Jerusalem. She went on,

> My generation and later generations were brought up to believe we were Arabs. But suddenly, under Sadat, we were being told we were not Arabs at all! Suddenly we were being denied our identity, we were being told, 'We are descendants of ancient Egyptian culture, our Arab essence is not important'. Sadat was saying, 'We Egyptians are the masters of the Arabs'; to me, this was almost reminiscent of Hitler. And then, suddenly, alliances changed: enemies became friends, friends enemies. So, this man was saying to us, 'You are to join the camp of civilization, you are to leave behind the primitive character of the Arabs and the undeveloped world. And you have to change alliances: break with the Soviet Union, and join with Israel and with the US.'
>
> Under these conditions your conception of self has to change radically. The younger generation had learned, for example, that the US was a force for imperialism – and even I, who am a bit older, well, I witnessed Hiroshima. But then Sadat, to support his sudden change of direction, had certain expressions, a certain vocabulary, officially prohibited in the newspapers, on television and radio – terms such as 'zionism', 'imperialism', 'Arab nationalism'.
>
> So, we were required to go against our own history, against our conceptions of what had made progress possible during modern Egyptian history since the French occupation.[2] This history, as we saw it, was based on struggle against occupation and on our fight for economic and social independence, our fight to establish our own industry and our own economy. If you look at our literature, our poetry, our sociology – in all branches of knowledge the core is this perpetual struggle for liberation against foreign domination.
>
> So Sadat was just taking the ground out from under us: we were obliged not only to deny our present but also to deny our past.
>
> Now all this was made palatable to many Egyptians by promises of prosperity at a moment when the Egyptian people were in a very bad state, when there were people here who were really and truly starving. The promises were that the new alliances would mean food and prosperity, and that less of our money would have to go for war. But this failed drastically, and it was this failure that exposed Sadat's vision as ideological propaganda, as totally false. Only the fulfillment of economic promises would have saved Sadat's vision. When people are starving, you can push them to abandon almost everything.

How had this situation changed under Mubarak?

> Well, Mubarak had no choice but to change these things, but he changed them only mildly, of course, because there were many commitments. But

at least we could return to being Arab. Because one of the things that doomed Sadat's policy to failure was his rejection of our Arabness, and the Arab rejection of us after Camp David. So, Mubarak had to change this.

At least he changed the tone. We aren't told anymore that we aren't Arabs. And in his own way, he is trying to improve relations with other Arab countries. And within the limits of his commitments he is doing this. Of course, at times he emphasizes Egyptian nationalism, especially when we are rebuffed by other Arab states. But you know, Egyptians are loved by other Arabs, even if at times they resent us. And it's not because we are better than they are, but because historically we are at a higher stage of development, and because of our geographic situation.

Latifa Zayyat then drew a clear relationship between these dilemmas of identity and the resurgence of religious movements.

You know, it is only by going back to the notion of identity that you can understand the growth of the religious movements. All through the history of modern Egypt, and during the Nasser period, we've had our feeling of identity and of belonging: to our country, to the Arab nation, to the larger identity of the Islamic 'umma. And it is only when you lose your national identity that you seek a new one.

So now there are two main groups seeking their identity in a religious construction. You have, on the one hand, the commercial bourgeoisie who are using religion for commercial purposes and who represent a very influential sector, with the support of Saudi Arabia and possibly even of the US, although on that I'm not sure. This bourgeoisie is a reservoir of support for the regime. And on the other hand you have the fundamentalists, mostly young, from the lower middle class, artisans, students, villagers. With national identity having broken down, they are seeking in religion a new identity, and using religious identity to protest against a disintegrating society, rejecting the values and the corruption of this society.

Part of the quest for identity involved an effort to distinguish one's own community and civilization from others. How would Latifa Zayyat characterize efforts in this direction? In particular, what were the various attitudes towards the West?

Well, on one hand we have people who say, 'We have our identity, anything foreign is alien to this, we have to keep this identity to be able to develop our society. We should not follow either socialism or capitalism but should depend on our own religion to guide us.' Within this group we have some enlightened people but we also have more extreme groups like the fundamentalists.

Then there is the group that believes absolutely in the interchange of ideas between our country and other countries, particularly with Europe, but who fail to see the significance of imperialism – that Egypt is a dependent country unable to make free choices in both internal and external matters. They tend to believe that Europe is the seat of civilization and that imitation of Europe is always a step forward. They mostly were part of our Egyptian renaissance in the 1920s and were educated in France. These people have always propounded the thesis that Egyptians are Mediterraneans, and not Arabs.

And finally there are those who are mainly oriented against imperialism and zionism, who accept the need for interchange between cultures and civilizations provided we have some power to choose what we think is good and reject what we think is bad. These people are mostly of socialist persuasion – I number myself among them – and I suppose this group, opposed as it is to a system based on religious authority, emerged as a reaction to the first group. Most of us believe that there are only two great traditions in the world today, the capitalist and the socialist. Within these traditions every nation has to develop its own special path and character. Take Nasser as an example: he was a socialist, not a follower of the Soviet Union, but his genius was that he was a great Egyptian, and his socialism was empirical. Egyptians responded in a very special way to Nasser and the Egyptian street is a Nasserite street, although it may not always recognize itself as such.

Another Egyptian woman I talked to who was also concerned about pressures that might lead the Egyptian state to become a religious rather than a secular one was Nadia Ramses Farah, a professor of economics at the American University in Cairo and author of a recent book on relations between Muslims and Copts.[3] The secular/religious issue is a sensitive one in many Middle Eastern countries, and perhaps even more so in Egypt where more than 10 percent of the population, or approximately 6 million people, are not Muslims but Copts and where the power of the Islamic religious movements had discouraged many people from addressing this issue head-on. Nadia Ramses Farah was herself a Copt.

The question of secularism was, of course, tied directly to Egyptian notions of identity, and Nadia began by historically situating these two issues, focusing on the emergence of religion as an explicit political force.

To really understand what is happening, we have to put it in context. I think that during the Nasser period, especially in the 1960s, almost everybody agreed on one dominant ideology – Arab socialism.[4] This was a consensus, in part imposed by the state, but accepted by Egyptians because, among other things, it implied Egypt's leadership of the Arab world.

However, in 1967, after the war with Israel, this consensus collapsed and other viewpoints began to be heard, of which the strongest was the religious. After Nasser died in 1970, Sadat supported the religious forces in order to cut Nasser's social base and to create something to replace the Nasserist identity. By the way, I prefer to call it a Nasserist identity because it is so particular to Nasser – people accepted Nasser's ideology because of Nasser himself and perhaps they would have accepted it from no one else.

To compete with Nasserism, the new regime had to create a new consciousness. Sadat was not a figure charismatic enough to build an ideology on, so he made alliances with the groups that had been repressed by Nasser: mostly, the Communists on one side – he appointed a number of Marxists as ministers – and the Muslim Brothers on the other – he made agreements with Saudi Arabia, pardoning the Muslim Brothers who had left Egypt and allowing them to return.

But the real alliance that was forged was between Sadat and the Islamic groups and he began to give a free hand to the Muslim Brothers. He started to use Islam as the new ideology, the new ideology that would legitimize him and would crush the more secular Nasserism. As Sadat was forging this new identity based on Islam, he was also emphasizing Egyptian as distinct from Arab nationalism – and Islam plus Egyptian nationalism is a tandem that has a long history in Egyptian politics.[5]

The Islamic groups in the universities began to get a lot of support from the state – money, and even arms some people say; and the leftist groups were being harassed, put in jail, and were growing weaker. Of course, if you have the state supporting one group against another, well, that second group just doesn't have a chance.

At the same time, by the mid-1970s, labor migration to the Gulf and Saudi Arabia was increasing rapidly and this contributed substantially to the Islamic trend: the Saudis were providing financing for the Islamic laws, for scholarships to students, for writers to write, for intellectuals to be 'Islamic' thinkers. Saudi Arabia has always been very, very interested in preventing another Nasser from coming to power in Egypt. For them, Nasser was a worse fact than Israel, they do not bother about Israel. Nasser was really the big scare, so they're always pouring money into Egypt to prevent something like that happening again. And that coincided with the interests of the Egyptian state at the time.

The religious ideas weren't used only to legitimize the state, but were also used to gain the support of the poor. People who were very poor and who had the opportunity to migrate to Saudi or the Gulf were told that secularism and Arab socialism meant you would no longer be able to migrate and that the doors to the outside would be closed as they had been during the Nasser period. So, strong vested economic interests were promoting religion: Islam and private property, Islam and economic opportunity. The only way to attack all the Nasser achievements on labor rights and the development of the public sector was to attack public and state property and works, and this was done systematically during the Sadat period.

All this worked together to create a dominant ideology, a religious ideology. Everybody began to talk Islam, it became the priority on the agenda. The choice we faced was now no longer between Egyptian nationalism or Arab nationalism – the real battle was whether Egypt was going to be an Islamic state or a secular one.

However, the honeymoon between the state and the Islamic groups started to disintegrate, especially after the January 1977 food riots. January 1977 was the turning point, because for the first time the state seemed weak; the Islamic groups moved to the attack because they thought they had a chance to take over the state. But they underestimated the real strength of the military and the police.

Sadat at first tried to accommodate the Islamic groups because he didn't want to lose their support. But as the groups stepped up their attacks, Sadat had to react. Finally, he put everybody in jail. But that was his deadly mistake. Usually you play one group against the other, but this time he lost patience and put everybody in jail. This made the Islamic groups even more powerful. They became public heroes. And what made them even more credible was the credit they got for the assassination.

How was this situation developing under Mubarak?

Mubarak is stressing Egyptian nationalism more than religion. If you follow his speeches or pay attention to the television, you can now see more and more about our Egyptian identity, our culture from pharaonic times to now. What I feel is that there is now a mounting trend of Egyptian nationalism and that discussion about our identity is now more open. This does not mean that Islam as a basic element of identity is going to disappear, but I think it is good to have a situation that is not as monolithic as before.

At the same time there is also a very broad consensus, even among the Muslim Brothers, on democracy – because otherwise they are threatened. But also, associations such as the human rights and women's organizations, which have only recently emerged, have pushed the discussion farther: the consensus about democracy has now been pushed so that the secular trend has reemerged. Before, perhaps, they were talking about secularism but were using the term 'democracy' as a way to do this; now the issue of secularism is beginning to be addressed directly.

Were Egypt to lose its secular character and become a religious state, this would certainly mean a closer application of Islamic law. And it might mean, as well, a drastic recasting of the role of non-Muslim minorities in society. I recalled what Rachid Ghannouchi had said to me in Tunisia about the limited role that would be allowed to non-Muslims in an Islamic society as he conceived it. I asked Nadia how she thought this might develop in Egypt.

Well, whatever the Muslim Brothers or the other groups have written up to now about the 'peoples of the book' has been very disturbing: they adopt the classical position that 'peoples of the book' have to pay a special tax (jizya) unless they are willing to serve in the army, and are allowed certain communal rights – their own religious institutions, courts, and so on.[6] But certain positions are going to be closed to them – Copts will not be allowed to be government ministers and so on. In court, testimony by a Copt will not be accepted – it will have to be a Muslim's testimony – so you will not be able to have Coptic lawyers or Coptic judges. We may be allowed to have some Copts in nominal positions but, effectively, when you are talking about law and about rights, the treatment accorded to minorities will be very discriminatory. To say nothing about the application of Islamic punishments.

At least there are some people who, even though they support the introduction of Islamic law, are now saying that there must be assurances that the rights of Copts and of women will not be violated because of the application of Islamic law. Also, it should be said that as far as some of the Islamic punishments go, there is a general revulsion in Egypt towards harsh physical treatment like cutting off hands and things like that. These harsh punishments are really not accepted within Egyptian culture – you know, Egyptians are not fond of blood at all!

'THE NEW TRADITIONALISTS . . . SEEKING ISLAMIC SOLUTIONS TO MODERN PROBLEMS'

Much of the discussion I had been having about human rights, identity, the secular or religious nature of the state, had been phrased against the background of the growth of explicitly 'religious' movements with programs founded on the renewal and reinvigoration of religious sentiment in society. I wanted to talk to some Egyptians who were close to or involved in this effort. But this is a very complex terrain filled with people of many different persuasions, and I was certainly not going to be able to do more than sample some of these varied opinions. First of all, how might one characterize the varied trends?

One Egyptian described to me the variety of such groups in the following way: 'Basically there are three groups: those I will call the "new traditionalists" *(turathiyyun al-gdud)*, the old traditionalists like the Muslim Brothers and the traditional shaykhs, and the fundamentalists.' When I asked him to amplify on this, he added,

The new traditionalists were trained along the broad lines of rationalist thought as you know it in the West – although of course the West has no monopoly on rationality and obviously has its own irrationalists! But with the new traditionalists there is a certain common ground for discussion, especially because they are aware of and want to address central issues that lie outside the religious tradition, such as economic development, national goals, and so on. Their argument is that national goals, economic goals, can be best served by solutions developed within a religious perspective, although they do not feel bound by a literal reading of our sacred texts. So they are seeking Islamic solutions to modern problems. Some will even go so far as to argue that the Islamic notion of democracy actually means the separation of church and state, and the independence of the judiciary.

The old traditionalists on the other hand locate their aims strictly in a religious framework. So, they try to give content to notions such as justice and economic development by literal readings of the sacred texts. Compared to the old traditionalists, the new traditionalists have a harder time defending themselves, because they have to make an analysis of the social formation; the old traditionalists have it easier – they don't have to analyze society, only texts.

As for the fundamentalists, they really do not seem to be thinking things out in any new or systematic way. In their discourse, justice is still based on notions of charity; they don't call for change in the class structure and often make the implicit argument that, in fact, class differences are inimical to Islam. So, they are unable to deal with modern notions of rent or wages and can't deal with ideas about, say, agrarian reform. They haven't directed themselves to articulate the interests of the landless peasantry or the working class. Their social basis is among the petty bourgeoisie and some elements of la grande bourgeoisie.

If we accept this categorization for the moment – and this Egyptian had obviously given the matter much thought – I saw a number of reasons why I wanted to concentrate on what he called the 'new traditionalists'. On the one hand, the 'fundamentalist' trend has already received a large amount of attention in the Middle East and the West, in the day-to-day items of the mass media as well as in serious scholarly works.[7] But there was clearly much Islamic discussion taking place throughout the Middle East that was not 'fundamentalist' and that was not receiving its due in the West.[8] And the 'old traditionalists', while certainly reflecting a significant strain of Egyptian (as well as Tunisian and Moroccan) opinion, did not seem to be raising the kinds of issues that I was most interested in.

The 'new traditionalists', on the other hand, although definitely not the most numerous and certainly not the best organized set of Muslim intellectuals, nonetheless were engaged in thinking through the kinds of questions I was posing, and held out the most hope for interesting discussions. They represented a historically deep and vital strain within Islam, and were a force to be reckoned with in any assessment of current trends in the societies I was looking at. I had already had some discussions with people of similar minds in Tunisia – the 'progressive Muslims' of the *15–21* group, and hoped to be able to probe more deeply some of the relevant issues in Egypt.[9]

I outlined some of the problems that I thought would be most important to these thinkers, and I was able to spend considerable time with several of them – each quite distinct in his own way and some none too anxious to be thought of as part of a group with the others.

The problems I meant to discuss with them included the following: what would be the proper relationship, from an 'Islamic' point of view, between the rights of the individual and those of the community (sometimes referred to as the relationship between rights and duties), and how they would conceive of the notion of human freedom; how would an Islamic community deal with variety within it, and what would the attitude be towards pluralism and social justice; how, given the international hierarchy of power, would a nation like Egypt be able to move beyond its current dependent status; and finally, how might thinkers and intellectuals use the conceptual resources of Islam to understand current problems and move towards solutions.

I was able to discuss these topics (although not in this order) with an 'Islamic Marxist', a law professor who had written widely on 'new traditionalist' themes, a well-known Islamic philosopher, and a journalist specializing in contemporary religious thinking.

ᶜadel Hussein, referred to by a number of people I met as an 'Islamic Marxist', was a controversial figure among Egyptian intellectuals. Some people were unforgiving in their criticisms of him, claiming that he was opportunistically manipulating an Islamic vocabulary in order to get closer to power, that he was 'more concerned about winning immediate political battles than about the deeper intellectual problems that still needed to be solved'.[10] But there were also several individuals, including some on the left, who strongly praised ᶜadel Hussein's integrity and sincerity, even while saying that they disagreed with his positions. As one woman said,

> ᶜadel Hussein started out as a Marxist, but he is really a liberal by nature and believes strongly in equality. He seems to be growing increasingly disturbed about the position that women and non-Muslims would occupy in an Islamic society.

ᶜadel Hussein had just become editor-in-chief of *Shᶜab*, the newspaper of the Socialist Labor party, a party often taking 'militant Islamic' positions. At his appointment, some of the people I talked to mingled surprise that Hussein had taken a post thought to be too extreme for his known views with some hope that this indicated the party might be taking more 'progressive' positions in the future.

When I first contacted ᶜadel Hussein, a man in his mid-fifties, he had only recently recovered from a serious illness and had just begun his work at *Shᶜab*. We agreed to cancel our first meeting, planned for the late evening, when on my arrival he was clearly too tired to talk to me. But several months later, when I returned to Egypt, he was very welcoming, and we met one afternoon in his simple but comfortable apartment in Heliopolis, on the outskirts of Cairo.

I had recently looked over his book, *Towards a New Arab Thought* (1985), in which he asked how Egypt and the Arab world might gain greater control of their destiny in a world where the International Monetary Fund, the World Bank, and the great powers all perpetuated inequality between nations and dependence of the weaker upon the stronger. The book also criticized social science for its Western presuppositions and procedures and argued for the creation of an Arab social science.

When I asked him to explain his views on how Egypt could gain control over its present and future, he began by saying that, in the current world, he didn't believe that one country operating strictly on its own could achieve real independence. He went on,

> *I can't conceive of an independent Egypt without a broader framework of Arab unity. So we must see independence and Arab unity as the same question. Of course this doesn't mean that we should take no steps until Arab unity is achieved, but it should nonetheless be clear that Arab unity is an ultimate aim.*
>
> *Now, when I mean independence I don't mean isolation, I mean a situation where we have fair, equal relations with our international partners. And for this, you have to have some self-reliance concerning basic needs. Moving in this direction would improve the balance of forces between the two great powers and the rest of the world.*

How would he propose moving in this direction?

> *The challenge of dependency doesn't lie mainly in the economic sphere, but in the cultural, ideological sphere; this, then, should be the starting point. But no one can deny that our society is influenced by Western ideals, that most of our intellectuals are impregnated by Western ideals, and that the West is opposed to Arab unity. So, intellectuals who oppose Arab unity are a major force we have to contend with. In effect, these intellectuals are against our independence although they will not say this. Therefore, our effort to achieve independence is a difficult one: it is a struggle between those who are authentic and those who are dependent. And if a political party comes to power under the slogan of 'independence', it will be difficult for it to coexist with those who are seriously against our independence.*

ᶜadel Hussein's argument here seemed to reduce opposition between various political, philosophical, and ethical positions to an opposition between 'authentic' and 'inauthentic' intellectuals. He seemed to me dangerously close to demonizing his opponents, an attitude that can sometimes lead to the worst excesses. The implied threat in his last words made this even more disturbing. I suggested this to him and, while not rejecting the need for different points of view as such, he responded by challenging the view that more 'democracy', in the sense of a pluralistic political party system, was necessarily the only framework within which Egypt's problems might be solved. 'Frankly', he said,

> I do not think pluralism or a multiparty system is as operational as some people think; I am not optimistic about its future in Egypt. In the light of our past, and in the light of our obligations and commitment to an independent path, I think our main aim has to be to establish human rights and to deepen and enlarge mass participation in policy and public affairs, even where there is a one-party system. Our main battle should not be to substitute pluralism for the one-party system.
>
> Egypt's one-party system has had its own characteristics that may be specific to Egypt and may operate for the benefit of Egypt. For example, perhaps because of our long history as a unified state, the unity and existence of the state is not in question and the state needn't take extreme measures to fortify its position. Perhaps this is also related to the homogeneity of the society and the strength of the army. All this gives Egypt a good chance to find its own political system, the one most appropriate to its needs – and it may even be able to lead other one-party states to ameliorate their own systems.

ᶜadel Hussein's sanguine view of the virtues of a one-party system ran counter to the accent on democracy and pluralism that I had heard from many other people – their criticism of a one-party system was usually that it necessarily violated certain fundamental political rights, even though it might promote economic and social rights. I asked ᶜadel Hussein about this.

> Look, it is true that in Russia, for example, the one-party system crushed civil society; but in Iran they are trying to strengthen civil society, to create different centers of power. So it is not impossible to conceive of a one-party system that may be able to encompass society in a pluralistic way.
>
> But, of course, this idea is opposed by many people in this country, by many intellectuals. You know, you can have pluralism if the society has a basic consensus, what I call a 'grand strategy'. This kind of grand strategy rules the thinking in any truly independent nation, it rules the thinking of both the government and the opposition, controlling contradictions so that the country doesn't explode. But in a dependent country this consensus on grand strategy isn't there, or it is controlled by and is in the interests of dominant countries like the US. Our program must be to establish a grand strategy as a foundation for independence.

Wondering what role Islam played in his thinking on these subjects, I asked ᶜadel Hussein whether there was a relationship between the program for a grand strategy and Islam.

In order for our independence to be based on our own traditions, it must be based on Islam. But Islam is in no sense simplistic, and Islamic philosophy has a very complex, dialectical view of, say, the relationship between the individual and society. This remains to be worked out in detail but the theoretical model, in general, is that when there are serious societal problems, the needs of the society would be emphasized, and when things are stable the individual would be emphasized. As in the case of war: individual rights are not sacred, but there is a certain minimum that should be preserved. What is crucial is that there must be social and political structures that allow civil society to grow and flourish, that guarantee the strength of civil society. Here the private economic sector is very important – some form of mixed economy may be the best option.

Knowing his Marxist background, I asked ᶜadel Hussein whether he had always favored a mixed economy. He indicated that his positive appreciation of the private economic sector was a change from his previous more orthodox Marxist position, and resulted from his negative assessment of the Soviet experience.

ᶜadel Hussein's attempt to frame basic problems of the contemporary world in the framework of Islam, and his concern to have a political system that was dynamically related to civil society in a way that did not simply model itself on the Western pattern recalled for me some of the concerns of the *15–21* group in Tunisia, and I asked ᶜadel Hussein whether he was familiar with their work.

Although saying that their thinking was, in a broad sense, similar to his (an opinion I am not sure they would share), ᶜadel Hussein was nonetheless quite critical. 'The problem is that they are still influenced by Western thought more than is necessary. They contradict themselves on important things and adopt some non-Islamic ideas. These are not the kind of innovations *(tajdid)* that we need.'

When I asked him what kind of contradictions he saw in their thinking and what were some examples of non-Islamic ideas that they were using, ᶜadel Hussein, perhaps unprepared for such specific questions on thinkers who, after all, are not much discussed by Egyptian intellectuals, was unable to give any specific examples. He simply said, 'They are confused on many issues'. When I suggested that perhaps this was because the issues themselves were complex and confusing, he stated, 'As for me, I'm not confused on these issues'.

ᶜadel Hussein's air of certainty and his taste for a one-party system distinguished him from many of the other new traditionalists I talked to, most of whom stressed that they were only beginning to discuss these issues and were still far from finding any answers.

One of these was Kamal Abu al-Magd, a man in his late fifties, who had been a cabinet minister in the very early years of Sadat's rule but who, after leaving the Sadat cabinet in 1975, had become Dean of the Law School in Kuwait and was now a professor of law at the University of Cairo. He had been mentioned to me early in my research as a participant in 'moderate' Islamic discussions and quite capable of giving a broad overview of how this discussion was proceeding.

As Kamal Abu al-Magd described them, the new traditionalists had no organization of their own but were simply an *ad hoc* collection of like-minded individuals who were working on similar problems from a similar perspective and who tended to look for one another's work once it was published.

I first asked him upon what basis such thinkers were attempting to construct an Islamic vision of human rights?

There are several main elements here, but all have the following belief in common: that in bringing people to worship nothing but God, Islam liberates man from servitude to fellow men. This doctrine of the unity of belief (tawhid), of worshipping only God, thus becomes a proclamation of emancipation, of man's rights as inherent in his creation. There is therefore some similarity between this and Western ideas of natural rights and natural law.

What were the main consequences of this?

The first is that by adding religious interpretation and a religious source of validity to human rights, the status of human rights in society will be strengthened. Second, many writers refer to the fact that, in essence, Islam is a system of obligations and establishes and protects rights by commanding believers to fulfill obligations.

Third, Islam strongly blames those who do not struggle for their own basic rights and encourages people, if they are being denied their rights in one place, to migrate to places where those rights are better protected. And Islam disapproves of weakness in the struggle against violations.

Fourth, there is a new emphasis on Islamic injunctions for individuals to fight to protect the rights of others, and on Qur'anic verses that censure believers for not sufficiently protecting weak men, women, and children. All these elements can be used to support international efforts to protect human rights.

Did these ideas have resonance among the various Islamic groups in Egypt?

Well, you have to distinguish between several kinds of Islamic discourse.

On the one hand, you can see some of these ideas in the political sphere where the Muslim Brothers have formed alliances on occasion with the Wafd party and have then argued that democracy and human rights are essential cornerstones of a just Islamic society. As far as the 'angry young Muslims' go, which is a term I prefer to 'fundamentalists', they seem to be more concerned with issues like identity and authenticity, and tend to deemphasize issues like tolerance, pluralism, and the rights of others. In their zeal to distinguish Islam from everything else, they reject natural law ideas because of their Western taint. Then there is the discourse of some of the intellectual elite who seek to root themselves more solidly in the masses and to counter the negative effects of fanaticism, by using Islamic ideas to advocate tolerance for those who don't have the same ideas, or who aren't Muslims.

I asked Kamal Abu al-Magd whether he thought the emphasis on duties and obligations, and on the rights of the community, might have the effect of limiting respect for the individual's human rights, an argument I had heard frequently.

To the contrary. Perhaps from one point of view it may seem that there is no difference, since rights and obligations are two sides of the same coin. But the chances for the effective protection of human rights should be greater if you have a community of individuals competing to fulfill obligations rather than having a community of individuals fighting selfishly for their own rights. The difference lies not so much in protecting human rights but in social attitudes: people would be trying to give rather than trying to take.

For example, there are a number of Qur'anic verses relevant here, of the sort, 'If you forgive it is better for you', that follow a statement saying that you do have a right to vengeance or retribution if you want it.

Kamal Abu al-Magd's discussion of how the notion of human rights was being approached in contemporary Islamic thinking and the stress he laid on the need for individuals to think about their obligations rather than their rights seemed to lead naturally into the subjects of human freedom in Islam and, related to this, the latitude within the Islamic community for variety and difference. I also very much wanted to pursue the central question of what people took to be the crucial differences between the West and Islamic civilization.

I raised these questions with Muhammad ᶜamara, a religious scholar and philosopher and author of many books on Islam including a recent study called *Islam and Human Rights*. He had frequently been mentioned to me as one of the preeminent new traditionalist thinkers, and he was also characterized by several people as a follower of the Muᶜtazilite school.[11]

Muhammad ᶜamara received me in his home outside central Cairo. I thought it best to begin by asking him to situate his thinking with respect to other similar thinkers in Egypt as well as other 'progressive' Muslims, such as those of the *15–21* group. He answered,

> *As in everything, there are some similarities and some differences. You have to understand that my training is in Islamic studies, in philosophy, and I have perhaps a broader historical and philosophical view than some of the others. As far as the other Egyptian writers working in this vein, our basic similarity is that we are all thinking about the distinctiveness of Islam and are trying to bring about a renaissance of Islam, even though there are many differences between us. But these differences are healthy, because Islam is the ideology of the 'umma and within the 'umma there are bound to be many different viewpoints.*
>
> *As for the 15–21 group, I met one of them here in Egypt not very long ago. I am in basic sympathy with their views but there is one aspect that distinguishes my thinking from theirs, although this is perhaps not a major difference. They try to adapt Islam too much to some Western modes of thinking – they should put more of the spotlight on the distinctions between Islam and Western society. But they do put the spotlight very well on social issues, social justice, and human rights.*

The distinction between Western and Islamic ways of thinking was often invoked as though such differences were self-evident. To me they weren't and I asked Muhammad ᶜamara how he saw this distinction.

> *What I mean by distinction is not that they are enemies or that they are completely different. No, it is just that their multiplicity should be highlighted. In fact I have written a pamphlet on this, called 'Civilizational independence' ('Istiqlal al-aḥdari). One of the basic distinguishing factors of Islam is its moderation, similar to the balance (mizan) that Islam uses in its approach to problems. Islamic moderation, although sometimes taken to be the same as Aristotle's mean between two extremes, is actually quite different: it is a stance and way of conceptualizing that brings together elements of both sides.*

I asked him if he could give an example.

> *Take for example the human quality of courage: it synthesizes the rationality and wariness of cowardice with the daring of rashness. Generosity is different from stinginess and from giving everything away: it is a synthesis of giving and of being careful with your things.*
>
> *Also, on civil and social issues, the differences between Islamic moderation and other kinds of moderation are very clear. Take for example the nature of state power: in the West you have had either theocracy or a secular system that separates religion and the state. So you either have a religious state or a non-religious one. But in an Islamic system we have a*

civil regime where the 'umma, the people, is the source of power but bounded within the Islamic tradition.

The relationship of the individual to the group is another example of moderation. And the relation of matter to spirit. In the West you either have spiritualism, that is, a literal word-for-word interpretation and a view that the world is a product of divine inspiration, or a Greek rationalism that knows neither god nor inspiration. In Islam, we have the Qur'an which is a rational miracle – that is, it is a miracle that has the power to attract the mind.

So, in all these examples you can see that Islamic moderation is an attempt at synthesis of extremes, not a separation of extremes. It is comprehensive, while in the West you have either oneness, or dualism, or sectarianism. So, as far as culture and the understanding of the cosmos is concerned, there is a great difference between the West and Islam. But in the factual sciences that are based on empiricism, there is no difference.

How did the different way in which things were conceptualized in Islam work itself out with regard to human rights and notions of freedom and democracy?

In Islamic thinking, the freedom of the individual and the relationship between this and the general good is very closely linked to Islam's view of the human being. Islam has a moderate view of the human being's place in the universe, unlike the West which has an exaggerated view. Islam doesn't think either that the human being is the supreme being in creation, or that he is indistinguishable from the rest of creation. Man is the representative (khalifa) of God, and human beings have liberties that reflect their nature as God's representatives. These liberties are not absolute, they are bounded. So the individual as civil and social being is free, but all this is limited by the need for the freedom of the society. There has to be a balance between what is good for the individual and good for the group – they are not mutually exclusive.

'This', he stressed,

is very different from the Western view where, in the democratic state, the ruling class's interests take precedence; or where, in the authoritarian state, the state's interests take precedence. In Islam, the 'umma's interests take precedence, not those of the ruling class, not those of the state, and not those of the individual. So, in this sense, Islam has a moderate view of the individual: the individual is free in so far as it is of benefit to the community.

You also have to understand that Islam's view of liberty is similar to Islam's view of other freedoms. Liberty isn't merely a human right, because if that was the case the owner could sacrifice it. But in Islam liberty, like other human rights, is a duty in Islamic law, it is not something that you can just give away. Take for example, the protection of life (hifaz al-ḥayyat): this too is not just a right, it is a duty – you know that suicide is a crime in Islam. The preservation of life is therefore an Islamic duty under Islamic law, a duty that people must struggle to fulfill.

Muhammad ᶜamara had traced what he thought to be some crucial differences between Islamic and Western ways of thinking. But to do this, he seemed to me to be simplifying the variety within the Islamic community – simplifying, for example, tensions between the various Islamic nations and tensions within a nation such as Egypt, composed of groups that had sharply conflicting interests. I asked him about this.

The existence of classes within the 'umma is a real fact, and class conflict within the 'umma is a real fact also. The Islamic position is not to exacerbate these tensions, but to try to mitigate these conflicts and to bring the classes together in a union. So, the aim is not to replace one class by another, but to create a union of classes. Because each of these classes has a function in society.

The same picture applies to nations in the Islamic 'umma. If we don't use the racialist or fascist aspects of nationalism, nations should become like islands in an ocean, each contributing to the general welfare of all. In the development of the 'umma, we cannot deny that differences between nations exist, and how each nation can best develop is therefore a domestic matter: each nation's aim is to increase its own resources, but this should be in the framework of an integrated Islamic unity. In the future, at some time, equality will exist – there is a prophetic tradition (hadith) that says that when one believer goes hungry there is no money for anyone.

Remember that the reality of conflict in the current situation is caused by many things. These nations and current regimes are now aiming towards the realization of their own particular advantages, and are not working for the good of the 'umma. And they are ruled by vested interests and often are not even working for their own national good. And remember, first and foremost, this situation is the creation and the result of the actions by the Western powers.

Muhammad ᶜamara had already defended the view that a community as complex as the Islamic *'umma* needed to be tolerant of different viewpoints within it. But, I suggested, multiplicity and pluralism were easy to defend when all contending parties accepted the need to protect free and open discussion. But what about groups that did not think that a multiplicity of views was healthy for society?

Muhammad ᶜamara continued,

Yes, this is indeed a problem. It is true, there are such groups, and of course they take root as a result of the kind of unjust situation we now live in. But these groups are confused, and their big mistake is not understanding the differences between the basics of our religion (ᶜubudiyyun) and its details (furuᶜ). *In Islam this is a fundamental distinction. Muslims in the past and in the present haven't clashed about the original religion. As far as the basics are concerned, there are no differences. The differences arise over understanding what the 'state' means, what 'civilization' means, what politics is, what should be the social order, and so on. But these are details, not the basics.*

This distinction between details and basics was a frequent leitmotif in conversations I had about religion. But wasn't part of the problem that some individuals or groups took as basic, as mandated by religion, matters that Muhammad ᶜamara had glossed as 'details'? He answered,

Yes, you're right. The real problem arises when some people think their political views, for example, are part of the religious basics and that everyone must agree to them. But as far as politics is concerned, and laws, and so on, people have to think and exert effort to understand them, and therefore you must have open discussion. And on these details, on the matters of this world, we have to have multiplicity in so far as we talk about things of this world.

Let me give you an example. Take the concept of shura – *what you might call 'democracy' but more accurately meaning the expression of the general will.*[12] *This is basic to Islam, so all Muslims should be united on this. But the formal institutions to enact this* shura *may vary. So unity is necessary insofar as there should be a belief in* shura, *but there is no unity on how best to implement this. Our effort to find such a solution must allow a multiplicity of views to be expressed.*

Take another example: social justice. In society, capital and wealth belong to God. Man is the representative of God and is charged with increasing these resources. This is part of the essence of Islam. But the social order which determines wealth and resources changes from one situation to another.

Now, the extremist groups in our society may think that their views on these subjects have to do with the basic *questions of religion and they therefore may demand agreement with their views. But these matters are only matters of detail – their demand for agreement is not a deliberate confusion, but a product of too little thinking, too little knowledge. All learned Islamic writers see this clearly.*

And remember, too, that such confusion is not specific to Islam or to Islamic groups. There are some secular parties that would persecute and incriminate multiplicity, and silence people who don't follow their views.

So multiplicity in opinion has nothing to do with religion or secularism. It is a problem though: just like some people want to monopolize nationalism, others want to monopolize Islam. It is just that when we make the political into the religious, we turn differences of views into a matter of heresy (kufr) versus belief, whereas in fact we should be judging in terms of right and wrong, not in terms of belief and unbelief.

So there is a multiplicity between the two civilizations, as between all civilizations. And just as we criticize those Muslims who believe in the oneness of views, we also criticize those Westerners who think that their civilization is that of the future.

With these sharp differences both within and between Islamic communities so indelibly stamped upon the contemporary situation, it was nonetheless clear from what Muhammad ᶜamara had been saying that there were many conceptual resources within Islamic discourse to understand these differences. To what extent, however, could these resources be used to understand the changes societies were experiencing and to envisage solutions to current problems?

Some time after my talk with Muhammad ᶜamara I went to see Fahmi Howaidy, a well-known journalist and a specialist on current Islamic thinking and religious affairs. He was himself a participant in the new traditionalist current. I began by asking him whether he thought the new traditionalists merited being called a group. He answered,

Yes, they are a group, they understand Islam as a way of living, as a way of thinking, and see this as a way to help people to improve themselves and society, rather than as just something to practice in the mosque, as something that is simply between the people and God. In general the differences between the positions of these people are small, especially compared to the differences between them and say, the Jihad group.[13]

I suppose, broadly speaking, you should consider me as one of this group. As for a label, I prefer 'moderate fundamentalists' ('usuliyyun muᶜtadilun). But they are sometimes also called 'new traditionalists' (turathiyyun al-gdud).

I asked him what he thought of their force as a group.

A big problem is that moderate Islamic groups are not even allowed to organize, to develop their thinking, and to develop a program. A few years ago we officially requested the right to have an association of moderate Islamic thinkers, but this was refused, supposedly for security reasons. We have no concrete plans to make further requests, but there are some informal discussions with this aim in mind, and I am involved in these. At least we should be allowed to have an association, if not a political party. So, many of us are writing, giving lectures, and so on, but the moderates are not organized as a group.

Using an Islamic perspective, how would he begin to approach the problems of contemporary society?

In all these questions, in all Islamic fields, the essence is justice. As the Qur'an says, 'God orders people to serve the cause of justice'.

Now, to achieve a just society you have to start from shura.[14] *You have*

to give people liberty first, so that they can then decide their own future. Take the question of applying Islamic law – this is one of the main areas on which there is wide disagreement among Muslims. Many of the Islamic groups start from the prescribed Islamic punishments, saying that the first thing to do is to apply them. We say, the implementation of Islamic law has to start from shura *– because after all,* shura *is said in the Qur'an to be as basic an element in our relationship to God as prayer is. And* shura *not only refers to political freedom, but also should cover every domain of social life. But here in Egypt, for the moment, we are concentrating on the political domain.*

Now, how should shura *be operationalized? Well, that is another question, that is a question of detail. It is a question of foundations (ʾusul) versus detail (furuᶜ). For us too, it is too early to find answers to these details – the best we can do now is to begin to raise the crucial questions.*

What is imperative is for people to have a new attitude. In the Qur'an it says, 'God listens and sees.' Muslims must begin to heed this, everywhere – not only in the mosque but in their everyday life, in their education. These values are essential, and they must become part of the attitudes of the new generations. This is the way to build.

However, in addition to changes in ways of thinking about problems, and changes in attitudes, specific measures had to be taken if Egypt was to have any hope of surmounting its current crisis. I wondered whether Fahmi Howaidy felt that an 'Islamic' perspective was providing new insights into, for example, economic problems, given that there had been much talk recently about an 'Islamic economics' (just as there had been about an Islamic or Arab social science).

You know, there are some so-called Islamic economic projects, but these are really just flag-waving, rather than being truly Islamic. In the banking field, there have been some efforts, but too many mistakes have been made. I think you have to recognize that an Islamic solution can't come in just one field, you can't cut up life into domains. Even if interest (riba) were to be outlawed as it should be in the Islamic view, how are you going to force people not to deal with an international banking system based on interest? You can't take just one element and try to implement it without regard to what is happening around it.

To confront these economic problems real expertise is required. Some people ask, 'How do we solve the problem of US aid? How do we solve the problem of the World Bank?'. This is all not so simple, it requires special expertise to solve these problems of detail.

How, then, were these problems going to be solved? Was there anything about the approach to possible solutions that was 'Islamic'?

We have many resources in Islam to enable us to deal with the problems of change, with the obstacles that impede change, and with the need to adapt our thinking to changing circumstances. First of all there is the idea of gradual implementation (attadaruj), or implementation by degrees. As our learned men have said, 'You can never solve all your problems at once'. Remember, the Qur'an was sent to the Prophet Muhammad over a period of twenty-three years, not all at once but over quite a long period. Things were built gradually.

For example, take the case of the Qur'anic verse that outlawed drinking. It didn't say that drinking must cease immediately. There were four stages: first, 'drinking is not that good'; then, 'you shouldn't pray while you are drinking'; then, 'there are good and bad things in drinking, but the bad things outweigh the good'; and then, 'to be a good Muslim, you must not drink'. Another example? Islam is against idols and you will remember that twenty-one years passed after his first revelations before Muhammad destroyed the idols.

So, if God sent the Qur'an over a twenty-three year period, and if things are gained in stages, why must we be in such a hurry?

Also, there is the notion of necessities (darurat): things that we are unable to change even though they go against Islamic law. You know, when we contemplate changes there are some things that can't be changed immediately in the current situation. In this regard, there is a historical example that is often cited. Ibn Taymiyya was in Damascus in the Mongol period.[15] The Mongols were very cruel rulers, killing many people, many Muslims, even though they themselves were Muslims. Ibn Taymiyya was walking with friends through the streets of Damascus when they passed some Mongols drinking. A friend said to Ibn Taymiyya, 'Why don't you tell them to stop drinking?' Ibn Taymiyya answered, 'Because when they stop drinking, they may start killing again'.

Here is a clear case where you know what is forbidden (hram) and what is approved (hlel). Although it is easy to state what is right and wrong, it is difficult to apply it because you must take into account the problem of applying it.

This brings me to a third idea: there are things that are against Islamic law but were we to change them, the cost to the community would be too great. This is the idea of munkar. An example of this would be to try to implement the Islamic prohibition on interest.

After this outline of how, within an Islamic framework, a Muslim might both articulate the need for social change and remain reasonably flexible in trying to put it into effect, I wondered whether Fahmi Howaidy had had much contact with members of the *15–21* group in Tunisia who were working on similar questions.

Fahmi Howaidy answered,

Yes, I am familiar with their work, and know some of them personally. You know, we all agree about the need for innovation (ijtihad) and the need to take the general interest of society (meslaḥa) into account when we consider the rightness of actions. But to what extent, and on what basis? As far as the 15–21 group is concerned, I think they have perhaps gone a bit beyond what the Islamic limits should be: too far to the left, perhaps too far to the West, perhaps too much influenced by the French.

Could he be more specific?

First of all, they have gone too far in attacking prescribed Islamic punishments. They have made some arguments that not only should we not implement these punishments now, but we should not even do so in this century. They have also argued that although such punishments may have been right in previous centuries, this was no longer true. They argue as though we should no longer consider applying these punishments. For me, this dismisses the punishments too easily.

We believe, to the contrary, that we have to respect these punishments and to implement them, but according to the considerations that I have just outlined for you – we must work towards it and, at the same time, work towards meeting the needs of the people. If we take theft as an example, we must both move towards implementation of the Islamic punishments for stealing and we must see to it that people don't need to steal.

Also, while some articles in their journal say that the vote should be given to Communists, they also imply that some Islamist groups should be denied the vote because they are against progress. Why take these positions? I think it is just playing politics the wrong way.

And how would he deal with the problem of some Islamist groups that claim to have a monopoly on truth, and that seek to impose their ideas on others?

Well, you know, even if some of the Islamic groups are indeed against progress, even if they seem closed-minded, the problem is that they are forced into illegality and clandestinity. They are outlawed so they can't even have open discussions. If they were legalized, this would help everyone. For example, I'm sure that they move in such closed circles that they haven't even had the benefit of a discussion with someone with a deep knowledge of Islamic history and doctrine like Muhammad ᶜamara.

And then on a closing note he added, 'You know, we have to allow all these groups the right to make mistakes. Look, I've been a journalist for twenty-eight years and over that time I've made plenty of mistakes.'

Part II

Morocco: the individual, human freedom and democracy

5   Cultural obstacles?

THE INDIVIDUAL

A Tunisian acquaintance startled me one afternoon by saying, emphatically, 'In Tunisian society, there is no individual, the individual does not exist'.

His remark echoed, more starkly, what I had heard on other occasions in all three countries. It echoed, for instance, a remark made to me by a Tunisian journalist who, referring to the need to find a proper balance between the person, the state, and the institutions of civil society, had said that one of the main problems was that people believed they had no rights when they confronted the state – for example, when a person was taken to a police station he felt himself completely at the mercy of the state, with no defenses whatsoever.

And it echoed, too, what a Moroccan in his mid-twenties had said to me,

> One of our main problems is simply that in the political system of modern Morocco, the individual has no meaning. It is like in traditional society, where you are always seen as a member of one group or another, where you always have to be attached to some collective identity. In effect, the individual has no right or possibility to express his own personal opinions, without being accused of being in the service of a group.

Furthermore, a Moroccan sociologist had suggested to me, in passing, that in popular culture the notion of the 'individual' was so undeveloped that colloquial Moroccan speech had no common word that meant 'person, an individual', although there was a word for this in classical Arabic.[1]

These views were counterbalanced somewhat by an Egyptian law professor, who reinforced my studied effort to be cautious about such blanket statements by saying, 'It was the orientalists, particularly the French, who emphasized fatalism and the diminished role of the individual in Islamic civilization'. But a few days later, an Egyptian intellectual said to me off-handedly, 'If there is a clash between the needs of the group and the needs of the individual, the needs of the group should always take precedence'.

Many Middle Easterners argue that there are a number of broad cultural obstacles working against the promotion of human rights in their region; in particular, some argue that whereas a strong notion of the individual is absolutely essential if a belief in human rights is to take root, such a notion plays only a weak role in Middle Eastern culture. When people talked about the 'individual', they almost invariably linked it to ideas about human freedom and sometimes coupled these, as well, to ideas about democracy.

The general framework within which people formulated these themes was remarkably similar. The 'individual' – that is the autonomous individual, relatively free from prescribed obligations towards predetermined social groups and free to make his or her own decisions in life – was said to play a key role in Western liberal ideology and was closely associated with a capitalist economic system. Certainly the notion of 'economic man', free to satisfy his needs in the marketplace, was central to such a system, but this notion also had correlates on the social level – most people I talked to saw the individual in Western, capitalist societies as much freer from social obligations towards family, tribe, community, and society than were people in the Middle East.

To this model of capitalist society, exemplified by the contemporary West, people would contrast two other models: 'traditional' society, where the primordial bonds of family, tribe and community remain strong and constrain the individual's social behavior; and what I will call a 'purposeful' society, where people are motivated by an explicit social project, a (more or less) clear vision, where the needs of the society as a whole would take precedence, practically and ideologically, over those of the individual.[2] Although for different reasons and under vastly different conditions, in both these models the notion of the individual would be stifled and have weak cultural force.[3]

As it turned out, I was able to explore the notions of the individual, liberty, and freedom in most detail in Morocco. Before we turn to those discussions, let us hear the words of an Egyptian and several Tunisians (including the author of this chapter's opening remark) who have given the matter much thought.

'ON THE DAY OF JUDGEMENT . . . GOD SPEAKS WITH EACH INDIVIDUAL' (EGYPT, TUNISIA)

Did the Middle East and the West have different notions of the individual? If people thought such differences existed, to what would they attribute them?

I put some questions along these lines to Kamal Abu al-Magd, an Egyptian law professor. In particular, I asked him whether he thought that the West's vision of itself as a society that was built upon and encouraged individualism was perhaps something of a self-serving myth. He answered,

> *Well, this image is simplistic, but it does have a grain of truth, because you can't have a strong society without such strong notions of the individual. In the West, there is a long historical tradition of struggle that ended with the emergence of a system of protecting rights, and this helps creativity.*
>
> *Now, in Islam, there is of course the general principle of individual responsibility before God and before the community. For example, we have a prophetic tradition (hadith) that says, 'Foremost among martyrs is the man who stands up in face of a desperate ruler, who says "do this" and then is killed'; or in the Qur'an, 'Why don't you fight and struggle for the cause of oppressed women and children who have been evicted from homes and lands?' And again in the Qur'an, at the end of the chapter called 'The Cow', it says, 'No witness or writer should be made to suffer because of his testimony.'*
>
> *And there are injunctions in the same direction by some of the best known Islamic reformers. For example, Muhammad Iqbal argues that Islam doesn't ask people to deny themselves, but to strengthen their egos by being strong, working hard, undertaking difficult tasks. In one of his books he particularly focused on strengthening the individual ego and the collective ego.[4]*
>
> *But to a great degree an answer to this question depends on whether we deal with the conceptual level – here there are many texts in the Qur'an and Sunna that emphasize the individual as opposed to the community or the ruler – or with the practical aspects of society's domination by despotic rulers.[5] There is no doubt that in some Arab Muslim countries individuals are submissive, but this is a product of autocratic rulers and the long history of colonialism.*
>
> *So, I don't believe in any way that the source of these differences is religious. Why, if you compared the holy books you might find, if anything, that Islam gives more support to the individual. For example, you might argue that the concept of original sin confuses the issue of individual responsibility by taking away individual responsibility for acts.*

I sought more detail on how the notion of the 'individual' might be articulated within a religious framework from Salah ed-Din Jorshi, one of

Tunisia's leading religious intellectuals. Jorshi had been an important figure in the Islamic Tendency Movement (MTI); after breaking with them he wrote frequently for the 'progressive Muslim' publication, *15–21*.

Jorshi explained that one of the central motifs in Islam is the concept of the unity of belief (*tawhid*), based on a vision of one God, one Islamic community (*'umma*), and one final prophet. But Jorshi was careful to emphasize that to use this idea to reinforce the domination of the community over the individual and to encourage conformity – and it is often used in this way – was opposed to the basic message of Islam.

> *Look at the Qur'an: the Qur'an never speaks of people as 'the dust of individuals' – you know Bourguiba used these words. It speaks of believers and the community of believers. This is very important. But at the same time, it is dangerous because up until today our learned religious scholars haven't understood that within the community there are individuals. The community must not be a cage for the individuals.*
>
> *Because in Islam the individual exists: on the Day of Judgement, God does not speak with the 'umma, He speaks with each individual, He tells each individual 'You have done this, you haven't done that', and so on. So, at one and the same time there is the 'umma and there is the individual. And in order to have an Islamic view of freedom, of the individual, of human rights, you have to have a vision of the whole society and also of the rights of the individual, rights which have lost their meaning in our past history and in our past social and political experience.*

But, with many different individuals and many different viewpoints competing with one another, how could society move forward, take decisions, progress?

> *Although tawhid is based on the one god, the united community, the final prophet, this doesn't mean that there is only one way of thinking. Perhaps at the end of time there will be only one way of thinking but in the meantime we have to struggle, and that struggle must be carried out through dialogue. Because tawhid isn't a structure to be imposed upon the present, it is a vision of the future, it is a process, an effort to construct a just world. And this can only be carried on by a struggle within society, within history, within a world where there are contradictions. To say that we are Muslims isn't to say that we are all the same or that any of us knows the final answers. That's why we call ourselves 'progressive Muslims': because we believe that history moves forward, that there is progress, and that we can't mould the present or the future upon the past.*
>
> *This is why, for us, the social sciences are of great importance – we have to learn how to act within society for the development of society. And this is why, by the way, the thought of Ibn Khaldun is so important, because it marked the transition from philosophical and theological reasoning towards thinking about how man acts within society. [6]*

How was human freedom conceived of within this framework?

> God created the world, a world with certain aims, certain ends. In order for this world to have continuity it must have laws. Now man, who is God's representative on earth, is not God's remote-control robot, but is charged by God with changing the world for the better. Here the concept of freedom is central to Islamic thought because, first of all, God created man free. This is clear, and on this everyone agrees. And by the way, this also means that man is free to choose between religions, and even free to choose to have no religion at all.
>
> So, when we talk about the individual in Islam we are talking essentially about a creature who has been created with free choice and who is responsible for his choices. But this is not a limitless freedom, it is a freedom limited by the responsibility that each person has for his actions, because he is going to be judged, finally, by these actions. And that is why, when we talk of freedoms, and rights, we also have to talk of duties.

How was the concept of rights and duties related to human freedom, and to the idea of democracy? He dealt with the last of these first.

> The question of freedom and democracy is crucial, but how to put these into effect isn't obvious at all. Although we progressive Muslims are certainly against the current unity between the party and the state, we don't believe that the answer to this lies in individuals voting simply as individuals. The real democratic need is to find a way for the structures of civil society to have real power, to express their voice. But now civil society has been shattered: the Islamic brotherhoods, the mosque, the tribe, the educational system – all are dominated by the state. Why, in the countryside you can't even dig a well without first getting the state's approval.[7] So now we have a prior question – how are we going to reconstruct civil society?
>
> One of the problems in reconstructing civil society is that in Tunisia, today, everyone is talking of rights and freedoms. But if everyone thinks only of their own rights and freedoms, society will destroy itself, because we are a society that doesn't have everything, that is permeated by scarcity. We can't have everything we want, because we have to struggle against underdevelopment, against imperialism, against corruption, against many things. And that's why, at the same time that we talk of rights and freedoms, we have to also talk of duties and obligations, which are essential for us in this historical moment. A society that talks only of rights becomes not a society, but an archipelago.
>
> So we must also talk of duties. In Islam there is a whole philosophy of duties. We have the duty to ourselves, that is, we must respect our dignity as human beings, we must respect the rights of our society and of other people in it even though they may not be the same as we are, we have to respect the rights of others to think, to choose, to have property, to act, to

accumulate wealth, and so on. And also, within ourselves, we have the obligation to create clear and open ties with our fellows.

So, everything we do as human beings has many dimensions, not only affecting our individual social and material lives, but also has its effect on the society we live in. So, when I defend the right of, let's say, Marxists to meet, even if they don't believe in Islam as their religion, I do it while insisting that they must respect Islam as a culture – because there is a dialectical relationship between rights and obligations, between the individual and society, between myself, the groups I belong to, and the society as a whole.

I also wanted to pursue these issues with Abdelaziz Krichen, an agronomist and founder editor of the new Tunisian journal, *Mensuel*. He had made the categoric statement that opens this chapter, while lamenting what he thought to be a lack of creativity in Tunisian society; when I saw him again a few months after our first conversation I pushed him on this. He began,

Well, I've thought about this a lot – for me, the problem of the individual is the crux of many of the problems now facing us in Tunisia, and I could discuss this with you for several hours, if you have the time.

Krichen stressed that he hadn't come to this conclusion simply as a theoretical or academic exercise, but that this issue – how can the notion of the individual develop in society – had been a crucial one in his own life.

Well, let me start by saying that I began my 'adult' life, so to speak, my public life, in an extreme leftist movement, when I was a university student. This experience didn't take place in a vacuum within Tunisia, but was part of the upheaval at that time within the international Marxist-Leninist movement, the Maoist movement. The Cultural Revolution in China and then the death of Mao Zedong, the catastrophe in Kampuchea – all this led us all to call into question a number of things that we had been taking for granted.

As we began to question our central beliefs, and ourselves, I began to think about the whole experience of Tunisia from the 1960s to the mid-1970s – a period when the extreme left was the main political opposition in the country, especially among students and intellectuals. And all this questioning was to lead me to the centrality of the notion of the individual.

I began to see that in countries like Tunisia, feudal and mystical notions belonging to traditional society continued to dominate our thinking. Of course this was true for what you might call the 'modernizing' forces – Bourguiba and all his supporters who wielded state power – but it was also true for those of us who challenged the establishment, those of us who supported revolutionary ideologies of the Marxist-Leninist-Maoist type. Even we were reproducing, on another level of course, the essentially feudal and mystical ideas of traditional society. We were moving in an uninterrupted way from those traditional notions to totalitarian views that are still partly feudal and mystical. This happened on the ideological level, on the cultural level, and I would even say on the level of individual psychology.

In both configurations, in both the traditional and the totalitarian, it is always the group, the collectivity, that dominates, and never the individual. There is an entire culture, continuous throughout our history, that places the collectivity above the individual, the ends above the means. So, despite superficial differences between the political and ideological positions of the establishment and those of the opposition, there were no essential intellectual, moral, or psychological distinctions.

For a real transformation to occur, the problem of the individual has to be brought to the center of the stage. Not yet having done this, we still have no idea of what democracy is, what real respect for the human person is. But once we come to focus on this problem, a lot of other problems can be looked at in a new light.

From this perspective, I've tried to analyze some very different things, such as productivity in firms, technological innovation, relations between the sexes, relations between generations, artistic and literary creativity. Thus, for me attention to the individual has become truly a sort of focal perspective through which I try to understand this country's problems.

Could he give me a few examples to make this more concrete?

First of all there is the whole question of the entrepreneurial spirit, the creativity of individuals in society. This is definitely closely tied to the whole problematic of the emergence of the individual in a given society. Obviously, our society has to produce more, has to regain much of its lost energy, and it can only do this by encouraging the expression of individual creativity and enterprise. But don't get me wrong – I am not singing the praises here of capitalism, but I'll come back to that in a minute.

Let me give you another example – relations between the sexes. I may say a few things now that will make your hair stand on end: but just as there is no individual, and just because there is no individual in Tunisian society, real love isn't possible here either. And when I tell you that I've investigated this question, it also means that, being a part of this society myself, being right inside it, I have had to look deep inside myself. This 'investigation', if you want to call it that, can be very painful, if you see what I mean.

In saying something like 'love isn't possible', wasn't he exaggerating somewhat?

Just look at the marriage relationship. On the outside it seems as though the form of marriage has changed during the last thirty years: we no longer have the traditional extended patriarchal family, we now have the monogamous nuclear family. But still, it is never the individual who meets, gets to know, and chooses a partner. OK, when I say 'never', perhaps that is part of my tendency to exaggerate a little, but in general things just do not happen that way. It may be a modern marriage taking place in the municipal buildings, it may lead to a single family house and a monogamic nuclear cell, but behind all this there is the group, the extended family, deciding who the marriage partners will be. I'm not talking just about peasants here, or about workers or bank employees or bureaucrats, I'm talking also about teachers at the university. When you get married, it is still very often to one of your cousins, because the relatives agreed to this some twenty years earlier.

So I've come to realize that on the level of love, on the level of sexuality, there is a modernist discourse but it only serves to camouflage a very traditional social and psychological reality.

Now, this story of the individual has significant implications not only on the personal level, but in the political domain too, because it helps us see why all this discussion about democracy is just plain rubbish. After all, democracy is only really possible if people are conscious of their own unique existence, of their own special human value. And here, in general, that consciousness doesn't exist.

I remarked, alluding to what he had said a few minutes earlier, that all this could indeed be taken as an apology for capitalism and its notion of the independent, autonomous individual. Krichen responded quickly,

Again, don't get me wrong – I am not saying that all is well in those Western societies that have known a relatively long period of liberalism. Far from it. You know, one of our problems here is that many of us tend to overvalue the West while at the same time not knowing it very well at all. So we're often unable to criticize it, to think seriously about it, or to go beyond it.

But it does seem to me that in the West, at a certain period, because of certain historical conditions, the individual had opportunities to appear, to emerge, on the cultural level, on philosophical, moral, artistic levels, on the economic level, and to accomplish absolutely extraordinary things.

Krichen had few illusions about how these ideals worked themselves out in practice.

Certainly, in succeeding periods these opportunities largely fizzled out, and the American ideal of a society of free and equal individuals led to a mass society where people became clones of millions of others, where everyone was in a 'rat race', as you like to call it, motivated by the god of money. But that is another issue. So, I don't idealize the situation, but I do say that even if today in the West you have a mass society and before that you were immobilized in feudalism, at least you did have an intermediary *period that lasted two, three, or four centuries, depending on the country. Here in Tunisia we are going from one form of massification, of immobility, to another form of historical powerlessness, impotence, with practically no period of transition. And with the transition blocked, so is the emergence of the individual blocked.*

Then, trying to counterbalance the bleak picture he had painted, Krichen added,

Of course, maybe it is just this kind of blockage that allows us to have the possibility of casting the whole thing off, of breaking out of this mass society. Maybe we have much more of a chance than your societies have.

Was he optimistic about such a change occurring, I asked, where the individual would come to play a stronger cultural and social role? He answered,

I'm going to have to give you a 'gascon–normand' answer. It is clear that there are things in Tunisia, and in the Arab world in general, that are pushing for the emergence of the individual. But it is just as clear that there are things pushing in the opposite direction. And I'm not at all capable of predicting what we're going to end up with. Obviously, with my limited means, I'm trying to push things in one direction rather than the other.

Although I was not attempting to study the historical development of Middle Eastern society, it was also clear that the current situation couldn't be divorced from the historical conditions that gave birth to it and that still no doubt influenced its shape. If what Krichen and others had been saying to me was indeed representative and perhaps even true (in the sense that many leading intellectuals believed it to be the case) – that the notion of the individual was stunted – why was this so? Were the conditions that led to it still dominating the contemporary situation?

I was able to go somewhat more deeply into the cultural and historical roots of this issue with a well-known Tunisian sociologist, Abdelqadr Zghal. Zghal, in his late fifties, had first studied psychology and then sociology in Paris and is now one of Tunisia's senior and most widely respected sociologists. I had already read several of Zghal's writings, one of which was due to appear shortly in Krichen's journal. Some of what he had written in those articles directly addressed the question of the notion of the individual in Tunisian society.

Zghal had been thinking about the degree to which Tunisian society privileged the idea of the community over that of the individual. When he talked to me about this, he outlined his argument by comparing the Tunisian and Arab with the Western experience.

In the West, I think there was an evolution on the structural level that was parallel to developments on the level of values. Urbanization and industrialization were specific social processes that favored the emergence of the individual, divorced from communal ties, as a significant social actor. In the West this industrialization and urbanization had been preceded and was accompanied by debate on what I will call the 'sanctified' individual. So, there was a displacement of sanctity from the community to the individual, a displacement that happened relatively slowly, over a considerable period of time. And, remember, all this took place in a historical period, roughly from the seventeenth through the nineteenth centuries, when the European community wasn't threatened from the outside, when it was dominant.

Since the nineteenth century, Tunisia and the rest of the Arab world have been in a dominated situation, where their autonomy in making their own decisions has been constantly under threat, when it has not been taken away completely. This led to a renewed emphasis on the sanctified collectivity as our societies tried to mobilize themselves collectively to respond to this threat.

How was this history making itself felt in the present?

Well, more recently, during the colonial period and particularly since independence in 1956, the state has attempted to radically alter our notions of where authority should lie or, to put it differently, what are the legitimate sources of ultimate, 'sacred' values. Under the declared aim of modernization and development, the more specific political aim was to take power away from all its traditional centers – from the religious scholars, from heads of families, from leaders of craft guilds, from all traditional authorities – and to consolidate national power at their expense.

In Tunisia this has had complex effects. In the first place, of all the Arab world, we may have the best organized civil society. That is, there is a labor movement that is the most important in the Arab world; there is a women's movement and a human rights movement that are of long standing;[8] there is a tradition of organizations on non-traditional, non-tribal, non-familial bases in civil society, all of which are favorable to the expansion of the notion of the individual as individual.

So, the political decision to weaken traditional authority was relatively easy to take and put into effect, because of the strength of these civil society institutions, because these institutions were favorable to this step. But since independence, as the state seized more and more power and took over more and more domains, these civil society institutions have also been attacked and many of them have grown weaker and weaker. So, within Tunisian society we have a basic contradiction: civil society and its institutions favor the emergence of the notion of the individual, but this is blocked by laws and practices on the political level.

But you must also bear in mind that our recent political history has infantilized the individual, has given the individual no possibility to behave politically as someone who makes choices, who participates – that is, who behaves politically as an adult. Under traditional authority, although the individual had little or no political responsibility, at least those who held power shouldered the responsibility for it. But when those traditional authorities are destroyed, as in Tunisia, the individual is placed in the position of a child under a state authority that has only a minimal sense of its own responsibilities. All this makes very difficult the transition to a society where there is a full sense of the individual.

What was his prognosis for the near future? 'Well,' he continued, but now with a laugh,

it is difficult to be a prophet, especially in our part of the world. What is most probable is that whatever predictions we make, we will all fail to foresee what actually happens, because the future is usually more original than our imagination of it. But there are new institutions such as the Tunisian Human Rights League which is of fundamental importance and which is only able to organize and develop because the notion of the individual exists. The state accepts that. And there are the beginnings of a multiparty political system – stifled still of course – but this is also an indication that the individual as a forceful cultural idea is struggling to emerge.

But although these are clearly steps in that direction, the process may be contradictory – it contains elements that may damage this evolution.

Did he mean by this that a reaction to growing individualism might emerge from movements that sanctified the community – from religious movements, for example?

Yes, that is a possibility. But this may even come from movements that are against transcendent values, that are against politicizing religion, but that are also against the emergence of the individual in that they reject all forms of structuring civil society. We might then find ourselves under some form of monopolistic state power which, bad enough in itself, might also generate the conditions for an extremist religious reaction.

Many suggestive ideas had been brought forward by these speakers, yet the ideas were understandably often laced with ambiguities and contradictions as the speakers sought to give concrete meaning to the central terms of the 'individual', 'freedom', and 'democracy'.

Some argued that their societies had a weak cultural notion of the individual, but this was in the context of a system of religious belief that, according to some interpretations at least, gave the 'individual' and the notion of human freedom a fundamental place. Some argued that personal freedom was central to a society's creativity and capacity to progress, but others stressed how difficult it was to allow individual freedom much rein in historical situations where societies struggled against foreign domination and had to mobilize their members on the basis of collective purpose.

Some would point to the need to build society on a foundation of human rights, others would respond that too much emphasis on rights leads to selfish, even anti-social attitudes and that social cohesion can only be achieved by coupling notions of rights to notions of obligation and duty. And many, while subscribing equally to the term 'democracy', would still be seeking ways to avoid both the monopolistic domination of a totalitarian one-party state and the social anomie of a simple one-person, one-vote political process.

A number of these issues will be explored in detail in my discussions with Moroccans. But before turning to these, let us take a closer look at the nature of Moroccan society.

6   Independent Morocco

MOROCCAN COMPLEXITIES

What if we compared the greetings exchanged by two Moroccans when they meet, with those exchanged by two Frenchmen, or two Englishmen? A Frenchman will say, 'Comment allez-vous?', which implies, on the subconscious level, an idea of movement, of action aiming for something. An Englishman will say, 'How do you do?', which conveys a will to act and indicates what one does in life. As for the Moroccan, he will ask of his friend, 'Ach Akhbareck?', 'What is your news?', which shows a desire to inform oneself and marks one's attachment more to the form of existence than to its essence or to its aims. So this is what dominates our subconscious being.

(Benslimane 1985: 14)

These thoughts, recently published by a Moroccan with a long career spent implementing government programs and a wide knowledge of Moroccan society, were part of his effort to understand why Morocco had not yet fully adopted the ways of the 'modern world'. But to me these thoughts point not only to the pressing need individuals have to understand themselves and their society in situations of rapid social change, but also to the risks of starting from appearances – and questionable ones at that – to reach conclusions about 'essences', 'fundamental nature', 'national character' or, in this case, 'subconscious being'. One might readily have taken other terms of address – an English 'What's new?', a French 'Quoi de neuf?', a Moroccan 'Kif dair' (roughly, 'How're you doing?') – and inferred quite different underlying propensities, quite a different 'subconscious'.[1]

If I have become convinced of anything about Morocco in the many visits I have made there over the past twenty years, and about human society in general as a result of being an anthropologist, a professional student of human society, it is that all contemporary societies are extremely complex entities, full of contradictions, and impossible to reduce to 'essences' and simple stereotypes. Of course, it is also true that it is absolutely necessary to try to simplify, analyze, and recompose such complexities as part of the effort to talk about and understand societies – to say nothing of living within them – but it is best not to do this believing that one has found the one true answer, or submitting to the illusion that a complete understanding is within grasp, or even around the corner.

What, for example, in the instance at hand, is one to make of Morocco? The country boasts a monarch who, ruling since 1961, is the second longest serving head of state in the Arab world (after King Hussein of Jordan), and the most recent leader of a dynastic line whose history of continuous rule is among the longest in the world; a constitution and parliamentary system that, while certainly not challenging the palace's dominant position, provide a framework for a well-developed political party system; and a vibrant cultural and artistic life that is the envy of many Arab intellectuals and artists in other countries and seems to be growing richer by the year.

Yet, despite this apparent institutional solidity, Morocco has witnessed over the past several decades serious outbreaks of popular protest, leading on several occasions to many hundreds of deaths, has been the scene of several armed insurrections, and the King himself came within inches of losing his life in two separate coup attempts. Human rights have been seriously violated, grave constitutional crises have abounded – the country has been governed since independence in 1956 under three different constitutions – and, since 1975, Morocco has faced a continuing war against an independence movement in the Western Sahara.

Morocco's geographical and social situation adds to this complexity. Morocco is a moderately large country in area (with somewhat less than half making up the Western Sahara), larger than France, Germany, or the UK, but only about one-third as large as its neighbor Algeria. With a varied geography marked by four mountain chains, a climate that encompasses Mediterranean as well as arid desert zones, and a hetero-geneous population speaking at least two main languages (Arabic and Berber, the last of which has several mutually unintelligible dialects), Morocco cannot be said to possess a 'natural' unity.[2] Indeed, the Moroccan nation, temporarily unified first in the late eighth century but tested frequently since then as dynasties and local political forces vied for power, has not always rested on firm footing.[3]

And the contrasts continue. Morocco is a country with much rich agricultural land – it had been an important granary for the Roman Empire and exported cereals to Europe throughout the nineteenth century (well before France established its protectorate in 1912) – yet it now needs to import substantial quantities of cereals. And despite recently improving performance in a number of key sectors of the economy, Morocco still finds itself on the World Bank's list of highly indebted countries and in 1987 had a higher long-term debt to GNP ratio than either Mexico or Argentina.[4] It is also a country where the glaring disparity between rich and poor, even when not striking the casual visitor as harshly as in other poorer countries, is nonetheless a stark fact of life for those who live there.

MOROCCO UNDER HASSAN II

When Crown Prince Hassan assumed the Moroccan throne in 1961 upon the death of his father, King Muhammad V, he became the most recent in a line of Alawite rulers that had continuously ruled the country since the seventeenth century. The Alawites, who trace their origins back some forty generations to the Prophet Muhammad and are descended from Hassan, son of the marriage between the Prophet's cousin Ali and his daughter Fatima, had come from Arabia to the Tafilalet region in what is now southeastern Morocco in the beginning of the thirteenth century.

In the course of the seventeenth century, the Alawites were able to build a military and spiritual power that united most of the country. Although their rule from that time on was often challenged, the dynasty managed to forge and maintain a continuously unified Moroccan state – the only southern Mediterranean territory to remain independent of the Ottoman empire – and to constitute a political entity of some significance in the region.

The French interrupted Morocco's independent history by forcing Sultan Moulay Hafidh to sign the Treaty of Fes in 1912, following decades of colonial pressure and Morocco's growing indebtedness and weak leadership. A French protectorate was established over most of the country and other zones (the northern tier of Morocco, the Ifni enclave and Tarfaya area on the southwestern Atlantic coast, and the Western Sahara) were carved out for Spanish rule.

When Morocco regained its independence from the French in 1956, Spain also renounced her claim on the northern zone (but retains to this day the Mediterranean coastal presidios of Melilla and Ceuta); Tarfaya was returned to Morocco in 1958 and Ifni in 1969. A treaty between Morocco and Spain awarded most of the Western Sahara to Morocco in 1976, but Moroccan sovereignty in the area is challenged by the Polisario Front, an independence movement with bases in Algeria and receiving considerable, if sporadic, support from both Algeria and Libya.

Upon independence in 1956 Sultan Muhammad V instituted a

governing cabinet consisting of members of several political groups, but the palace retained most of the power.[5] Muhammad V's son Hassan was made chief of staff of the Royal Armed Forces and led the battle against unrest in the Rif mountains in northern Morocco in the late 1950s.

In 1957 the Sultanate transformed itself into a hereditary monarchy from what had been, in principle at least, an elective one, and accordingly the ruler's title was changed to King. Political parties began to gain some strength and the Istiqlal (Independence) party – the strongest grouping to emerge from the nationalist struggle – led the governments during the first three years of independence. However, serious tensions within the Istiqlal party soon developed and the standing leadership, under Allal al-Fassi, was challenged by a socialist wing led by Mehdi Ben Barka. In 1959 this wing broke away from the main party to form the National Union of Popular Forces (UNFP – l'Union nationale des forces populaires).

The palace was able to play upon these divisions and in 1960 King Muhammad V dismissed the government he had allowed the UNFP to form, asserting its incapacity to rule. The King now became the government, arrested members of the UNFP, banned the small Communist party and, promising a constitution by 1962, appointed Crown Prince Hassan as prime minister. After Muhammad V's death in 1961 Hassan II fulfilled his father's promise and in December 1962 a referendum on the palace-written constitution was overwhelmingly approved (despite a boycott by the UNFP).

When Crown Prince Hassan assumed the throne in 1961 at the age of 32 he laid claim, as had his predecessors, to a double legitimacy: political, in prolonging Alawite dynastic rule and religious, in fulfilling the ruler's function as 'commander of the faithful'. It was never a foregone conclusion that these two sources of legitimacy, powerful as they are, would be strong enough to secure Hassan's rule against challengers. Supporters and opponents have frequently invoked other possible sources of legitimacy – ruling 'justly', developing the country economically, enhancing the quality of life, protecting the nation's territorial integrity – to either buttress his rule or attack it.

In the first years of Hassan's rule Morocco faced some serious external problems as well as internal ones. In 1963, in a dispute that was to fester for many years, a six-month border war broke out between Morocco and newly independent Algeria over territories that had been part of pre-colonial Morocco but had been attached by the French to Algeria while both countries were under French control. Relations with Algeria worsened still further when it was accused of supporting a 1963 plot against the monarchy, and also of supporting radical members of the UNFP, including Ben Barka.[6]

The first parliamentary elections held under the new constitution, in 1963, led to victory for pro-palace political parties led by Ahmed Reda Guedira, then a royal counsellor (and still one of the men closest to King Hassan II today). But this parliament appeared incapable of solving the country's serious economic and social problems, and feelings of social and political crisis grew very sharp.

On 23 March 1965 serious rioting broke out in Casablanca. Police and army action against the demonstrators led to more than 400 deaths. Hassan attempted to form a government of national unity to weather this crisis but after the UNFP and other leftist parties refused to join, he declared a state of exception and suspended the constitution for what was to be a period of five years. Early in this period, in October 1965, high-level Moroccan officials participated in the kidnapping in Paris of UNFP leader Ben Barka who disappeared and was never seen again.[7]

A new constitution, drafted by the King, was approved in a referendum in 1970, and parliamentary elections again gave a strong majority to pro-palace parties. However, in July 1971 a group of disaffected army officers launched an attack on the King's palace at Skhirat on the outskirts of the capital city Rabat, during a diplomatic reception. More than fifty guests were killed, and the King himself was held at gunpoint before convincing his captors to free him.

The coup was unsuccessful in its main objectives – the coup's leader, General Medbouh, was killed in the attack and ten other officers were later executed – but Hassan's image of invulnerability had been seriously damaged. A major reorganization of the army was initiated and repression of the left, particularly of members of the UNFP, hardened.

The 1970 constitution was suspended and in early 1972 a new constitution was adopted, again prepared under the supervision of the King and approved in a national referendum. This constitution is still in effect today.

The first elections due to take place under the new constitution had to be postponed after another nearly successful attempt was made on the King's life in August 1972, when his airplane was attacked in full flight by its escorting jets. This failed attempt, led by Minister of Interior Oufkir, had the same paradoxical effect as the first, both shaking the King's rule to its foundations yet strengthening it by reviving the popular view that Hassan possessed the special blessedness or grace – *baraka* – that should inhere in true religious leaders.

The uncovering of an insurrectionist plot in March 1973, attributed this time to Libyan involvement, led to another election delay, and to more arrests and repression on the left and of UNFP members. Under this pressure the UNFP split and the dissidents, under the leadership of

Abderrahim Bouabid, formed the Socialist Union of Popular Forces (USFP – l'Union socialiste des forces populaires), which was to become in ensuing years the main opposition force on the left.

Elections under the 1972 constitution were finally held in 1977. The constitution establishes a parliament, two-thirds of its members to be elected by universal direct suffrage and one-third indirectly by professional associations, communal councils, and trade unions. The constitution also establishes an independent judiciary.

Under this constitution, Morocco is a 'democratic and social constitutional monarchy' with Islam as 'the state religion guaranteeing to all the free exercise of their faith', and the principles of political and legal equality of men and women, freedom of opinion, expression and association, and freedom from arbitrary arrest are all clearly affirmed. However, these freedoms may be considerably limited, but 'only by law'.

In this constitutional monarchy, the King retains the lion's share of power. He is the commander-in-chief of the armed forces, signs and ratifies international treaties, has the power to name and dismiss the prime minister and other ministers, to appoint all judges, to dissolve parliament by decree and retain all law-making powers when parliament is not in session. He also may declare (and terminate) a state of emergency and exercise all powers of government during the emergency period. In addition, provisions in the penal code provide severe penalties for insults to the King and for challenges to the monarchical form of government. The most important regional officials – the governors – are appointed by the King and through this the King's power stretches deeply into the fabric of local communities.

In the period leading up to the 1977 elections new political parties were founded, including a reborn Communist party, and trade union organizations, some newly formed, entered into association or renewed their ties with the political parties. In the elections, 'independents' supporting the palace won more than 55 percent of the seats; and pro-palace politicians also dominated the next parliament, elected in 1984.

The 1984 election, originally planned for 1982, had been delayed for two years because of the war in the Western Sahara; elections planned for 1990 were also rescheduled to take place in 1992, to allow time for a UN-directed referendum in the Western Sahara to be implemented. These delays underline the clear fact that the most significant national issue during the last two decades has been Morocco's pursuit of its claim to the Western Sahara, a claim voiced early on both by the King's father and by the widely respected leader of the Istiqlal party, Allal al-Fassi. Within Morocco, Hassan II's pursuit of this claim has gained him, on this issue at least, almost unanimous support, despite widespread international opposition.

In mid-1974 Spain decided to put the future of the Western Sahara to a referendum of its inhabitants. Morocco brought its own territorial case to the International Court of Justice at the Hague and, although the Court's decision did not support Morocco's view that it had full sovereignty over the area, it did give the Moroccan government some grounds to claim vindication. With Spanish action hampered by the lingering death of Franco, King Hassan showed the strength of Morocco's commitment by mobilizing 350,000 Moroccans in November 1975 to stage a 'Green March' into the territory. This peaceful invasion forced a final agreement, negotiated in February 1976, between Spain, Morocco, and Mauritania, with Morocco and Mauritania dividing the former colony between them. Mauritania later abandoned most of its claim.

Algeria always strongly opposed the integration of the Western Sahara into Morocco and has given substantial material support to the area's independence movement, the Polisario Front, as well as providing territory and funds for refugee camps; Libya has given substantial support to the Front as well. Algeria's diplomatic aid helped secure recognition of the Polisario Front's Saharan Arab Democratic Republic by more than seventy states and the Organization of African Unity.

Towards the end of the 1980s, after more than a decade of inconclusive fighting, Moroccan military and internal political and economic measures began to bear fruit. Morocco progressively expanded the wall of sand it built around key areas until the wall circumscribed almost all of the region and, by injecting massive funds the government encouraged significant immigration from northern Morocco as well as settlement of the Western Sahara's nomadic populations. Together these measures appear to have led, as the 1980s end, to *de facto* Moroccan sovereignty over the region.

The UN is currently in the process of organizing a referendum to determine the fate of the area, but disagreements over the modality of this referendum have caused a number of delays so far. In any event, it is unlikely that Morocco would agree to referendum conditions that would seriously prejudice its interests and whatever the referendum's outcome, it is difficult to imagine Morocco accepting any loss of control over the area.

From the mid-1970s to the present, the palace's leadership on the Western Sahara issue secured a broad national consensus, a consensus that not only strengthened Morocco's military effort but also reinforced the King's position after the threats of the early 1970s. Opposition political parties have actively supported the King's policy on the Western Sahara, and the few individuals or groups taking the risk of either siding with the Polisario Front verbally, or arguing that the Western Sahara was not truly Moroccan, have paid dearly for this in long prison terms (and have often been refused pardons given to other political prisoners).

With a strong political consensus having been reached over the Western Sahara, the economic situation has generated most national discussion and controversy, and the poor (although recently somewhat improving) performance of the Moroccan economy has been the crucial internal problem the country has faced in the last decade.

Morocco's economy is run along 'liberal' lines although the public sector remains important. The government has made a strong commitment to a program of privatization, but it has been proceeding cautiously in this area. According to recent figures, the state holds 100 percent of the capital in 140 enterprises, is majority shareholder in 160 companies, and owns between 1 percent and 50 percent of stock in 387 firms.

Morocco's population has been growing at a rate of 2.7 percent in recent years – a relatively high rate characteristic of many Third World countries – and its urban areas are growing even more rapidly. The productive sectors of the economy have not been able to keep pace with this rate of growth: growth rates in industrial and manufacturing production were much lower during the 1980s than the 1970s, and although agricultural growth during the 1980s was higher than that of the economy as a whole, the increase has not enabled Morocco to avoid having to import large amounts of cereals. In addition, unemployment remains very high and the formal economy seems unable to absorb more than one-half of the 250,000 Moroccans who enter the labor market every year.

Morocco's main trading partner continues to be France, which both buys from and sells to Morocco approximately three times the amounts of Morocco's second most important trading partners. France also is far ahead in the list of foreign investors, with Spain second. The European Community (EC) as a whole buys almost two-thirds of Morocco's exports and provides just more than half of its imports.

Morocco's production and trade characteristics leave the country with a substantial trade deficit, food imports alone often accounting for more than 20 percent of the value of exports and oil imports for approximately another 20 percent. A portion of these deficits is met by remittances from Moroccan workers abroad (although these have been static or decreasing lately) and by recently growing tourism income. Nonetheless, with weakening phosphate prices – Morocco is a major world producer and exporter of phosphates – and some rises in oil prices, the trade gap has recently been growing at an alarming rate.

All these factors contribute to Morocco's serious debt problem. With a long-term debt equal to 117.9 percent of GDP in 1987, and with the servicing of such debt requiring approximately 30 percent of the revenue from the export of goods and services, Morocco places eighth on the

World Bank's list of the most heavily indebted Third World countries. Morocco has often had to engage in negotiations to reschedule these debts, and has been implementing a structural adjustment program under the advice of the IMF.[8]

Whatever the effects of such adjustment programs may be on the economy in the long term (and it is far from proven that IMF recipes do lead to successful outcomes), popular discontent with living standards and conditions has triggered numerous protests over the last decade – peasants in land disputes, workers in factory strikes, university students in strikes over study conditions and levels of financial support, to name just a few. In the most tragic of these, in June 1981, trade union demonstrations turned into mass protests; a violent response by the police and army killed more than 600 demonstrators in Casablanca. On another occasion, in January 1984, serious unrest broke out throughout much of Morocco following implementation of a number of IMF recommendations, including reductions in subsidies and substantial price rises in basic commodities. Official figures put the death toll at twenty- nine, but unofficial estimates were much higher.

Although Islamist groups have undoubtedly had some role to play in these outbursts, and although they are certainly present among the poorer sections of the population, such groups do not have the broad support in Morocco they have gained in Egypt and Tunisia. This is due in part to the religious legitimacy of the King and in part to the efficiency of the secret services in infiltrating and controlling such groups and in disciplining their members.

Recently there have been some positive economic signs but these threaten to be short-lived. There were several good agricultural years at the end of the 1980s (particularly when contrasted with radically depressed cereal and livestock production during the disastrous drought of the early 1980s) and this gave support, as the decade ended, to the official view that relatively positive economic performance was in prospect. There has also been a general increase in exports overall, inflation seems under control at less than 5 percent, and GDP growth for 1989 was predicted to be about 6 percent. However, figures for 1989 are reported to be much worse than those for 1988 with growth down to 1 percent from the previous year's 2.5 percent and the trade deficit having doubled.[9]

Although many aspects of this recent performance are encouraging, it will be difficult for Morocco to sustain them. Given the proven irregularities of climate and their often dramatically negative effects on agricultural production, it is unlikely that recent positive performance in this crucial sector can be consistently maintained. Also, Morocco's access to the EC countries – its primary export market – is threatened in its main agricultural exports, citrus fruits, by stiff competition from the southern European countries. These factors, together with the irregularity of oil prices and Morocco's increasing need for oil (the largest item on Morocco's import bill and threatening to grow much higher with repeated devaluation of the Moroccan currency), as well as the sluggishness and unpredictability of the phosphate and phosphate derivatives market (Morocco's largest export earner), mean that any recent gains can only be taken as fragile.

While the economic situation has been precarious, Morocco has nonetheless experienced, particularly during the second half of the 1980s, something of a cultural renaissance. Many cultural, academic, literary, and political journals have established themselves as serious contributors to their respective fields and many Arab authors have come to see Morocco as a major publishing center, especially since the decline of Beirut.[10]

As the general pattern of its economy suggests, Morocco has been politically pro-Western and Hassan, recognizing the importance of the EC for Morocco's future, has expressed a strong desire to have his country accepted as a full member. He has made every effort to keep Morocco's relations on an even keel particularly with France (not only Morocco's most important trading partner but also host to a Moroccan community of more than 600,000 immigrant workers and their families) and Spain (where the problem of the Mediterranean coastal presidios of Ceuta and Melilla, still under Spanish rule, has flared in the past and may do so again at any time).[11]

Under Hassan's leadership, Morocco has played an important role in Arab diplomacy, hosting several Arab summits, including the important 1982 Fes summit that elaborated guidelines for settlement of the Israeli–Palestinian dispute. Hassan is also head of the tripartite Arab heads of state committee for the Lebanon, and the special Arab League committee to further the peace process in the Middle East; and in 1989 he was named the first president of the newly formed Arab Maghreb Union.

Throughout the 1970s and the 1980s Morocco, as a result of both its debt problem and the war in the Western Sahara, has been heavily dependent on foreign good will and aid, most of which came from the US, France and the other EC countries, and the Arab oil states. Morocco was willing to risk strong opposition from the US when it joined Libya in a 'union' that lasted from 1984 to 1986, to counteract alliances being formed between Tunisia and Algeria. However, Morocco broke this union when conditions no longer required it and Hassan was then particularly prompt in placating the US by inviting the then Israeli Prime Minister Peres to Morocco in June 1986, despite some internal opposition and disruption of relations within the Arab world.[12]

7   Moroccan voices

'FIVE YEARS HERE, IT'S LIKE A CENTURY'

The notions of the individual and human freedom, and the related idea of democracy, were stressed more in my discussions in Morocco than elsewhere. Was this a sign that Morocco, more than Tunisia and Egypt, was shifting from a 'traditional' system of primordial loyalties where the 'individual' and notions of freedom and liberty existed in inchoate form, towards a 'modern' one where, under the pressures of urbanization and industrialization in a liberal economic mold, the individual was coming to assume greater cultural force and liberty and democracy were becoming more explicit motives in social behavior?

I had few illusions that such broad comparisons would be of much help in understanding the complexities of Moroccan life today. But even had I expected a clear association between a liberal economic system and a strong role for the individual and a fuller exercise of human freedom, these expectations would have been put to rest in one of my early conversations with Jamil Salmi, an economist and social analyst in his mid-thirties, who, in addition to having published an important study on the education crisis in Morocco, had just written a long essay on human rights in liberal society.[1]

Jamil began by suggesting that it was very difficult to tie 'freedom' to any particular societal model.

> Look, it is true that the private sector is really in favor in Morocco right now – people within the government and economic managers all think that the private sector has the most to offer. But let's face it – whatever lip-service they may give to 'freedom', 'democracy', and so on, they really do not care about it at all. There may be a few people in this system who will say, as individuals, 'we need more freedom', but mostly they are saying things like, 'the Moroccan people are not ready yet for democracy and freedom, they are not yet mature enough'. Basically these people are just thinking of a certain kind of limited freedom, a limited economic freedom.

But let me say also that after having studied this closely, I see that you can't go simply from criticizing the capitalist firm – that is, saying that the worker is exploited, that his freedom is an illusion – to praising the socialized, nationalized firm. We have both here in Morocco, both private firms and nationalized ones, and I think you can say that workers are as unfree and exploited as much in one as in the other.

At least in the capitalist firms there is one advantage: the firms must be profitable. This can in some circumstances operate as a check on the managers and can give the worker some small power, in principle. But as far as giving freedom to the workers, neither form of firm seems to me to be unequivocally the best.

Perhaps the ideal firm would have some deep form of worker participation within some kind of cooperative ownership structure, but we are all a long way from that, in Morocco and everywhere else. And here, of course, the ideological discussion is not very advanced. All you really hear is a dispute between a basically egalitarian socialist position where you take from the rich to give to the poor, and a liberal position to which some welfare concerns have been added, where you talk about giving to the poor without taking from the rich. That level of discussion doesn't get us very far.

Was there any place where such discussions seemed to go beyond simple ideology?

The only people who seem to me to get beyond this empty discussion are women and their discussions of women's liberation. Their notions of freedom and so on try to go beyond these economic structures. But of course then they often get attacked from the left, facing the traditional argument that socialism should come first and women's liberation will follow; to say nothing of facing attacks from the right, which accuses them of breaking up the family, weakening the structure of society, and so on.

Jamil's last remark, in fact, made me recall a meeting I had had with a Moroccan religious scholar who had been teaching for fifteen years at the Faculty of Law at Muhammad V University in Rabat. The religious scholar, a man in his early fifties who had received all his education in Morocco, had suggested that,

In the West, you see human rights and the rights of the individual as more important than the rights of the family. In fact, it is this expansion of the rights of the individual that is one of the causes of the decline of the family in the West. And this emphasis on the rights of the individual over those of the family was reinforced by the various international human rights conventions adopted after World War II.

And he went on,

In our societies, it is hard to struggle against this – there are so many forces at work leading in this direction – our economic system, the increasing employment of women and the changes in the woman's way of life. I don't know if we can find a way out of this imbalance, but we must try not to allow the expansion of the individual to go so far as to weaken or even destroy the family and our other social institutions.

Jamil had phrased the issue of freedom in terms of the economic structures and orientations of contemporary Morocco. The individual, as he saw it, was so exploited economically and socially that the emergence of a cultural notion of the 'individual' as a powerful force in society was at best a secondary concern. The religious scholar had expressed his fear that the emphasis on the individual was sapping the strength of social institutions and particularly of the family.

Perhaps one way to get an insight into the relationship between notions of the individual and personal freedom, and the strength of social institutions such as the family, was to try to understand directly how someone growing up in a relatively constraining family environment came to a sense of self.

This was one of the subjects I talked about with Fatima Mernissi. I had known Fatima for quite some time and knew she had grown up in a conservative and restrictive family. But Fatima had nonetheless succeeded very well in marking herself out as an individual in Moroccan society: now in her late forties, she is a sociologist with an international reputation and currently a professor at Muhammad V University in Rabat. Fatima had obtained her first university degree from the Law Faculty in Rabat and then received her doctorate from Brandeis University in the United States. She is the author of a number of books on Moroccan and Arab society and at the time I talked to her she was working on a study of the political role of women in Islamic history.[2]

Fatima began to talk first about her personal experiences as a young girl growing up in a bourgeois family in Fes, a city with a long history and well known as the seat of Morocco's *haute bourgeoisie*. During her childhood in the 1940s, women were first beginning to gain access to and more freedom in public space, and were beginning to shed the veil.

How did she herself experience this situation as a young girl – how did she feel its constraints and its benefits, how did these contribute to her notion of her own self?

Fatima began, 'For me it all revolves around the question of space, space and confinement.' I asked her to elaborate. 'You know', she said,

we were in a big, extended, patriarchal family, and in that family there were two worlds. When my father was there, there was 'the law' – we had to behave, be silent, be obedient. But when we women were alone it was a completely different world, the opposite of hierarchy. We wouldn't worry about praying, we'd just talk and laugh. When the weather was hot we'd be sitting around half nude – we'd just be having good times.

But it was my parents who controlled all my relations with people. I had no right to have friends, not even girlfriends, outside of my family, outside of my 'tribe' as you might say.

You know, this continued into my teenage years – around the age of 12 or 13 real friendships start to form. Of course, as far as boyfriends went, that was out of the question but that didn't create a problem for me, because I took that for granted. But the most painful were friendships that I was forming with other girls in my school classes. My mother would break up these friendships – break them up because perhaps a male cousin of mine would tell her that the girl's family had a bad reputation, or that he'd seen us standing and talking at the bus stop, or that he'd seen this girl talking with a boy. This was when I realized that I was in a kind of prison where they could break my relationships just like that. I would try to defend my friendships but there was nothing to do, they'd break.

I wondered whether there had been any problem about her attending school.

No, not at all. But that's because I was born at a time when the nationalist movement opened schools for women in Fes, and it was the big fashion to send your daughter there. And then, of course, we all used to go around singing about 'liberty' – that word was in all the nationalist songs. And my father used to have us perform – he'd put me on the table to perform, to sing songs that I'd learned at school when I was just 5 or 6 years old, or to recite verses from the Qur'an. Like a little thinking dog!

And I never had to wear the veil either, because that was around the time, during and after World War II, when women began to wear the jellaba – you know, the jellaba was originally a man's gown.[3] It was also around this time, in 1946, that our Sultan Muhammad V made an unforgettable gesture with his daughter. He was in Tangier, speaking in Tangier, and he took off his daughter's veil, he took off the veil of Princess ᶜaisha. And he had her read a political speech about change, about the need for change in our country. The Sultan was a model for my father, so my father was pleased when I began to study and even when I began to make speeches myself.

Shedding the veil was a big thing – a little bit like when women began to wear pants in Europe: the veil is awkward and clumsy, the jellaba is much freer. And with the jellaba the woman gained much more access to public space. I know that my mother had a battle with my father over the jellaba – he wanted her to wear the veil, but she just stuck to the jellaba and because he loved her very much, there wasn't much he could do.

How did she manage to develop as she did, given the limitations imposed by her parents and by the society around her?

> *Of course, even within this structure, we did find ways to expand our world and even to fool around a bit with boys. You know, in my large family there were a lot of girls and a lot of boys too. We used to play games with one another. I remember one – there was an immense trunk on one of our third floor terraces. There were six or seven of us, adolescents, maybe we were 10, 11, or 12 years old. And I was in love with one of my cousins – but all the girls were in love with him. Well, what was the game? It was called, 'Bride and bridegroom'. We'd get one of the boys and one of the girls to go into the trunk together, and we'd have them stay in there together for three or four minutes. But you know what's amazing? I've asked my cousins about this recently, and none of the boys remember, but the girls do. The boys have completely obliterated it from their memories.*
>
> *So, you have to realize that in our feminine world, there was a lot of freedom. And the women in my family, for example, were very strong, I never saw a woman beaten. And when the women wanted to, they could certainly do a lot of shouting and yelling.*
>
> *But this feeling of confinement was always there. I remember that I was forbidden to go into the gardens that were near the secondary school. You know, in spring, in Fes, the gardens can be so beautiful – the smell of the flowers, the jasmine. And there would be five or six of us girls, we'd love to go to the gardens so we could feed the silkworms. We'd climb up the trees to get these special leaves, and then collect them to feed the silkworms – we'd learned all about this in school – how it goes from caterpillar to butterfly, and so on. We were all crazy about this at the time and we'd each gotten our own silkworms to nourish.*
>
> *At first, my brothers would help me collect the leaves. But then I wanted to do this on my own and my parents wouldn't let me. And the gardens were so wonderful. I was saying to myself, 'My God, how can they prevent me from doing this, I mean, I am not doing sex or anything like that'.*
>
> *But no, it was forbidden. You go to school and you return, you have no possibility to go elsewhere. So again you were confined, again it was space that defined your sense of self.*
>
> *So space became for me a kind of obsession – confining me to a certain space defined my friendships, decided for me that I couldn't go to a movie, or to a garden, or to the beach. You know, even now that feeling is still with me – even now that I have a little bungalow at the beach. Sometimes I still get harassed on the beach, and it makes me think of this question of confined space. I used to get so angry about it. It was this anger that pushed me to leave Morocco in the first place.*

Fatima then talked about how her experience in the United States had affected her sense of self and her attitude towards Morocco.

There were a number of important things about my experience in America. First of all, when I went there I couldn't believe the freedom I had, I just couldn't believe it. I mean, no strings, no strings at all. But after about six months I started to feel a malaise, because it seemed to me that I wasn't feeling passionate about what was around me, there was nothing that really affected me in the guts. And that is really why I came back to Morocco.

The anger that I had originally felt in Morocco now began to turn to passion when I realized, after I had been in the US, that of all the societies in the world the one I really loved with passion was this one here, Morocco. Of course we have a lot of problems, but my God we have so much potential. For example, one of the things I realized while I was in the US was how much more difficult it was to change society there than here. If I had to struggle in the US against the image of women that is presented on the television and in advertisements – well, it seems so much more possible to change that image here.

Just look at how rapidly things have changed already. When I was a girl, I was still mostly confined to the house and there was still sexual segregation – for example, I didn't have the right to go to the library, or to the theatre, or to the swimming pool with my friends. But for my sister who is just two years younger than I am things were very different. I couldn't go to the swimming pool, but she could, and now she has become a champion swimmer. But that's Morocco. Five years here, it's like a century.

With her anger having turned to passion, how did she channel this passion?

Ever since I started writing, from about the age of 27, I no longer felt the same anger in my life. In fact, now, I have trouble relating to women and men who are angry. And I see that passion is a more fundamental axis around which my life revolves. There is a great difference between passion and anger – anger is an infantile state where you are out of control and can't control anything; passion gives you drive, it is with passion that you can change the world.

And what most needed changing in Morocco?

Well, now that I've been back here for something more than ten years, for me there is one issue that runs across the whole spectrum of life: the problem of democracy. The right to say what you want, to go where you want, to organize – you know, the people's fundamental rights. This is a primary problem, a primary woman's problem, a primary man's problem.

Was she not angry about that? 'When I was angry about these things, my attitude was, "Morocco now is a ruined society, it's finished". Now, with passion I think more about how we can change it.'

Fatima had been talking about how she defined herself as a person, what kinds of motivations she had, and how these motivations had developed against the background of her own upbringing, her own society, her own culture. The character of the socio-cultural context had also been suggested, from different perspectives, by Jamil Salmi and the religious scholar.

However, what seemed to be missing from these discussions so far was a sense of the cultural background against which the struggle for the 'individual', for 'liberty', for 'democracy' was taking place. I wanted to see if that cultural background could somehow be brought to the foreground; then I would be able to turn to the question of how these issues were articulated in contemporary Moroccan political discourse.

'IF YOU ARE A NAIL, SUBMIT; IF YOU ARE A HAMMER, HIT'

I was discussing this cultural background one day with the Moroccan sociologist, Muhammad Guessous, when he mentioned to me that, among his many other activities, he had been trying to understand Moroccan culture by analyzing about 10,000 Moroccan proverbs he had been collecting over many years. He had been focusing on three aspects: the person – what are the fundamental motivations and needs that make up the human being; the universe – what is the nature of creation and the place of the human being within it; and society – what is the proper and actual structure of society and how should and do human beings behave within that structure. Perhaps, he suggested, his analysis might be useful to me. I couldn't resist the opportunity.

However, an analysis of proverbs is problematic on many levels and Muhammad was well aware of such problems.[4] But we both thought, nonetheless, that such an analysis, if used carefully, might shed some light on subjects of interest to me. Muhammad began,

Taking into account the problems in analyzing proverbs, I think we can still find constant themes running throughout these proverbs. There are also great similarities between these themes and those you find in popular songs – if you exclude the modern, commercial songs that we have all around us these days.

Now, if we take all these proverbs together as a corpus, I have found that almost all of them can be put into three major chapters: one is what I would call a kind of theory of the universe – a cosmology – that is, what is the universe made of, what kinds of forces control the universe, and so on; the second chapter would be the nature and theory of the human being – an 'anthropology' in the classic sense of this word – what is man, what are man's innate abilities, what are his propensities, what are his limits, what are the effects of his actions; the third chapter is what I call a

kind of practical ethics – if we take the world for what it is, and man for
what he is, what are we to do? How are we to behave? What must we
expect from life in this world? And, most particularly, how does all this
apply to behavior in the political realm?

Muhammad took more than six hours, spread over several days, to
present his argument, liberally sprinkling in proverbs he thought were
apposite. He would refer to his notes from time to time (he had asked me
before our discussions to give him some time to look over his materials)
but most of his presentation, of which I am only giving a summary, was
delivered as though the material was part of him.

Although his proverbs were often very interesting in themselves, his
analysis interested me just as much – less perhaps for any 'truth' it
conveyed about Moroccan culture as such than for what it said about how
some people thought about Moroccan culture and about the role of the
individual, liberty, and democracy.

He began with the cosmological section.

Generally speaking, the world in these proverbs is described as irrational,
incomprehensible, not amenable to human understanding. Second, the
world is random, capricious: you cannot predict, you cannot control, you
cannot influence it. Third, the world is malevolent: the power of evil in the
world is much stronger than the power of good. Fourth, there is not
enough good in the world: it is scarce and it is not evenly distributed. Fifth,
all of these characteristics seem to be growing more extreme, things are
getting worse over time: more irrational, more beyond control, more
malevolent, more unequal.

One very interesting aspect of this cosmology is that the proverbs
sometimes show conceptions of God that challenge the orthodox Islamic
view. You know that in Islamic theology the forces that rule the world start
with God, an omnipotent, transcendent, all-powerful God, a God without
rivals. This vision holds for the proverbs and for the Qur'an.

But in the world of the proverbs God sometimes shows some very
peculiar behavior. You beg him, he does not do what you want; somebody
does not need a thing, he gets it; you need things and you do not get
them. For example, 'God gives hard beans to those who do not have
teeth'. Or, 'The orphan cries and God adds to his misery'. Remember that
in the Qur'an the orphan is among the first to receive alms, and that the
Prophet Muhammad himself was an orphan from a very young age.

There are many, many proverbs in which God is described as
somebody peculiar, who cannot be trusted. In other words, something is
wrong: it is as if God had other things on his mind. Of course, the
cosmology also includes many kinds of magical forces, spiritual forces,
demons, that can be described as arbitrary, capricious, malevolent – but
what I said above relates to the way God is talked about.

Now, when we get to the 'anthropology' we again find several themes, themes that cover a general description of what it is to be human, and also a theme of decadence.

First of all, man is seen pessimistically, as somebody who is naturally vulnerable, incapable of knowing by himself what is true and what is false, what is just or unjust; he is naturally egotistic, tends toward vanity, tends to be more unjust than just, and will do more harm than good. Basically, people never change their character: you might think you're going to improve things, but you'll only end up making them worse.

Let me just give you a few examples. 'He ran away from a hill, he fell into a well'. Or, 'You can only change your friend for someone worse than he is'. Or, to take a harsher proverb, 'You can beat a prostitute until she pees, but what is in her head will never come out of it'.

Man tends to value things according to wealth, rather than according to their spiritual or moral worth. And no one can be trusted any more, not even your own family. For example, 'Fill his throat with food and he will forget that he is a believer'. Or, 'The pigeons I have raised have run away from me; the flowers I grew have been picked by someone else'.[5] Or, 'Your paternal uncle will blind you, your maternal uncle will kick you out of his house; run away from your blood before it curses you'.

The idea that human beings are very limited is joined to a theory of decadence – man's limitations are becoming ever more limited. This leads to a kind of critical attitude towards the present: the golden age is behind us and in the present all the things that make life worthwhile are lost or are disappearing. There is no trust anymore, no longer any respect for honesty, for good moral behavior, for piety. There is respect only for falsehood and, more and more, for money. An example: 'Gone is that time with its people, and this new time has come with its axe; and whoever speaks the truth, they break his head with it'.

Muhammad now summarized what he had said so far before turning to 'practical ethics'.

Up to here I think you now should have the following picture. You have on the one hand a world which, as I said, is random, malevolent, uncontrollable, where the amount of evil is increasing, the amount of good decreasing – a vast world, like a giant. And in the face of this you have a man whose inner capacities are limited, who is by himself and incapable of defending himself, who in the face of the world is a tiny, tiny thing.

Of course, as an aside, you know that it is on just these grounds that all theology books justify the notion of prophets. After all, why did God send prophets? Because man, by himself, would never have been able to find the truth. And then why did God have to keep sending one messenger after another? Because man is stubborn – look at the story of Noah, look at the story of Adam, of Abraham, of Isaac – prophets had to come one after the other.

So, now we come to the third section – practical ethics – asking, I think, the following questions: what can you therefore expect in this world, with the world as it is, with man as he is? What kind of behavior is appropriate in this sort of world? And how does this apply to political behavior?

In general, what I find from the proverbs is the argument that if you take man as the small thing that he is, and the world as immense and dangerous as it is, you must conclude that pain, hardship, losses, problems, are the normal, natural, and necessary stuff of life. Happiness is impossible, fulfillment is impossible.

The best a person can realistically expect is to minimize evil. Evil is necessary, natural, unavoidable – it will keep happening to you – and the best you can do is to do certain things to protect yourself. The wise man is the man who does not expect good things in this life but who takes precautions to minimize the evil. The fool is the man who expects more out of life – he will usually end up getting his head cut to pieces.

So, then, how should you act to attain a good life, to minimize the evil? The answer, when you piece it together, is actually very logical, like a formula, like a syllogism. But the elements in this formula, although each necessary, are not sufficient, and each must be added to the others.

Let me start it from the beginning. In order to minimize evil, you need to work, and you need to work hard. This is a strong, peremptory statement, as if God were saying to man, 'Work, O man, and I will help you. But first, man, you must do your part'. So, there is a cult of work, a high value put on work. But – and there is always a 'but' – work alone will never guarantee the much desired minimization of evil.

What do you need in addition? You need worship. There is a direct association between work and God. And, in fact, you know that whenever you begin to work, whenever you begin a job, you must say, 'Bismillah' (In the name of God).

However, even God plus work is not sufficient. God may forget you, he may be too busy for you. So you also need intermediaries to intercede between you and God. You need holy men, you need patrons. You need a broker or you need magic to mediate with the natural forces.

But even this is not sufficient. Because even with all this you may, so to speak, enter the mosque with your shoes on, you may be so isolated from the world of other men, from the world of social relationships and kinship ties, that your behavior is untrained, undisciplined.

Now, in addition to these conditions – work, religion, mediation, social relations – there are two other requirements. First, there is the state of mind – you need to be realistic and to know your limits. Here we have proverbs like, 'He who is frugal will feed his hunger quickly'. Or, 'You would better be cursed by your parents or by God than be a big eater'. You have to be able to distinguish between dream and reality. You have to always be on your guard, mistrustful, and never take anything for granted – what you see outside the house is not what is inside, what you see in the face is not what is in the heart.

And finally, there is luck, chance. That's it, just pure luck. As in the saying, 'Luck is given by God to whomever He wants'. This idea of luck is a bit like the belief in hidden treasures, like in the love stories where the boy meets the girl and the girl turns out to be a princess. But you also have to know that this last step in the ladder of success is also the first step of the fall, because the next step can bring you all the way down to the bottom. The princess can just as quickly turn out to be a child of nobody, the big man can become the smallest, and all in the blink of an eye. As the proverb says, 'He fell from the top of the minaret to the bottom of the well'.

Now we reach the part that should interest you the most – how do these practical ethics apply to the political domain? There is one part that I'll call analytical or descriptive – it analyzes what power holders do and what can be expected of them – and a second part that is normative, asking what the appropriate type of political organization is, what kind of relationships people should have with the power structures as they are. Finally, there is a third part that is more prospective, dealing with the likely evolution of such types of power structures.

If we start with the first part, what is most striking is its realism on the one hand and its pessimism on the other. Generally political power is seen essentially as a source of evil and harm, and those who hold power tend to be unjust, to break the law, and to play with other people's lives. Generally the tone of the proverbs is quite bitter, they convey a sense of fear and betrayal. Injustice is the rule, the abuse of power is the rule; the proper, adequate use of power is the exception.

Let me give you a few examples. 'Only the powerless are not despotic.' Or, 'He who defeats a rat, cuts its tail' – in other words, if you are victorious, it is normal for you to be cruel to those you defeated.

Now, if this is the general behavior of power holders, how should ordinary people behave, from their own point of view? Let's look at this over the long run and the short run. Over the long run, people appear to live for the day when they will be able to avenge themselves, when the roles can be reversed, when those who have humiliated and threatened them can themselves be humiliated and threatened. And remember – those who are up today will be down tomorrow. So, you must just wait, and the times will turn.

For example, 'If the times are just, one day will be for you and one day will be against you'. And one of the best, 'The son of power is an orphan' – meaning that power is not socially guaranteed, you may have a protector and power today and nothing tomorrow.

And patience is necessary, too; you must wait and your time will come. 'The rat who is too nervous is a godsend for the cat'. And, 'The only thing that comes fast is death'.

But while waiting, what must you do? You must keep your distance from those in power and you must work together with your fellows. On keeping your distance, 'He who frequents the blacksmith will see his clothes get all black'. And 'Who dares to tell the lion that the lion's mouth smells?' On working together, you find proverbs such as 'A dispute between dogs is a godsend for the wolves'. Or, 'Little sticks can burn a big stick'. Or, 'Little animals in a pack can beat a lion'.

Over the short term, you must be quite realistic, never expect anything from those in power, and depend on yourself not on them. 'With my own bread under my arms, nobody will hear me shouting or crying.' Of course, at the same time, you must show outward respect: 'The hand you want to cut, kiss it until the day you can cut it'.

And this is all mixed with a healthy dose of skepticism. Perhaps a new leader has come, promising all kinds of nice things. Many proverbs say, in effect, whoever in power promises and whatever they promise, don't believe it. For example, 'Your smoke has blinded me, but your food has never come'. Or, 'He took me all the way to the sea and brought me back thirsty'.

There remains one last thing: what kind of power would one have wished to find in this life? What would legitimate power, appropriate power, be like?

First of all, the proverbs seem to show a longing for a strong power. For example, 'The stick is the only thing that will prevent rebellion and dissidence'; or, 'An unjust government is better than bad citizens'; or, 'Starve your dog and it will follow you'. So, the general rule seems to be: if you are going to be eaten, let yourself be eaten; but if you can eat others, then eat them. And the reverse side of this is, 'It is better to be eaten by a lion than to be picked to death by dogs'.

What we see here then is fertile ground for despotic behavior, because society can't do without rulers. And we need strong rulers, because otherwise things are likely to go berserk.

Did he take this to mean that the individual was completely dominated, that there was no room for personal freedom, that the democratic impulse was absent? Muhammad answered,

Let me just say what I said a bit at the beginning. First – these proverbs are not univocal: they have many meanings and many of the things I have mentioned could also be interpreted in other ways. To give this corpus some measure of its real complexity, you have to see it as having three structures at least: an actual structure – the meanings that are clear, manifest, dominant, most frequent; a potential structure – the range of possible variations in meanings; and a counter-structure – the meanings that challenge and contradict the dominant meanings – like the atheistic streak, the critique of religion, the critique of the Prophet.

For example, take the notion of the hustler. There are a number of

> *proverbs with characters whom you might call 'the hustler' and 'the sucker'. The hustler uses the same formula – religion, effort, mediation, social relations, state of mind, luck – but takes them as tools and uses them to his own advantage; the sucker goes by the same rules but takes them too seriously, takes them as principles, as destiny, and suffers for them. It just shows that within the culture there is always a counter-culture – the hustler can use morals, ethics, religious beliefs, and your good intentions, and gain his own ends and trick you out of yours.*
>
> *But remember, even in this counter-culture, if you really follow the story to the end, the hustler will eventually fall into pieces. Always, in the end, nobody is cleverer than life.*
>
> *So, it is only when you take this all together – the actual structure, the potential structure, the counter-structure, as well as all the many complexes and configurations of behavior – that you can begin to get any idea of what 'Moroccan culture' is.*
>
> *This 'fundamental' culture is widely shared, widely shared just because, with all these different ingredients you can make many different blends. Out of all this, different groups and different individuals can each find the cocktail that suits them and communication can take place between high and low culture, between the spoken and the written word, between the intellectuals and the ordinary people, between the rulers and the ruled, between the generations, between men and women, between social classes, between countryside and city. And this may be what constitutes the cultural continuity that marks Morocco.*

I asked Muhammad again whether, on the basis of his analyses, he could draw some lessons as far as the notions of the 'individual', 'freedom', and 'democracy' were concerned.

> *Now, the lessons I see from all this? On one level, I think that a positive lesson from this corpus is that it preserves a certain autonomy of the person in a situation where the state seems to be taking over everything. And, to the extent that the corpus also contains a critique of modern times, of the present, this also amounts to a critique of the state since today the state controls everything. And there is also the notion that there is a person who does not feel fulfilled, who does not feel he has accomplished enough in a world where values are being lost.*
>
> *And secondly, in only very few places do I find any kind of expression for a moderate view of power, such as in this proverb, 'The best rule is one that neither leaves the wolf hungry nor makes the shepherd cry'. Nowhere can I find any real support for democratic structures. The best you'll find is an undemocratic despot, but one who is weak, mild, not too oppressive, subject to checks, counter-balances, and so on.*
>
> *Really, the dominant view is the one you find in many proverbs that show fighting over who'll be the boss rather than a struggle for democracy or equality. For example, 'I would rather live for only one month, as a cock,*

than for two years as a hen'.
Let me give you one final proverb that I think sums most of this up: 'If you are a nail, submit; if you are a hammer, hit'.

The intricate interweaving of themes that Muhammad had brought forth from the proverbs not only displayed the originality and analytic power of his own thinking, but also showed how a set of apparently fixed forms of social expression could carry conflicting messages and how a complex cultural system could unite people on one level while also, on another, providing them with symbols and a vocabulary that might be used as weapons in their struggles against one another.

While showing the cultural context against which notions of the individual, freedom, and democracy, might emerge, Muhammad's presentation did not address (nor was it meant to) the question of how political action itself might invoke these notions and how these notions might be used to articulate various political positions and various political programs. These were some of the questions I was able to address in my next series of interviews.

'LIBERTY IS A VEIL AMONG VEILS'

Jamal Zyadi, a sociology graduate in his late twenties, had been a student of Muhammad Guessous; Guessous had recommended him very highly to me. While Guessous' influence on Jamal's thought was perceptible, Jamal had made his own comprehensive study of the notions of liberty, freedom, and democracy in the political thought and action of contemporary Morocco; in addition, he was a committed political activist in his own right.

Jamal found himself in the same predicament as many other recent university graduates – he was unemployed and, despite his obvious intellectual dedication, was unlikely to find a position in a university system in crisis. It did not help that, from a working-class family and having spent all his university years (and indeed his whole life) in Morocco, Jamal did not have the highly valued French or American university diploma obtained by many of the sons and daughters of the Moroccan elite. Nor was he socially or politically well connected in a way that, for some people at least, helped them attain university teaching posts.[6]

As it turned out I was to have many hours of discussion with Jamal and I learned to appreciate the qualities that had pushed Muhammad Guessous to recommend him to me: he had an intimate knowledge of the wide readings he had done, a direct experience of political action (Jamal was an active member of the USFP), an ability to empathize with thinkers whose views he nonetheless opposed, a gift for turning his sometimes enigmatic formulations into pregnant ones, and a strong critical spirit.

In one of our first talks, Jamal had given me some of his general ideas about the central importance of the concept of liberty in Moroccan life today. He began,

> The theme of liberty, the question of liberty, in modern Morocco penetrates all social and political currents. But this widespread, explicit demand for liberty is only the top of the mountain, and it hides behind it the many different forms this demand takes. For liberty is like a body that heightens desire, it is like a lost capacity. Why? Well, let me try to explain it to you.
>
> The call for liberty in Morocco is open and clear. People say it without detours. One reason for this is because the idea dominates people's consciousness; another is perhaps because people here are better able to express the need for liberty than elsewhere in the Arab world. But liberty is in no way a new character on our stage; it is a veil, a veil added to other veils, a veil among veils. You know Nietzsche, in his Zarathustra, says that we discovered the 'you' before we discovered the 'I'. But in Morocco, and I think it is the same in the other Arab countries, we transfer our attention from one 'you', to another 'you', to another 'you', and we never come to focus on the 'I' – on what we ourselves are as makers of our own society, and on what we are each as individuals.
>
> Now, how can the notion of liberty advance in a situation where there is the almost total absence of 'the individual' as an idea, as a value, as a guide for conduct? It is clear, you know, that all the calls for liberty in modern Morocco have one thing in common: they keep the individual under a shadow. For example, we never hear demands that political prisoners be released simply because as men they have a right to liberty. No, it is always in terms of big words, grand ideas, like 'the interests of the nation'.
>
> The classic cause offered for the absence of the 'individual' – that the intermediary groups in traditional Moroccan society tied the person to them and did not allow the individual an independent existence – is well known. These intermediary groups guaranteed a certain freedom of action, but within clear limits.
>
> Also, in the century preceding colonization, we were already facing external threats. That century allowed Moroccan society to become conscious of itself, but it was a consciousness in opposition to the external threat. Both during the struggle against the threat and during the later struggle to throw off colonialism, the Other was an outsider, a foreigner.
>
> But with independence, the Other is now no longer the Frenchman, the Spaniard, or the Englishman. The Other is now a Moroccan. But – and

here is the point – even though this Other is a Moroccan, we tend to view him as a foreigner, as not a member of the group, as not reflecting our own essence, but as something that must be eliminated, that must be cut off from us.

This is all deeply rooted in Islamic society. You can see it in our history, you can see it in our popular stories. We do not want believers or brothers to fight one another. But they do. And when they do, we are willing to accept it only on the condition that each sees the other as the devil.

I asked Jamal whether he could give me a specific example.

OK, let's take a political party in Morocco, a classical political party. Usually, it will not admit publicly that there are disputes, that there is dissent within the party; it will only admit these disputes when it expels the dissenting group, or expels its leaders. So, there is liberty, the freedom to express yourself. But either the words will be absorbed as a new fashion, or wiped out by an accusation that there is some intrigue behind it, or lead to expulsion. So underneath the apparent liberty there is a kind of order that is itself contrary to liberty.

This is a general pattern that repeats itself from party to party, from social group to social group – you can see the same thing happening now with the religious groups. And that's what I mean when I say that the open discussion of liberty is like one veil among many veils, all of which keep us from discovering the 'I'.

After this introduction, Jamal and I discussed how we might best proceed. We decided to begin by discussing a recent work by a leading Moroccan intellectual, Abdallah Laroui, that examined the historical roots of the idea of liberty in Arab society and tried to explain why the notion had achieved such importance today. Then we would move on to discuss the ideas of liberty and democracy put forward by two pivotal figures in contemporary Moroccan political life: Allal al-Fassi, a major representative of reformist Islam and a leading figure in the struggle for Moroccan independence and in the immediate post-independence period; and Mehdi Ben Barka, a leader of the socialist left in the immediate post-independence period until he was kidnapped and disappeared in 1965. Throughout this, Jamal would try to give me his own ideas and criticisms, and we would reserve a period at the end for him to sum up the importance of the notion of liberty in today's Morocco.

Abdallah Laroui was for many years a pre-eminent Moroccan intellectual of the left and he has written several influential books on Moroccan history and on the contemporary situation of the intellectual in the Arab world. In 1981 Laroui published a book, *The Concept of Liberty (Mafhum al-ḥurriya)*, exploring the notion of liberty in Arab society, and this book was frequently referred to in discussions I had with other Moroccans.[7]

In describing Laroui's project to me, Jamal would talk mostly without referring to his notes; when wanting to quote Laroui directly he would read from sections in his notebook that he had copied from Laroui's book.

In *The Concept of Liberty* Laroui addresses a problem that is central both to anthropology and to today's human rights discussion in the Middle East: to what extent can concepts developed mainly in one society be applied to another? Laroui tries to apply the notion of liberty as it was forged in the West to understand Arab Muslim society – but this same problematic would be applicable to other human rights concepts and to the explicit notion of 'human rights' itself.

After exploring the Arabic language historically for notions of liberty and finding no words that convey the Western meaning of socio-political liberty, and then examining the religious tradition where freedom and liberty are seen as aspects of the relation between the person and God, Laroui spends most time examining social practices that might exemplify socio-political liberty, even though the term 'liberty' (or an appropriate Arabic translation) might not itself be used.[8]

Laroui argues that liberty was indeed socially practiced, although not explicitly formulated, well before the Middle East felt the Western colonial threat and influence. He locates this practice in four different domains of social life where the central authority's capacity to dominate was circumscribed: in the peasantry, which displayed a significant potential for revolt against the ruler and thus kept despotism and absolute power within certain bounds; in corporate groups of various sorts – clans, families, occupational guilds – which protected to some extent their members against both the Sultan's arbitrary orders and the full brunt of outside economic forces; in piety, which the believing Muslim sees as liberating one's superior side from one's inferior side, freeing oneself from the slavery of nature; and in union with the Absolute *(attasuf)* (as in the mystical Sufi orders), where one seeks complete identification with the Absolute and freedom from external influences, be they natural, social, or psychic.

However, as a result of the threat from the West and the need to protect itself against the European colonial incursion that started in the late eighteenth and early nineteenth centuries, Arab Muslim society underwent profound transformations. The independent groups within the state – the peasantry, the corporate groups, and the Sufi orders – came to be seen by the state as internal enemies that had to be disarmed. Even individual religious piety lost much of its liberating force as the state came to exercise increasingly tight control over religious scholars. As the relative independence of these domains was eroded, the individual became increasingly vulnerable.

Laroui can thus explain why the word *hurriya* propagated itself so quickly in the sense of socio-political freedom as the colonial threat and presence made itself felt: Arab Muslim society was prepared to accept the idea of liberty because, before the colonial incursion, it already had the practice of it. And Laroui goes on to say that 'although the Arab world will come to use foreign expressions, the content of these expressions is born from within the reality of traditional Islamic society'. As we approach the present, as the state threatens to dominate everything, and as all human experience becomes political experience tied to the state, the term in the socio-political sense becomes ever more significant. And the dialectic of liberty is set in motion. 'Each time that the domain of liberty as reality is restricted, the force and precision of liberty as symbol is strengthened.'

Having traced the notion's development from its historical foundations into the present, Laroui sums up by stressing that

> the word liberty, hurriya, has become the symbol of everything one demands; it has put an end to preceding symbols ... it is among the most commonly used terms, as though the contemporary mind can't do without it ... it shifts its meaning from liberty for Muslims from the foreign danger, for the Arabs against Turkish domination, for the craftsmen against the monopolies, to liberty for the woman against the old practices, for the student against the old pedagogy, for literature from archaic styles, for freedom of the mind from myths.

As Jamal had presented Laroui's arguments, it was easy to see why 'liberty' had evolved into a term of great emotive value, as have many other terms today (among them 'human rights' and 'democracy'). But this inflated rhetorical usage made me uneasy. How, I wondered, were these and related notions embedded in the actual struggle of Moroccans to secure their independence, to secure better conditions in their daily lives? How had the notion of socio-political liberty been used and wielded on the public stage?

To explore these questions, Jamal and I first began to talk about the reformist Islamic figure Allal al-Fassi.

Allal al-Fassi, born in 1910 in Fes, was educated in that city's (and Morocco's) most prestigious center of Islamic learning, the Qarawiyin, and came to adulthood at a time, in the late 1920s and early 1930s, when reformist Islam was at its height in Morocco. This was also during the period when the French colonial authorities promulgated the Berber Decree (1930), attempting to draw a legal distinction between customary (supposedly Berber) and Islamic practices, and so to divide the Berber-speaking populations from the Arabic speakers. Both of these elements gave great impetus to the nationalist movement. Allal al-Fassi, frequently in prison or exiled as a result of his nationalist activities – the Protectorate authorities considered him for a long time to be their number one enemy – was a leading figure in this struggle throughout the period leading up to independence in 1956.

After independence, al-Fassi was a government minister for a time, but spent most of the period until his death in 1974 working within the Istiqlal (Independence) party. With all governmental power in Morocco effectively wielded by the palace, a measure of al-Fassi's importance can be readily seen in his ability to move his party to positions, over the opposition of many of its own members, that were against the policies of the palace and that the party never again adopted after his death: for example, he led the party to reject King Hassan's constitution in the early 1970s, and he forged an alliance between the Istiqlal party and the main leftist opposition party, again against the wishes of the King. He was also instrumental in pushing his party to confront fundamental national problems, like the problem of the educational system.

Jamal began,

The first point to keep in mind when talking about Allal al-Fassi is that among all our Moroccan Islamic reformists, Allal was the one most familiar with Western thought. For him – and I wish I could say as much for many of our other thinkers – in order to reject a system of thought you first have to know it. He is a reformist who can easily refer to Descartes, to Marx, to Rousseau, even to Nietzsche. A second point is that his thought has two sides: a religious vision of society that sees the continuity of Moroccan society with an Islamic tradition, and a critical vision of the West. This critical vision is based, as we will see, on what you might call a 'liberal' conscience.

For Allal all the true values, such as work, and liberty, and rationality, are essential elements at the heart of Islam. If Muslims have at times lived in situations that were, so to speak, anti-liberty, or anti-work, or anti-rationality, this has nothing to do with Islam, but with the corruption of Islam by local practice and traditions. There is, for Allal, a pure, true Islam; and there is an Islam that is second-hand.

But Allal faces a difficulty: he sees that in his world, the world of colonial Morocco, the good values of work and liberty and science come from the Christian countries, the colonial powers, the countries of the atheistic West. But Allal doesn't believe that these true values have their origins in Christianity, which he sees as a religion of false values.

For Allal, then, the aim was not to borrow what you wanted or needed from the West and then reject the rest; the aim was to recognize the origins in Islam of these central values, and to encourage the nationalist movement in Morocco to translate these values concretely into the *nationalist struggle and eventually into independent Morocco.*

Both these aims led him to two new emphases: instead of focusing on a Moroccan Islamic community, or on the tribal community, or on the national domain of the Sultan, Allal promoted Islamic law (shari^ca) and its purposes (maqasid) as the basic point of reference for the believer. This meant that the primary community of reference became the Islamic community, the 'umma. But perhaps even more importantly, Allal didn't judge whether an action was Islamic or not by returning to a hadith or to a Qur'anic verse.[9] He believed, instead, that Islam and its law had certain purposes, and that it is in the light of these purposes that the meaning of Qur'anic verses must be interpreted, that the meaning of the Prophet's words must be judged, that an assessment of actions must be made.

I remarked to Jamal that this was not the first time in Islamic thought that inferential rather than literal meanings of sacred texts had been elaborated, and how important this theme had been throughout Islamic history as a way for human beings, living in concrete social situations, to understand and draw lessons from a sacred text specifically referring to a different concrete situation. Jamal responded,

Yes, it isn't the first time that anyone did it, but it is very important just the same. Allal constructed criteria that aren't explicit in the Qur'an or in other privileged texts, but that are behind everything, that are in effect the purposes for which the Qur'an was given by God to the Prophet and to the believers.

I was particularly interested in this notion of aims or purposes, which had come up in other contexts in other countries, and in how this was related to ideas about the person, the individual. I asked Jamal if he could elaborate on this.

For Allal, man is before everything else an animal, an animal composed of two principal elements: on the one hand an animal side, an emotional side; and on the other, a human side, a 'disposition' (fetra) to realize one's human nature. Realizing this disposition means, for Allal, recognizing that you are free, that is free to choose Islam and the fundamental aims of Islam as your own. Now, for Allal, man cannot attain his humanity completely on his own. This is why God had to send his prophets, so that man becomes able to make this transition from the animal to the human.

Now, what is the purpose of humanity? Allal says, 'God created the earth and the universe. He put into the hands of man the task of improving this earth. The reason why God created the universe was to transfer his responsibility to man on earth.' You can summarize this a little schematically: you can only fight your animal nature and gain access to your human nature first, by belief in God; second, by believing in man as an honored creature, charged by God; third, by assuming God's mission

– improving the earth in the interests of man.

So for Allal the fundamental aim of the Qur'an, of Islam, is to make of man the representative of God on earth, responsible before God for improving the earth, for carrying out God's charge, and for doing this by acting with justice. For Allal, then, the representative of God on earth isn't the ruler, or the learned man, or the religious leader – no, it is man himself, man as man, man as worker, man as free.

The notion of man rather than the ruler as God's representative had important implications for the idea of democracy as well as giving, potentially at least, a significant role to the individual. In al-Fassi's thought all this seemed hinged to the idea of justice and I asked Jamal how al-Fassi meant this term to be understood.

For Allal, in order for man to act justly, he should not be content with the mere surface appearance of Qur'anic law – God didn't make these laws and then tell men to judge by appearances, by explicit content. No, he charged man to do what is just, to try to realize one's responsibilities as God's representative on earth, even if this means going against one's self. Even if the surface appearance of Qur'anic law seems to be in one's favor, one should act in accordance with the deeper aims of Islamic law, even if these deeper aims go against one's self.

You have to understand the central role played by justice in Allal's view of Islam. As Allal sees it, justice in the history of Christianity emerged as a product of revolutions and social transformations that took place outside of the church. These struggles created institutions and laws to guarantee justice, outside of religion. So, justice is something outside the church. For Islam, it is the contrary. Allal says that in Islam, justice is the practice of Islam's law, its legal precepts, its laws. Justice isn't a legal theory independent of Islam. And it doesn't depend on the mere appearances of the Law. Justice, in Islam, resides in the belief that man is charged, that he has a mission. This is the purpose of Islamic law in the light of which justice exists.

This notion of justice seemed a bit vague – and I recalled Muhammad ᶜamara in Egypt talking about justice as 'moderation' as 'the synthesis of extremes'. Was this the same for al-Fassi?

Now, in Islam, when talking of justice, everyone talks of the center, the mean (al-wasat, al-kelmat al-wasat). Hassan II talks of it and the religious leaders talk of it as synonymous with justice. But Allal reminds us that this center, this justice, is not the 'center' of finding the middle of two propositions or of two courses of action, as many people will say. For Allal justice means knowledge, sincerity in witnessing, and judging in accordance with the purposes.

It is also important to see that for Allal, Islam is absolutely synonymous with liberty, because it is only through realizing his human disposition that man becomes free, that is free to choose between good and evil. For Allal you can't say that the concept of liberty is in Islam. No, for Allal, Islam is liberty. One can even say that for Allal, the theory of liberty – that is Islam – plays the same role as the theory of the proletariat plays for Marx. For Marx, the theory of the proletariat in fact creates the proletariat as a class conscious of itself, that is the theory leads a mass of individualized, objectified human beings to gain conscience of themselves as commodities, and therefore to work for the destruction of the commodity nature of human beings.

For Allal, it is the theory of liberty, that is Islam – the view that man is free and can therefore choose God's mission – that leads man to become free. Because when we say that man is charged with God's mission, it is the exact same thing as to say that man is free. Because man can only be charged when he is free, free from his animal nature, but also free to choose, to believe or not to believe.

Now, for Allal, Islam – the realization of liberty in human experience – is the real beginning of human history because from then on man can do either good or evil, is free to do either good or evil, is responsible for his actions and can decide his actions himself.

To see this better, look at what Laroui says about Allal. He calls Allal an Islamic reformist who doesn't reject the liberal notion of freedom. I think you have to add to this that for Allal, despite the great significance for him of liberal freedoms – freedoms he indeed considers sacred – they are only appearances, they are only limited liberties, in limited domains, pieces of liberty. What Allal is looking for is total freedom.

What did this mean, 'total freedom'?

If you did have a society where total liberty was in effect, you would have a society that saw liberty very differently from the way it is seen in the West where you only have pieces of liberty, limited liberties. Where total liberty was in effect, these liberties would be felt not as rights but as duties.

How did Allal (and Jamal) see the contrast between rights and duties, a contrast that I had heard several times already in other countries? Jamal went on,

The difference is that rights give you the feeling of having a claim, of being able to demand and to take, whereas duties give you a personal obligation. Without this personal obligation, there will be no liberty. It is like for justice: without the feeling of personal obligation there will be no justice because people will just hold on to the appearances of the texts, they will manipulate the texts for their own personal ends rather than invoking the purposes of Islamic law even when these go against their own immediate interests.

At this point I wondered if Jamal could sum up Allal and explain why so many Moroccans responded to his person and his leadership. Jamal answered,

> *First of all, his force came from his Islam. For Moroccans, a man who wears a turban and a jellaba and who still has the power to talk to the West not as a student to a teacher, but as a teacher to a teacher – well, that was already something. And remember, just as Allal was fighting against those traditions that he believed left Morocco vulnerable to foreign conquest, so was the newly urbanized population of Morocco fighting against those traditions too, and Allal's support was mostly in the urban areas.*
>
> *Of course, Allal's view of tradition had many nuances. Allal says that religion doesn't erase everything that preceded it, that religion doesn't seek to erase all the habits and traditions that precede it. For him the need is for religion to dominate, not to erase, prior practices. And it will dominate not by the sword, but by its truth, its rightness (l-haqq), because Islam constitutes progress for humanity.*
>
> *So the urban masses considered him an anti-colonial Islamic symbol, but also an innovative symbol who fought against outdated and weakening traditions. In the countryside he was seen as the Muslim who could defeat the West on its own terrain: he could talk about democracy, about shura (mutual consultation), could give lectures – and for the people, this was better than a westernized Moroccan wearing a suit and tie.[10] And also, he was a militant who took many risks in the fight against colonialism, and many Moroccans admired him for that.*
>
> *But you know that Allal never dominated the national scene as a thinker or as a political figure. He dominated as a symbol. And as a symbol he was used and exploited even by his enemies. On the level of his thought and his actions, he was always attacked from many sides. Many of his contemporaries didn't believe that Islam was the source of values such as work and liberty, and they believed instead in force, in modernity, in the efficiency of the colonial power. They used Allal only in so far as it helped them get the support of the masses. And the generation that followed him has deformed his thought and his action even more.*
>
> *So, Allal has been accused of being a reactionary not only by the French, but also by many Moroccan secular leaders and political figures. But in several respects he was really a very progressive figure in Moroccan culture. First of all, he opposed the dominant view of religious scholars for whom the patrimony, the Islamic legacy, was untouchable; Allal believed, to the contrary, that this legacy was incapable of providing solutions to current problems, and that it had to be criticized in the light of the fundamental aims of Islam, aims that were based on human liberty.*
>
> *Second, Allal led the revolt of the reformists against the reactionaries, against those who wanted to preserve traditions, who wanted to keep traditional society the way it was. Allal believed that in order for Islam to dominate in the contemporary world, traditional institutions, traditional ties*

and restrictions, would have to be weakened or dismantled. In doing this, Allal expanded our frame of reference to the Islamic community, instead of restricting our vision to the Moroccan Islamic community, or to the tribal community, or to the Sultan's domain.

Allal thus argued against both the Islamic and secular legacy of traditional religious scholarship and Moroccan social history, seeking to replace these with a vision of a progressive Islam.

But there was another line of thought that, together with al-Fassi's, contested the palace's domination of political power, contested what Moroccans call the '*Makhzen*' complex.[11] This was the secular, socialist line represented by Mehdi Ben Barka, who had led a breakaway group from the Istiqlal party in 1959 to form the National Union of Popular Forces (UNFP – l'Union nationale des forces populaires) that soon became the dominant political party of the left. Ben Barka, in subsequent years, became an internationally recognized political leader until he was kidnapped and disappeared in Paris in 1965, with the complicity of high-ranking Moroccan and French officials.

Jamal began again,

For me, Mehdi Ben Barka represents the current of political thought that takes colonial modernity to its logical extreme. By the way, though, when I use the words 'modernity' and 'tradition' you should understand that I always put them in quotes because these terms simplify very complex phenomena and often mean different things to different people. But they are the terms everyone uses so we have to use them too.

For Mehdi, Morocco's main misfortune isn't colonialism. For him the heaviest burden and the greatest danger result directly from Morocco's struggle for centuries to keep foreign invaders at bay: the war machinery and the barriers, both material and cultural, that protected Morocco for so long against foreign invaders were also the barriers that made it impossible for science, for example, to penetrate Morocco. So, for Mehdi, traditional society is the root cause of our backwardness; the great evil of colonialism was that it didn't extend its modern forms to encompass all of society but worked night and day to keep Moroccans underdeveloped and imprisoned in tradition.

With this in mind, what does Morocco's independence look like to Mehdi in the late 1950s? Independence appeared to him to be pushing Morocco back to the pre-colonial period but with one new element, national consciousness, that could provide the springboard to escape from backwardness.

His notion of 'national consciousness' has great bearing on our theme of democracy because, for Mehdi, 'democracy' means getting what he calls the 'conscious element of the people' into power, not keeping it excluded from power. Without this participation, the state will be cut off from the people.

Of course, one of the things that unites him with other political figures is that they all begin with the elite. Whatever they call it – whether they call it 'the conscious element of the people', or 'the leadership', or 'our militants', it is always the elite that they are talking about. But with Mehdi, although there is this emphasis, what distinguishes him from the others is his insistence that the building of the nation would never result from governmental decisions unless the government learned how to involve the masses. For this, he talks about getting the masses to control their elite, 'immersing' the leaders in the people. Mehdi Ben Barka is, in this, a little like Mao before Mao.

Unfortunately, after the UNFP broke away from the Istiqlal party in 1959, Mehdi was no longer able to pursue his vision of building a national consciousness capable of making the transition from tradition to modernity. Why? Because, on the one hand, he saw that there was a race, a race between the Makhzen, which wanted to return to the kind of power structure that existed before 1912, and the opposition forces that had no other choice but to build on the colonial heritage and try to expand the modern order to encompass the whole society.

In this race, Mehdi saw that a cultural politics that tries to address all of society and to slowly build society's political consciousness would be too slow and would lose any chance of gaining power. So Mehdi, rather than directly calling into question traditional society, postpones this question not simply because like all the other political leaders he is obsessed by the race for power, but because there necessarily is a race for power. We all know that thinking doesn't develop in the abstract, but it develops in an historical and political context. How much more true this is when the thinker himself is a political leader! The tragedy is that with Mehdi you really have the feeling that he had significant potential for very fertile, productive thought. But in a large measure this potential was wasted, just as a backward society wastes so much of its resources.

Also, this matter of putting traditional society in question is postponed because at this time there was also the need to struggle against neo-colonialism. By the way you know, don't you, that it was in fact Mehdi who invented this term, 'neo-colonialism'? So, the struggle against neo-colonialism began to take more and more of his effort, in addition to his struggle against the Makhzen. At this time, his influence in Morocco was beginning to wane, and he began to devote himself more and more to world politics, and to spend most of his time in France.

If his influence in Morocco had diminished to this extent, why then was he still considered such an important figure in post-independence Morocco?

First of all, because he calls 'traditional' society into question. This is more important than most people think, but he was practically the only

Moroccan political leader who was willing to see traditional society and the traditional ruling structure of the Makhzen as the cause of our backwardness.

Second, his conception of neo-colonialism. The entire Third World was gaining its political independence at this time, but people had a very rudimentary notion of independence, thinking that once foreign troops had been evacuated colonialism was over and done with. But Mehdi stressed that political independence wasn't real independence, but only created the possibility that real independence could be achieved. Real independence required a struggle for economic independence, cultural independence, and so on. And also, he stressed the importance of looking not simply vertically, at the relationship with the former colonial power, but also horizontally, at other former colonies. He was one of the first, you know, to talk about working for the kind of solidarity that we now call 'South–South' solidarity.

And third, there is the very important issue of self-criticism. Now Mehdi, like many of his contemporaries, was often in favor of purely technical measures, and in fact he was mainly a positivist in his approach. He looked at society as though it was the patient and he was the doctor. But this poses a very great problem, because if the patient is sick and the doctor isn't, then this is essentially a non-democratic relationship. So, in the doctor–patient relationship there is no self-criticism, because the patient can't heal himself or else he wouldn't be sick, and the doctor doesn't have to criticize himself because he's not the one who is sick.

But despite following this metaphor, which assumes that the doctor is immune to the ills of his own society, we find Mehdi Ben Barka insisting on the importance of self-criticism, insisting that the doctor too is sick. And he does this over a long period, starting already in 1956, arguing for a deep self-criticism of the party and its practice and attitudes. In particular, he talks about the very dangerous disease of being dominated by the aristocratic spirit.

I have to insist on Mehdi's courage in analyzing this problem, although he never had the chance to carry this out in the Istiqlal party, and he was often on his own on this issue within his own party, the UNFP.

So, if you want to sum this up, although Mehdi Ben Barka was on the political stage for much of his life, he had a number of key ideas that were against the normal current of political thinking. First of all, there was his view that traditional society was at the origin of our backwardness. None of the political leaders nor political militants took this seriously at the time and most people today avoid questioning it because it has become risky to do so. Second, there was his emphasis on neo-colonialism, and his idea that real independence required concrete action not simply in the political sphere but in the economic, cultural, and social fields. Most people came around to this view at least theoretically, even if they were not able to accomplish much concretely. And finally, there was his emphasis on self-criticism, particularly his ideas on public self-criticism, which everyone, even those within his own party and even those closest to him – the trade union militants and so on – rejected.

Now, all those who followed Mehdi, what do they follow? Well, they might follow everything else that he said, but they all leave aside the self-criticism. And those on his own side who rejected him, did so primarily because of his emphasis on self-criticism. But with all his faults and all his limits, Mehdi continued to emphasize self-criticism right up until the end. In fact, he published his own self-criticism in 1965, just a few months before he was kidnapped.

The tragedy is that, on the left, there has never been a militant since Mehdi who has said anything that wasn't already said by Mehdi. Just as, in Allal's milieu, nothing new has been said since he died.

Jamal and I, in discussions that had taken place over several days, had passed in review much of Moroccan history, both in the distant and the more recent past. Now, in our final session, I asked him to sum up how he assessed the meaning of liberty in present-day Morocco.

In general I believe that the question of liberty in Moroccan society today has two sides: an explicit side limited to political, economic, and juridical domains, and a latent side that concerns all of society.

For me the problem is not at all what you hear many researchers say – Europeans, Americans, and even some Moroccans – that the problem of liberty in Morocco is the problem of how to transfer a Western juridical system to Morocco, a society supposedly unsuited to such a system. That is not the problem at all. The real question is whether the kind of political and legal liberty that is related to so-called 'modern' institutions – the constitution, parliament, the separation of powers, elections – expresses our real societal needs, or just the needs of certain sectors of our society. By this I mean that the demands for freedom of opinion, of assembly, of association, of expression, certainly respond to real, authentic needs – at the very least, political parties require them if they are to have any power or weight on the political scene. But do these kinds of demands touch all the actors on the Moroccan stage?

I believe that they don't, I believe that these kinds of partial demands for liberty only affect a limited sector of the population, and a limited domain of life in Moroccan society. They don't reflect our society's global needs. Today, when we speak about the need for liberty, it is a need that refers mainly to the needs of the privileged classes, and the discussion is limited primarily to political liberty.

I asked Jamal what he meant by the 'global needs' of Moroccan society, above and beyond those that he termed 'partial'.

The real problem today is to reconstruct, to reorganize the entire society – not simply to establish an order, whether it be Makhzenian, or Islamic, or socialist. And this is why the basic problem in Moroccan society today is one of liberty – not partial liberty, but societal liberty. Because this liberty is intimately tied to the capacity of this society to reconstruct itself. We are talking here about the freedom to exist, the freedom of this society to create and maintain itself as a human society.

But what did Jamal mean by this rather grandiose formulation – 'the freedom to exist ... as a *human* society'?

All right – what does this mean for the simple individual? You know, among the vast majority of people – the peasant, the clochard, the unemployed, the youth, the women – you don't even hear the word 'freedom' expressed so much, though of course if you ask them if they want freedom, they will all say, 'Yes, I want to be free'. But for me, what I hear, and what expresses their desire more accurately, is the phrase you hear very often, 'I want to be at my ease' (je veux être à l'aise, bghit rahat l-bal). That expresses it best. People need societal security, it touches all the aspects of being human.

So, when I am talking about the freedom to be a human society, it means the freedom to be able to give meaning to life, to consolidate one's attachment to other people, to get married and raise a family without fear. You know, it isn't so much that we lack political security here, or economic security – what we lack is basic human security, it is basic societal security.

You know, I'm not talking about poverty, I'm not talking about unemployment, I'm not even talking about the occasional explosions of popular anger as in 1981 and 1984. Those are just little fires underneath what is a permanent conflagration.

Let me give you an idea of what I mean. Take Qsar al-Bhar, the section of Rabat where I live. A large part of the population there feels like a piece of wood – they feel unable to do anything because at any moment the police may pick them up and do with them what they will. Why? Well, perhaps because they have no papers; but more basically, because they have no existence, no power. Their daily lives are not the lives of normal, full human beings. They constitute a big majority of the urban population and their days are filled with violence, not just from the state, or from the police, but among themselves. They are brutalized, their human society has broken down.

I could give you other examples. Take the family that comes from the countryside, where it had social ties, feelings of respect towards one's elders. After a while, in Casablanca, the father finds no work; he becomes like a garbage can, gets no respect from anyone. His son starts to bring in a little money, but starts also to spend it on wine and movies. The daughter starts to go out on the street – not, like the primary school textbooks would have it, to go to her job, but to prostitute herself. And, in a lot of families, the father even knows this, the brother knows this, but they allow it and even depend on it. The moral system, the system of self-respect, is destroyed.

You know, this is one of the reasons for the growth of Islamic groups. People aren't necessarily taken by their hypotheses. But many people for whom the modern sector has been a disappointment – failed students, unemployed teachers, women without husbands – find solutions to their problems in the Islamic groups. And these groups revivify people, give them new hope, give their life a meaning. So these groups are not simply political groups, or economic groups, or religious groups but are, so to speak, all of that – they are societal groups. In fact, these Islamic movements are an expression of the vital will of Moroccan society to maintain and perpetuate itself.

So the real danger in this concentration on partial liberties, is that those who put forward this view put it forward as though it was the fundamental societal need, the fundamental need of the youth of the country, of the unemployed, of the peasantry, of the women – we're talking here of probably more than 80 percent of the society.

Why had the political parties apparently been so blind to the needs of the vast majority of Moroccans, and so unable to develop effective political programs?

You have only to return to the immediate aftermath of independence and look at the attitudes of the Moroccan leadership. One part of the leadership saw many positive aspects to colonial rule and wanted those aspects extended to all Moroccan society. Another part of the leadership – and here I mean primarily those who rule, who are part of the Makhzen – only wanted to retain the violence and administrative powers that the colonial system introduced, and wanted to reject aspects like political institutions and citizens' participation in power.

Because of this, the struggle after independence became primarily a struggle for power. We can ask the question: why were the nationalist movement and later the political parties in Morocco unable to build society from the bottom up, unable to begin and carry forward the construction of civil society? The answer is simple: it is because the parties did not see this as their task, they existed instead mainly as channels toward power. This power, politicians assumed, would naturally enable them to solve the problems of society by imposing solutions from the top down.

Really, we can now talk of a Moroccan establishment, a Moroccan regime that embodies the two main contending political forces – the Makhzen that is against the expansion of freedom in the political domain, and the parties that are for limiting this demand to the political domain. This was the trap that the parties fell into, the progressive as well as the non-progressive wings. The dispute over liberty became the dispute over who was competent to lead this particular regime, and the parties made the mistake of substituting their particular problem of gaining power for the more general problems of the society at large.

Was there any chance that developments within the ruling elite might in fact lead to a fulfillment of the aims of societal liberty?

It is absurd to think that it is through the action of the state that one will achieve a global societal liberty. Remember what Laroui has shown: historically, liberty was outside of the state and constituted limits upon the state. But now so much of what you hear about liberty amounts to asking the state to award liberty to its people. But this is a fundamental contradiction: one of the main functions of the state throughout Moroccan history has been just the opposite – it has been to limit liberty.

Let's not misunderstand the nature of the Makhzen, of the Moroccan state. As it exists in Morocco today, the state's project includes imposing its will through violence. Of course, this is not unique to Morocco, it is a situation common to many states. Yet regimes that have this despotic project have never fully succeeded, can never fully succeed in becoming completely despotic. It is not only perhaps against human nature to submit completely to domination, but it is even more true that human beings do not fully control their own behavior – even if they want to submit fully, there are parts of them that are beyond their own control.

The problem is that to a great degree fear dominates, and the fear among the people of the despotic project gives great force to this project, gives it greater historical reality than it would otherwise have. So, to think that a regime such as ours can impose the reconstruction of all society, can dismantle and reassemble it according to whatever plan – modernization, or traditionalism, or whatever – is an illusion: it can only approach this reconstruction in a partial, incomplete manner.

But, in fact, the project of the regime is completely opposed to such total reconstruction, because whatever it tries to introduce, it does so through violence. Even the notion of democracy is used as a whip to beat the population. Instead, the state's dominant tone should be much more modest: something like, 'we hardly know what the problems are, we have great difficulty reorganizing and reconstructing, and so on'.

Did Jamal feel that intellectuals had an important role to play in finding solutions to current problems? He answered,

Intellectuals themselves participate in this despotic project sometimes despite themselves, sometimes quite consciously. I would say that in Arab societies, danger doesn't come only from the political elite that controls power. It comes also from the intellectuals. Because the intellectuals, instead of really posing the question of the whole society, and instead of recognizing that their own role in discussing such questions can be only very small, actually pose problems in such a way that they can be the only ones to envisage solutions. They pose these problems in a partial, incomplete, sectoral way. And in this, they can be seen as the greatest hypocrites – they accuse the rest of the elite of hypocrisy, but refuse to recognize their own.

All this goes back to what I said earlier: that all the propaganda for liberty in Morocco poses great dangers to liberty in Morocco. I'm not saying that the need for freedom of expression isn't a real need. What I'm saying is that focusing exclusively on this and other limited needs poses a real danger for societal liberty because, relevant only to limited sectors of the population, these limited needs hide the question of how societal liberty can be achieved, how society can reconstruct itself so that life for people within it has full human meaning. And all the efforts to talk about liberty – research programs, political programs, and so on – if they neglect this fundamental question they are missing the boat.

But beyond this, the real problem with this focus on the state, on power, and on partial liberties, is that it hides the responsibility of the total society for the absence of liberty, it avoids the critique of the 'I'. The question of liberty must relate not simply to political liberty but must also question those who limit the question in this way. This question would constitute a real danger for the 'I', not only for all of us as Moroccans, but more particularly for our ruling elite.

So, at the bottom of this, underlying everything I have said so far, there is another idea – it is what I will call historical cowardice. We have cowardice here of many sorts: the cowardice of looking ourselves in the face, the cowardice of calling ourselves into question, the cowardice of fearing to raise the question of liberty to ourselves who are calling for the question to be raised, the cowardice of confronting the real nature of our own society, of our own traditions.

This cowardice, in essence, takes our own history and makes it into a monster. Too much of our thinking about liberty is historical analysis. This thinking says: we have lived in societies that haven't allowed the individual to emerge, or we have lived under colonial domination, or we have experienced profound economic backwardness. But thinking too much in this way creates these monsters: they appear as external forces upon today's citizens, and allow us all to avoid our responsibilities for the characteristics of our present-day situation. How can we have the notion of liberty if we are not willing to assume our responsibilities in the present?

Jamal clearly did not believe that the answers to the problems posed by the reconstruction of society were going to be provided by the state. In fact, one of the dominant themes in his talks had been the need for citizens to assume responsibility for the present, the need to reconstruct society from the bottom up, to 'carry forward the construction of civil society' as he put it.

The task of constructing civil society came up again and again in my talks in Tunisia, and it is to these that we now turn.

Part III

Tunisia: organizing for human rights and the rights of women

8 Constructing civil society

A HUMAN RIGHTS CHARTER

In Tunisia in early 1985 Muhammad Charfi, a member of the executive committee of the Tunisian Human Rights League (LTDH – la Ligue tunisienne pour la défense des droits de l'homme), told me the following story.

> During our last national congress in March 1985, there was an incident involving Serge Adda – he's a staunch human rights activist, and he's a Jew. He was running as a candidate for the executive committee, and at the congress he was elected with a large majority. But on the last day someone took the floor and said, 'What? The Palestinian people are being oppressed every day – are we going to allow a Jew in the national leadership of the League?' Well, there was a terrible uproar.
> From my point of view, what followed was perhaps the best half-hour in the history of the League, at least in the last eight years that I know it. Because there was an immediate reaction to the attack on Serge Adda's Jewishness, an unplanned, totally spontaneous, and practically unanimous reaction against the person who had raised the objection, against the person who had said, in effect, 'because someone's a Jew he's suspected of being a Zionist and an oppressor of the Palestinians'. The debate gave a powerful reinforcement to all of us who want the League to be truly anti-discriminatory.

The LTDH, formally founded in 1977, had by 1985 become a significant force in Tunisian political life. In the preceding three years it had repeatedly called for a general amnesty for all political prisoners and prisoners of conscience; intervened with the Minister of Interior on cases of suspected torture and held a national day on the theme of torture in 1983; made public statements and established a commission defending freedom of the press; called for the abrogation of exceptional courts and unconstitutional legislation; and mounted a successful national and international campaign in the spring of 1984 that led to the commutation of all death sentences handed down in trials following the 'bread riots' of January 1984. The LTDH's achievements were all the more remarkable given the early problems the organization had had, the practical and objective difficulties people in the Third World face in forming such organizations, and the rather disappointing experience that had been had by a similar organization in Morocco.

Yet its continued success was in no way assured. Although the League grew significantly in the years following 1985, it remained exposed to attack on a number of fronts. Some of its vulnerability, of course, resulted from its very nature as a human rights organization and its obligation to take a public position on almost every controversial issue. Other problems arose from its own organizational needs – how could it remain immune to groups that might seek to infiltrate, undermine, or dominate it? And some problems seemed to be the result of its own success – how could the League remain strong and independent when one of its presidents had accepted a cabinet position in government and when its next president, Muhammad Charfi, was himself named minister of education less than two months after becoming head of the League in March 1989.

Of the many tests the LTDH faced over the decade of the 1980s, perhaps the most exacting was its attempt through much of 1985 to solve many of the above problems by elaborating a charter. Later in this part we shall be following this effort in some detail but, when I first discussed this matter with Muhammad Charfi in mid-1985, neither he nor I could possibly foresee that over the next few months the issue of the charter was to precipitate a crisis unlike any the LTDH had known before, with concerted press attacks on the League from the outside, and an accentuation of deep divisions within it. Together, these threatened, if not the very existence of the League, then certainly its effectiveness. As Muhammad Charfi was to say to me months later when the crisis was somewhat under control, 'Those weeks, when the charter problem reached its zenith, were some of the worst weeks of my life'.

A WOMEN'S MAGAZINE IN TUNISIA

In April 1985 a new bilingual (Arabic and French) monthly magazine appeared in the kiosks of Tunisia. On the cover of *Nissa* (Woman), Tunisia's first feminist journal, was the title of its feature article, 'Women, rape, and the death penalty' (in which the author argued against the hasty introduction into the penal code of an amendment that recommended the death penalty in certain rape cases). *Nissa*'s feature articles over the first year included discussions of the problem of illegitimate children, the personal status laws in Tunisia and Egypt (provisions regarding women's rights in both these laws were then under attack), the Israeli bombing raid on the PLO headquarters in a suburb of Tunis, the pros and cons of sexually segregated activities, the risks of childbirth, and feminism.

Seven issues in its first year – a substantial accomplishment, one that largely fulfilled the hopes expressed in its opening editorial that *Nissa* would be

> *a place for personal testimony, information, reflection and debate, open to women and men alike ... committed to respecting diverse points of view provided that ... they aim to promote more harmonious and satisfying relations between the sexes and to establish the foundations of a more free and equal society.*

Yet, from the outset, *Nissa* was plagued by difficulties. These surfaced in the magazine itself when, in its fourth issue, under the title 'Our disillusion', four of its co-founders accused some of their colleagues of undemocratic practices, of restricting the free expression and diversity of opinions that had been a primary aim of the journal. In their view, this had led to a journal that, 'far from exposing the reality of woman's oppression, only gives comfort to a moralizing and paternalist attitude'. With this, the four co-founders ended their collaboration and resigned from the magazine. The responding editorial denied the accusations of anti-democratic practices and the desire to impose 'a specific orientation', and reaffirmed the journal's main objective, to 'communicate with the reader and to participate in the construction of the image of woman that no longer hurts or shames us'.

Nissa lasted only several more issues, publishing its eighth and final issue in early 1987 in an impoverished format that symbolized its unhappy end. I was to spend considerable time trying to understand why such a promising enterprise had ultimately failed.

When I spoke in early summer 1989 to the woman who had been *Nissa*'s directrice, she admitted that the experience had affected her deeply, two years after *Nissa*'s last issue had appeared. As were several other women I met, she was now more interested in writing in a subjective mode – novels, memoirs, and personal testimony of one sort or another.

But she was, at the same time, continuing to be active in women's organizations and, in general, the turn toward personal testimony did not seem to indicate, neither for her nor for other women I talked to, a turn away from organized activity. A number of women who had been involved in *Nissa* were trying to form an association called 'Democratic Women', some had joined the LTDH and participated in its own Women's Commission, and some were active in local organizing and social welfare work.

The various responses to *Nissa*'s demise were probably best exemplified for me in the words of three former *Nissa* collaborators. One said to me, 'I still join many of these efforts to organize women, but I do it gritting my teeth, with bitterness. But I do everything now with some bitterness, bitterness towards others but towards myself too.' Another said,

> What we really need now is to think deeply about how to attack our society's problems – problems that are both men's problems and women's problems. There are the big political problems, of course, but there are also the daily problems that we have to learn how to approach. And for this, it is absolutely essential that we learn how to listen to other people, even to people like the Islamists who radically disagree with us.

A third added,

> Our new organization, the 'Democratic Women', may have been refused official permission the first time around. But that isn't going to stop us. We'll still be out there demonstrating and taking positions when the need arises, whether we've been legally approved or not.

THE QUESTION OF CIVIL SOCIETY

The question of how society organizes itself at the level between the family and the state is of crucial importance for the power of citizens to affect public life, in the face of what to many seems the encroaching and almost omnipotent power of the state.[1] How and to what extent do people with similar ideas come together to form groups and associations, to publish journals, hold meetings, lobby, create public pressure, attempt in any of various ways to put their ideas into the public arena in an organized manner? How can they try to influence particular decisions and more general matters of policy? How can they associate in a way that gives them more say in and more control over their own lives and the life of their community?

Morocco, Tunisia, and Egypt each have special laws and procedures governing the formation of associations. Despite some differences, these laws greatly resemble one another and require, in essence, that the individuals desiring to form an association submit a formal request to the government, usually to the Ministry of the Interior. Upon favorable response to this request (or in some cases, in the absence of a negative response) the association acquires legal existence. Until then it is not permitted to hold formal meetings or to publish a journal (although, in so-called 'liberalizing' periods, the group may be 'tolerated' by the authorities and allowed to carry out some of these activities without official authorization). Of course, in either status, either with the authorization or without it, the association is likely to be under constant observation and potential threat from the powers that oversee it, and control or harassment from above becomes more onerous the more controversial are the group's aims.

Over the last decade, among those highly controversial aims that have motivated people to form associations, to construct 'civil society', in Morocco, Tunisia, and Egypt, are the protection of human rights and the rights of women.

It is not surprising that people would seek to associate and organize around these issues, given the demonstrable incapacity of existing state structures to resolve the tensions and conflicting perceptions in these domains, and the almost daily violations of fundamental human rights and women's rights that people witness or experience directly. Contributing to the organizational momentum in both areas is the increasing internationalization of the human rights and the women's movement, and the growing numbers of urbanized, well-educated men and women in all three countries.

By the late 1980s in Morocco, there were already three human rights organizations, at least one women's rights organization, and several new journals devoted to women's issues *(8 Mars, Kalima)*; in Egypt, the Arab Human Rights Organization and the Arab Women's Solidarity Union had been founded during the decade and were on a reasonably firm footing, and Cairo was the seat of one of the Middle East's strongest professional organizations with a human rights orientation, the Arab Lawyers Union.

In Tunisia such developments had perhaps had the greatest national impact, and the Tunisian Human Rights League and the various efforts to form a Tunisian women's movement had had a marked effect on Tunisian life. The high level of national impact in Tunisia was due no doubt in part to the way the organizations themselves had developed and to the particular nature of Tunisian culture and society, as well as to Tunisia's relatively small scale and the relative ease with which associative activity could be put into operation and coordinated.

The Tunisian Human Rights League's effort to elaborate a charter, and the effort to launch and produce the woman's journal *Nissa*, need to be seen against the background of Tunisia's situation over the last few decades. After briefly looking into that background, we shall turn respectively to each of these efforts, while also trying to set them within the context of similar initiatives in Morocco and Egypt.

9   Independent Tunisia

A CONSTITUTIONAL *COUP D'ETAT*

Tunisians awoke on the morning of 7 November 1987 to hear on their radios, or via word of mouth, that the previous night Prime Minister Ben Ali had deposed 'President-for-life' Habib Bourguiba, the man who had led Tunisia ever since its independence from France in 1956. Some Tunisians described the change as a simple *'putsch'*, others saw it as a 'constitutional *coup d'état'*. In any event, in producing medical reports attesting that Bourguiba was physically unfit to continue as president, in taking over without bloodshed the position of president and head of state (and then, in April 1989 standing unopposed and being elected president with 99 percent of the vote), Ben Ali effectively followed constitutional forms and did much to ensure that the continuity of the Tunisian political system would not be put at risk.

As I landed at the Carthage airport outside Tunis in early summer 1989, I thought back to my first visit to Tunisia some fifteen years earlier and to the numerous trips I had made there in the last years of Bourguiba's rule. I remembered particularly the contrast between those two periods: the positive mood of the early 1970s when healthy improvements in the Tunisian economy, coupled with the strong performance of the Arab armies during the October 1973 war with Israel and the concerted economic action the Arab oil states had taken, nourished in many Tunisians the hope that a brighter period lay ahead; and the dark depression and sense of despair that prevailed in Tunisia in the mid-1980s as Tunisians saw their economy stagnate and, finding themselves unable to change the course of events, watched passively as President Bourguiba acted in an increasingly willful and arbitrary way.

The frustration Tunisians felt seemed often to turn upon themselves as they muttered, in effect, 'Well, if we are unable to do anything about this, then perhaps this is what we deserve.' It is not surprising, then, that with the government seemingly paralyzed by Bourguiba's behavior and Tunisia's problems growing more critical by the month, many Tunisians were pleased with Ben Ali's seizure of power, especially once it became clear that this was not leading to upheaval and instability.

But as Ben Ali took over, all the major institutions of Bourguiba's Tunisia remained in place, in particular the political party that Bourguiba had founded and that controlled most of Tunisian public life. With Ben Ali himself an outstanding product of this system – he had already served Bourguiba as director of military security and minister of interior before becoming prime minister just a month before deposing him – it was not clear whether the new president would have the will, or the power, to make substantial changes in the system he had seized from Bourguiba's hands, the hands that had done so much to shape it.

BOURGUIBA'S TUNISIA

France displaced Ottoman authority in Tunisia in 1881 and controlled the country as a protectorate until 1956. During the 1920s and 1930s the nationalist movement gained wide support among Tunisians and began to adopt more militant positions. In 1934 Habib Bourguiba founded the Neo-Destour (New Constitutional) party and, in the ensuing two decades, the Neo-Destour became the leading force in the nationalist movement with Bourguiba, imprisoned many times by the French and often in exile, becoming one of the dominant figures in that struggle. During the early 1950s the campaign by Tunisian militants and French repression grew increasingly violent, pushing France, already under similar pressures from Algeria and Morocco, into negotiations.

Bourguiba, held in prison by the French, emerged as the primary figure, the 'valid interlocutor', in negotiations that led to France's agreement in 1955 to grant Tunisia autonomy, over the opposition of a number of other Tunisian leaders, including Salah ben Youssef, who supported full independence. However, with Morocco shortly thereafter achieving full independence in its negotiations with France, Tunisia's demands changed accordingly and Tunisia achieved its independence on 20 March 1956, eighteen days after Morocco's.

Bourguiba was to dominate political life in Tunisia for the next thirty years. He was elected President of the National Assembly of newly independent Tunisia in 1956 and, after the abolition of the Tunisian monarchy in 1957, was proclaimed President of the Republic. Then, following promulgation of the constitution in 1959, he was the sole candidate for a presidency elected by popular suffrage. In 1975 Bourguiba was made president for life by constitutional amendment.

The Tunisian constitution of 1959, establishing Tunisia as a republic with Islam the state religion and Arabic the national language, provides for a presidential system and a one-house chamber of deputies, with elections on both levels held every five years. The 'first past the post' electoral system cemented the Neo-Destour party's control over national political life – the party had already established its leading role during the independence struggle by forming a strong popular base (400 local cells were in operation as early as 1937: Toumi 1978: 182). It was able to expand and solidify its position after independence, forming sections and branches in all Tunisian localities, in many of the professions, and within all major Tunisian institutions.

With its unchallenged control of government, the Neo-Destour (under its successive names) has been to all intents and purposes the only fully legal political party in Tunisia since independence. The government has tolerated other political groupings from time to time and sometimes allowed them to participate in elections, but the party, able to call freely upon the government's repressive measures such as imprisonment, forbidding public meetings, confiscating newspapers, and so on, welded an identity between it and state institutions that in effect created a one-party state.[1]

Bourguiba – president, head of state, and head of government – was also the head of the party. In 1969 he established the post of prime minister, largely to provide for an immediate successor to the presidency in the event of a vacancy (the prime minister was also the secretary-general of the party). After naming the prime minister in 1970 Bourguiba continued to name and dismiss all ministers (including the prime ministers) and neither the prime minister nor cabinet ministers, and certainly not the president, were responsible to parliament.

Bourguiba sought from the outset of his rule to present himself as the personification of the Tunisian nation and his leadership as a natural reflection of a special, organic tie between himself and the Tunisian people. He would frequently refer to himself as 'the father of the nation' and to Tunisians as 'my children', and the notion of 'one nation, one leader' became one of the bywords of the regime. However, his domination of the Tunisian political system was as much built upon his ruthless suppression of opponents as upon his claim to unite the nation, and some Tunisians may have thought ironically of this when President Bourguiba was referred to as 'the Supreme Combatant' – a title he had achieved during the nationalist struggle.[2]

Tunisia followed an *ad hoc* 'liberal' economic policy during its first years of independence. However, when economic problems persisted, President Bourguiba appointed Ahmed Ben Salah to the planning ministry in 1961 and charged him with infusing new spirit and raising productivity in the manufacturing and agricultural sectors. A former labor union leader and then minister of social affairs (where he had instituted a social security and health service), Ben Salah introduced a cooperative system and a socialist orientation that still remains associated with his name (it was during his tenure that the Neo-Destour party changed its name to the Destourian Socialist Party: PSD – Parti socialiste destourien). A charismatic figure, Ben Salah soon came to represent for Bourguiba a threat to his own leadership. In 1969, with economic performance still lagging behind expectations, Bourguiba dismissed Ben Salah, and had him arrested and tried the following year. He was sentenced to ten years in prison, but he escaped after serving less than three.[3]

With Ben Salah's dismissal, Tunisian economic policy took a more 'liberal' turn under the first prime minister Hedi Nouira (prime minister from 1970 to 1980) and continued in this direction under his successors Muhammad Mzali (1980–6) and Rachid Sfar (1986–7).

Tunisia was, in the early 1970s, a country of some 5.5 million people (47 percent of these were urban dwellers, and 50 percent were under 15 years old) and its landscape was dominated by its capital city Tunis (concentrating 17 percent of the national population). There were also a number of smaller but vital commercial and manufacturing centers, such as Sousse and Sfax, farther south along the Mediterranean coast.

By the early 1970s, less than twenty years after independence, Tunisia had some significant achievements to its credit. In 1956, less than six months after independence, a Personal Status Code (PSC) was promulgated; this and a number of complementary laws gave to women substantially greater rights than they had under previous strongly Islamic provisions. Under the new laws, marriages required only the consent of the couple involved and polygamy was prohibited (under Islamic law fathers have a say in choosing a daughter's marriage partner and men may take up to four wives, all of whom must be treated equally); men could no longer divorce a wife by simple public repudiation but had to follow a civil procedure; women gained the right to initiate divorce proceedings; adoption was made legal; women gained the right to choose to work and gained some improvements in their inheritance rights as well (although here the basic elements of Islamic law were retained, such as a sister's share in the father's estate being one-half of a brother's).

The Tunisian economy, based primarily on agriculture and on moderate phosphate and oil extraction, had been making considerable progress too. Tunisia had managed to double its per capita GNP between 1970 and 1976 and increased salaries over the same period by more than

60 percent. Tunisia was allocating substantial resources to education, leading to advances that were·the envy of many Third World countries. The number of primary school students between 1962 and 1977 almost doubled, secondary school students almost quadrupled, and the number in university education increased more than seven-fold. The proportion of females in the student population increased noticeably too.[4] Also, tourism became a major earner of foreign exchange as Tunisia profited from the advent of mass tourism by building a solid infrastructure and becoming an attractive Mediterranean resort not only for visitors from the former colonial power, France, but also for Germans and other northern Europeans.

Taken together, all these initiatives had made Tunisia seem, to Western eyes at least, a stable, moderate, progressive, modernizing society, a society that provided a notable and welcome exception to the common stereotypes applied to the countries of the region.

However, the tensions in Tunisian society – between the one-party state and democratic forces, between people in favor of a liberal economic system and those arguing for a more egalitarian, socialist orientation, between people who believed that politics and public life should be primarily secular and those who argued that Islam should be given a more significant place in Tunisia's ruling institutions – were often just beneath the surface. As the economy deteriorated toward the late 1970s and then worsened into the 1980s, these tensions erupted, sometimes explosively.

Throughout the 1970s students in both the universities and secondary schools were highly politicized, with various Marxist, Leninist, Maoist, and Trotskyist groups contending for hegemony. As the decade ended, Islamist groups were growing more powerful and, during the 1980s, it was not rare for the university campuses to be scenes of dispute, at times violent, between student groups arguing over whether students should be permitted to break the fast in public during Ramadan, or whether Islamic dress should be permitted for women students.

Islamist groups made their appearance in the army as well and although their numbers were by all accounts small, they were harshly repressed by the authorities. One Islamist group, however, the Islamic Tendency Movement (MTI – Mouvement de la tendance islamique), began to make a serious bid for mass support in the late 1970s, widened its base throughout the 1980s, and continues to be an important political force today.[5]

There was serious agitation in the trade union sector too. The trade union movement had been an active participant in the struggle for independence and had worked closely throughout this period with the

Neo-Destour party. After independence, as the party moved to gain control over all aspects of Tunisian life, its relationship with the General Union of Tunisian Workers (UGTT – l'Union générale des travailleurs tunisiens) became increasingly strained; although at times the UGTT did act in close concert with the party, at times it acted independently, and on occasion directly opposed government policy.

By the late 1970s the UGTT had emerged as a strong political force in its own right and the general strike it called in January 1978 led to violent confrontations with the police and army and to many deaths. The government, consonant with its broader aim of weakening and even dismantling opposing forces and institutions in civil society, stepped up its efforts to control the UGTT: UGTT president Habib Achour was in and out of prison numerous times and his public disputes with Prime Minister Mzali throughout the early 1980s grew increasingly acrimonious (in part, it was mooted, because both men were harboring hopes of leading the country once Bourguiba had left the scene).

These tensions – from the left, from Islamist groups, from the trade union movement, from students in the secondary schools and universities, and fueled by many Tunisians on the streets frustrated by the difficulties of their daily lives – exploded most dramatically in January 1978 when the UGTT called a general strike, and in late December 1983 and early January 1984 when 'bread riots' broke out on a national scale to protest reductions in subsidies on basic goods and the attendant rises in prices. Approximately 400 people died in the unrest in 1978, and in January 1984 the number of dead was close to 100.

By the mid-1980s Tunisia's situation had deteriorated in almost all respects. Not only had population continued to increase rapidly (in 1985 the population was estimated at over 7 million, was continuing to grow at an annual rate of 2.5 percent, and would reach 8 million by 1989), but also the economic situation had worsened: income from phosphate production was falling, oil imports rose as decreasing oil production fell farther behind rising domestic needs, tourism from the West stagnated as did transfers from Tunisians working abroad. Agricultural production had recovered somewhat from the droughts of the early 1980s but in 1986 drought again led to crop failure.

The economic crisis and the consequent social tensions were taking their toll on the spirit of many Tunisians. In addition to other problems, conflict between the government and the Islamist movements seemed beyond resolution. In March 1987 Rachid Ghannouchi, head of the MTI, was arrested and MTI supporters came out to protest in large numbers, leading to violent clashes with the police and more arrests. In late March Tunisia broke off relations with Iran, accusing it of supporting terrorism in Tunisia and encouraging Tunisians to commit terrorist acts abroad. Throughout the early summer months there were periodic clashes between Islamist protesters and the police, and by mid-summer some 2,000 MTI supporters were reportedly under arrest. Throughout this period there were frequent accusations that Islamist detainees were being tortured by the police.

In early August several bombs exploded in tourist locations in Tunisia. In the publicity and trials that followed, harsh sentences were called for by Bourguiba and several death sentences were handed down. In a number of public statements at this time, Bourguiba made it known that he would sanction no compromise with Islamist forces and called for vigorous governmental action. Many Tunisians feared an uncontrollable confrontation, and many had simply lost patience with what they saw as Bourguiba's intransigence and no longer had taste for the incessant intrigues in his palace at Carthage.

All of this discontent fueled Ben Ali's seizure of power on 7 November 1987 and, in the heady days immediately following the takeover, years of frustration were transformed into enthusiasm for the new beginning. This spirit even affected some of the more skeptical intellectuals I knew, one of whom said to me in the summer of 1989,

It is good to change horses because even if the new horse turns out to be no better than the old one, at least we enjoy a period of hope and possibility while we move from one horse to the other.

CHANGING HORSES

The period of hope and possibility may have lasted about a year. There were indeed a number of positive developments in the early months of the new regime. Ben Ali made a strong verbal commitment to human rights shortly after assuming power, and promised new laws concerning freedom of the press and the right to form political parties and associations. Provisions concerning prison conditions and incommunicado detention after arrest *(garde-à-vue)* were improved, Tunisia ratified without reservations the International Torture Convention, and finally passed a general amnesty law in June 1989 that awarded full civil and political rights to individuals who had been deprived of them during the Bourguiba period. Many exiles were encouraged to return and some did (including Ahmed Ben Salah), and negotiations were initiated for the return of some of Bourguiba's better-known opponents (among them Driss Guiga and Muhammad Mzali).

But there were also several waves of arrests and accusations that torture, particularly of Islamists, was being practiced. Many people were growing increasingly critical of some legislative and administrative initiatives: the new Press Law, for example, although stipulating that offenses would now be decided by the courts rather than by the administration, still empowered the authorities to confiscate issues of political journals, and these provisions were invoked on a number of occasions after 7 November 1987. The Ministry of Interior was now required to act upon applications for associations and political parties within three months of submission but the ministry was still rejecting many new applications.[6]

By the summer of 1989 there was a mixture of malaise and frustrated expectations in the discourse of many Tunisian intellectuals. Despite some new initiatives, the government seemed unable to make headway concerning Tunisia's serious economic situation. Exports had shown good growth but imports were rising even faster (in part because of a high food import bill), and the trade gap was widening. Income from tourism was down, largely because of a 30 percent drop in the number of Libyan tourists who seemed to be forsaking Tunisia for Egypt as relations between Libya and Egypt improved.

As a result, Tunisia continued to face a serious debt problem – its debt service ratio stood at 24 percent for 1987 and threatened to go higher over the next few years. These problems had led the government to mount a major campaign to attract private investment and facilitate investment procedures, and this program was showing some success by 1989.

However, the lives of most Tunisians had not yet seen the benefits of these programs and the structural changes necessary to transform the Tunisian economy significantly had still to be made. The Tunisian currency, the dinar, had lost more than 40 percent of its dollar value over the previous few years; unemployment still remained very high at about 500,000 or 15 percent of the work force, and a first round of substantial price rises in basic consumer goods was imposed in 1989 with every likelihood that further rounds were in the offing.[7]

Discontent was also growing on the political front. Elections held in April 1989 again demonstrated the iron hold the president's party had on government. Renamed the Constitutional Democratic Rally (RCD – Rassemblement constitutionnel démocratique) the previous February, the governmental party offered an electoral pact before the elections that would guarantee a small number of seats to opposition parties if they agreed not to challenge RCD candidates. The opposition refused and in the event the RCD won all 141 seats, amid accusations of electoral irregularities. Despite gaining no seats, Islamist candidates standing as independents won 13 percent of the votes overall, up to 20 percent of the votes in some constituencies, and 30 percent in the constituency where its leader, Rachid Ghannouchi, stood as a candidate.

Towards the end of 1989 there was renewed activity on the left, with some talk that a united front might emerge.[8] There was also talk in governmental circles, as well as in the press, that President Ben Ali might seek to form a presidential political party distinct from the RCD, in an attempt to inject new life into the political system. However, as of mid-1990, he had not made any significant steps in this direction.

Ben Ali has by and large followed the pattern set by Bourguiba for Tunisia's international relations, including continuing Tunisia's role as one of the West's most reliable allies among Arab Middle Eastern countries. With a community of approximately 300,000 Tunisians living in France, Tunisia has retained very close ties with the former colonial power, which is by far Tunisia's largest trading partner and accounts for approximately one-quarter of its imports and exports. Approximately 70 percent of Tunisia's trade is with countries of the European Community.

In the Maghreb, Tunisia is wedged between two geographically much larger and more materially wealthy neighbors – Algeria and Libya. Its relations with Algeria have for the most part been fraternal, but relations with Libya have been stormy.

In the early 1970s the Libyan leader, Colonel Mu^cammar Qadhdhafi, in power since 1969, suggested that the two countries form a union. There are strong objective arguments in favor of close ties between Tunisia and Libya: most simply, the relatively numerous and well-educated Tunisian labor force might combine productively with Libya's oil-rich but people-poor economy and generate greater wealth for both countries. In early 1974 Bourguiba seemed on the verge of signing a treaty of union with Libya but, after the strong opposition of then Prime Minister Hedi Nouira (and from the US as well), finally changed his mind and rejected Qadhdhafi's proposals.

Over the next decade and a half, talk of unity and cooperation between the two countries has alternated with hostile and angry exchanges, with relations hitting their lowest point first in 1980 when Libya was accused of backing a short-lived revolt in the southern Tunisian town of Gafsa (thirteen of the participants were sentenced to death and hanged); and again in August 1985 when Libya abruptly expelled from its soil some 30,000 Tunisian workers.

In 1983 Algeria and Tunisia signed a twenty-year treaty of concord and friendship, a treaty that was countered in 1984 by the Morocco–Libya union that lasted until 1986. In February 1989 Tunisia became one of the founding members of the Arab Maghreb Union (along with Libya, Algeria, Morocco, and Mauritania).

Tunisia, priding itself on its Mediterranean, African, and Middle Eastern identity, plays a special role within the Arab world, often operating as a bridge and meeting place for Western and Arab interests. Although Bourguiba at times took positions that were unpopular with his fellow Arab leaders, such as supporting recognition of the State of Israel (expressed during a visit to Egypt in 1965 and leading to popular protests in Cairo and Beirut and a cooling in his relations with Egyptian President Nasser), he kept Tunisian policy broadly in step with the policy of other 'moderate' Arab states. After the Camp David agreements and the expulsion of Egypt from the Arab League, Tunis became the seat of the League's headquarters after their removal from Cairo; and after the Israeli invasion of the Lebanon in 1982, the PLO moved its headquarters to Tunisia as well.

Another sign of Tunisia's special role in the region was its hosting of the seminal meeting that led to the founding of the Arab Human Rights Organization (AHRO). In April 1983 thirty-five Arab intellectuals, academics, and professionals met at the Tunisian resort of Hammamet to discuss human rights in the Arab world, and to draw up a legal framework for a committee that would monitor human rights in the region.

Tunisia also has become the home of the new Arab Institute of Human Rights (grouping the AHRO, the LTDH, and the UN Center for Human Rights), founded in 1989, that aims to promote observance of the Universal Declaration of Human Rights throughout the Arab world through publications, documentation, seminars, and training sessions. Tunisia also hosted, in June 1989, the founding meeting of the Maghreb Human Rights Union, grouping the human rights leagues of the five North African countries that form the Arab Maghreb Union.

Throughout the late 1970s through the 1980s perhaps the main issue for Tunisian society, above and beyond the question of who would succeed Bourguiba and how that succession would take place, has been the relationship between the state and the institutions of civil society. During the Nouira and Mzali years the state put many of the institutions of civil society under pressure and there was some hope that, under the new President Ben Ali, the state would reduce its efforts to dominate civil society institutions. But this hope is as yet still-born.[9]

Two fields in which Tunisians have been making serious organizing efforts over the last two decades are human rights and the rights of women. The problems faced by militants in each of these domains have been very different, their constituencies are diverse although not always distinct, and the success of these efforts has been very uneven. But efforts in each field reveal much about the tensions, trends, and potential of Tunisian society and also about the nature of human rights in the Arab world.

But these were vital issues in Morocco and Egypt too, and I had been talking to some of the key people in human rights and women's organizations there about the problems they faced. It will perhaps help us see the Tunisian situation more clearly and understand the Middle Eastern situation better if we first talk briefly with some people having related experiences in Morocco and Egypt.

10 Organizing for human rights

'A HARMFUL TRADE-OFF' (EGYPT)

I began to address the issue of human rights organizations in Egypt when I had several talks with Saad ed-Din Ibrahim, then the secretary-general of the Arab Human Rights Organization (AHRO). The AHRO had been formed in 1983 as a result of a meeting in Tunis of concerned Arab intellectuals from many different countries and many different political persuasions. By the time I first saw Saad in 1985 and 1986, the AHRO had solidly established itself as a credible voice for human rights in the Middle East. By the end of 1989 it had branches and associated groups in Egypt, Kuwait, Jordan, and North and South Yemen, and was organizationally tied to human rights leagues in Morocco, Algeria, Tunisia, and Lebanon. It also had formed branches in the UK, France, and Austria for Arabs residing in those countries.

Saad has his fingers in many pies and his feet in many offices – in addition to his position in the AHRO, he was a professor of sociology at the American University in Cairo, a part-time advisor to the kings of Jordan and Morocco, and a prolific writer with many books to his credit. He was also a frequent contributor to Egyptian newspapers and his columns were often picked up by newspapers in other Middle Eastern countries.

Saad began by outlining the development of the human rights movement in Egypt.

The issue of human rights became potent among intellectuals in Egypt only after 1967. Before that, under Nasser, the need to liberate Egypt from foreign domination and to socially develop the country dominated our attention and we allowed human rights considerations to remain in the background. This in itself was probably a reaction to the so-called 'liberal' period in Arab history, from about the 1920s to the 1940s, which had led to little concrete achievement. Arab thinking during the liberal period was subject to the criticism not only that it had been imported from the West, but also that it was the privilege of only a small number of people from the upper social classes.

As long as the social achievements were steady after the July 1952 revolution and during the Nasser period, people were willing to accept the trade-off of human rights for social development. But our defeat in the 1967 war against Israel made everyone think again, made us call everything into question. Most importantly, many people began to believe that the defeat itself was a symptom of fundamental problems: that the lack of internal criticism and the harshness meted out to critics of the establishment were at the root of our defeat and were stifling our capacity to go forward as a society. People began to realize not only that this trade-off wasn't necessary, but also that it was a harmful trade-off.

So, from 1967 until the mid-1970s there was great ferment of activity, and many new groups started to take shape, often under the rubric 'democracy'. And the three or four years after 1973 gave us even more hope, after the relatively good performance in the 1973 war and the formation of OPEC.

The mood in Egypt at that period clearly mirrored what I had remembered of Tunisia, although Egyptians had certainly experienced the swings of mood occasioned by the 1967 and 1973 wars more sharply than did Tunisians. As Saad went on, the surface parallels with Tunisia continued, even though the underlying causes often differed.

But then, as the years passed, the civil war in Lebanon dragged on and on, grew worse and worse; the Camp David agreement failed to address the issue of Palestinian national rights; and Arab resources were squandered. This led to great disillusion in the late 1970s. At the same time, many Arab regimes were becoming more repressive, including Syria, Iraq, and Libya. Here in Egypt repression also became more harsh under Sadat and began to affect more classes of people and more people altogether. Israel's invasion of the Lebanon in June 1982 really marked the low point.

Saad went on,

During this period, the Arab Lawyers Union (ALU) became more active on human rights issues, and human rights organizations started to form, including a few human rights groups in Egypt that were sponsored by or were very close to the establishment. In general, the establishment groups were rather inactive and most of them broke down after a time because many of the individuals involved could not put aside their political party loyalties. But at least there emerged from this ferment a core group of people of all political persuasions who were convinced they could sit down and work together.

Add to this the fact that in September 1981 Sadat arrested many people from across the political spectrum, including many who had been involved in the human rights effort. Now they were all in prison together and were all subjected to the same kind of repression. You know, perhaps this didn't change any of their ideas very much, but it changed their idea of how political discourse should be carried on, and showed them how necessary it was to find new ways of dealing with ideas that were opposed to their own.

It was shortly after this, in 1983, that many of us interested in promoting human rights in the Arab world held two conferences, the first in Tunisia and the second in Cyprus, that led to the founding of the AHRO. Crucial for the success of these initiating steps was that we Egyptians showed an increased willingness to be self-critical. I think the other Arabs responded to this very positively – it improved both their view of Egypt and their attitude towards the entire human rights effort.

Among other things, Saad had pointed to the general need for an appropriate social and historical context if a human rights movement is to work and grow effectively. But he had also pointed to a more specific problem, the relationship between a human rights association and other groups operating in the public arena, in particular political parties.

The Egypt-based AHRO and the ALU had perhaps been able to keep this problem at bay, in part because of the international character of both organizations. The success of Moroccan human rights associations in this regard was much more problematic.

'EVERYTHING HERE IS STRUCTURED BY THE POLITICAL PARTIES' (MOROCCO)

In the 1970s the Istiqlal (Independence) party had formed a Moroccan League for the Defense of Human Rights. The League at times raised important human rights issues in Morocco, but it was always closely tied to Istiqlal party policy, was never able to establish an independent mass base, and was largely kept in operation through the work of one man, the lawyer Muhammad al-Qebab.

In 1979 another opposition party, the Socialist Union of Popular Forces (USFP – l'Union socialiste des forces populaires) and some of the smaller groups on the left encouraged the creation of what many hoped would be a broadly based human rights organization, the Moroccan Association for Human Rights (AMDH – l'Association marocaine des droits de l'homme). The AMDH began with great enthusiasm and made important contributions to the Moroccan human rights situation during the early 1980s. It then began to experience serious problems and remained paralyzed for several years.

In 1988 a new organization, the Moroccan Human Rights

Organization (OMDH – l'Organisation marocaine des droits de l'homme) announced its intention to promote human rights awareness in Morocco and to work to improve the human rights situation there. It experienced some harassment from the authorities but by 1989 it had been officially accepted as a legal association. It has now become affiliated, along with the LTDH and fledgling human rights associations in Algeria and Mauritania to the new Maghreb Human Rights Union, formed in June 1989 in the aftermath of the creation of the Arab Maghreb Union.

Over the decade of the 1980s, of the human rights organizations in Morocco the experience of the AMDH was certainly the most eloquent.

Abderrahim Jamai, a Moroccan lawyer from Kenitra, now in his midforties, had been one of the founders of the AMDH when it began in 1979 and was still on its executive committee when I spoke to him in the late 1980s. I had known him well for some years and had watched him move from a committed defense lawyer in political cases to a broader human rights consciousness. Abderrahim Jamai is short and stocky, and full of energy. I would usually see him late in the evening after he had had a long day's work; he might be dressed in his track suit, coming to me right after his karate practice.

He first gave me some historical background to the development of human rights consciousness in Morocco, and then went on to discuss some of the problems the AMDH was facing.

> *I think that the reasons we began to agitate for human rights in the last few years have to be sought not only in the last few years, but in all that has happened here since the colonial period began in 1912. But, to keep our story somewhat short, after independence in 1956, as we all made our effort to construct a new, modern Morocco, many of us began to see that although much had happened on many levels in developing our society, little advance had been made on the level of human liberties, of human rights.*
>
> *Some of us concluded from this that for Moroccans, the question of our fundamental rights had to be posed on all levels. Because without this, the current crisis would continue – of course, this crisis isn't simply today's crisis but has been with us for a long time – and people would continue to feel they have no role to play in the construction of this society. People must be free if they are to give their full effort, if they are to achieve really positive results, either in the short or in the long term.*

Had there been any problems in promoting the notion of human rights, had the notion itself encountered much resistance?

> *Of course one of the problems that we faced from the beginning is the*

way in which the whole notion of human rights has been manipulated by the powers that be. When Carter or Reagan, for example, defends human rights, we know very well who are the human beings whose rights he is defending: it certainly isn't an African or an Asian or a Palestinian. Today he may talk of human rights but tomorrow he won't defend the rights of women and children who are killed by aggressors, or won't defend the rights of Blacks in the United States, or will support the racist regime in South Africa, or drop millions and millions of bombs on Vietnam or on Nicaragua. That becomes part of government policy. But remember, when I talk about Carter or Reagan or the American government, that's only one part of the picture; I'm not saying this about the American people, or about their non-governmental humanitarian organizations.

Had people in Morocco welcomed the formation of a human rights organization?

Well, first of all, how do we push people to believe in human rights, how can we struggle to get people to respect human rights? Let me give you a concrete example. In creating the AMDH in Morocco, it has been very difficult to get people to see the difference between a human rights organization and a political party. Even now, after our association has been in existence for almost a decade, people still do not distinguish between working in a political party and working in a human rights organization. For me, a human rights organization has to be distinct from any political party. You know, there is another Moroccan human rights organization, affiliated to the Istiqlal party. Well, there is no doubt that it does some good work, but it can't have a broad moral and social force because objectively it is tied to a political party and must follow the line of that party.

You see, one of the real problems in forming an independent human rights organization in Morocco is that, in one way or another, everything here is structured by the political parties. Some of these parties argue with those in power, others are just waiting their turn to wield power, some just shift back and forth between one attitude and the other. Even our association was able to get started only with the aid of some political parties, a few of the parties on the left. But from that moment, we all recognized the need to fill the most responsible positions with people who were known to be neutral, and who were without political ties.

What had the association been doing, specifically, to promote human rights?

We had lots of good ideas at the outset. We were going to have major educational programs in human rights, we were going to have special study days, and even self-education seminars. Some of these got off the ground and a number of them were actually quite successful.

But then, with a frustrated air, Abderrahim was led directly to discuss some of the fundamental organizational problems the AMDH was facing and which, as he said to me later, he was not sure the organization would survive.

But for us to be successful as an organization you have to sustain your activity, you can't just come and go like the oued *[a river that flows powerfully during the rains but may disappear during the dry season]. A big problem was our lack of organization, and the lack of people with the time and willingness to do the work. You know, there were always a lot of political party militants available to do this work, who really wanted nothing better than to do this work. But we didn't want to call on them. So we didn't have enough people for this problem, or for that case, or for this or that region.*

And we also needed specialists to study certain situations; the question of work, of the child, of the woman, of health care. Party militants can't do this kind of work. What we need is an organization not made of party militants but made of people who can give scientifically, juridically, politically, who can give a certain kind of weight. We don't need people with political convictions but we need people with a kind of human conviction, people who empathize with the problems and pains of other people.

But perhaps an even more critical problem emerged at the very beginning and was in part a product of our own early success. We were attracting a lot of new members. And a good number of these were people whose merit lay not in their political positions but in their humanitarian spirit. Well, if that had continued we would have created something stronger than any political party. And so the parties themselves, to say nothing of the governmental authorities, not only didn't give us support, but began to cause us problems.

Add to this the events of June 1981, and then the events of January 1984.[1] And in between these major events there were little events. This created serious problems for us: a great demand from many different quarters and ideological currents for the association to act, and an increased sensitivity from the authorities toward our activities. So, the next thing we knew, our annual congress was prohibited and some of our members were arrested and harassed.

As all of this was occurring we were facing the problem of how to control our membership. If we were going to remain independent and be seen as independent, well, we couldn't expand too quickly, we couldn't let every one join who wanted to. To remain in control of the work you have to have a pretty tight structure.

How could we do this? There was a great influx of people, especially young people, and all the divisions in the student movement, for example, began to be reflected inside the association. All the different ideological groups in the society at large began to show up in the association. So, for example, at the time of the elections to our national congress each trend, tendency, or little group was doing everything it could to get places for its adherents.

And this problem – the one of being threatened with atomization into little groups – is the critical problem that has in effect paralyzed the association for some time now. And not only is it reflected on the national level of the association, but also on the level of our local sections.

Over the years that I have talked to Abderrahim Jamai and other members of the AMDH, it was never clear that they would indeed be able to surmount these difficulties. For example, when the president of the AMDH resigned in 1985, divisions within the association made it impossible to agree on a successor. Abderrahim and others I spoke to wondered whether it made more sense to try and start entirely anew, or to persevere and try to revitalize the AMDH.

As the 1980s wore on the association remained paralyzed, as a result of a combination of the factors Abderrahim Jamai had outlined: the lack of organization, the undermining by political parties and small ideological groups, the reflection within the association of divisions in the larger society, as well as harassment from the authorities.

From both the Egyptian and Moroccan experiences some of the problems facing human rights organizations were clear: in addition to the obvious ones of official repression (and this should not be underestimated), there were also the more subtle ones of creating the proper social and cultural climate, recruiting competent, committed persons, and avoiding being caught in the web of political manipulations.

How was the Tunisian Human Rights League facing up to these problems?

TUNISIAN VOICES (1): 'AFTER ALL, WE'RE NOT ASKING TO GOVERN THE COUNTRY'

If Moroccan human rights organizations tended to exist along political party lines, and Egyptian ones to have a more regional or international orientation, the Tunisian Human Rights League (LTDH – la Ligue tunisienne pour la défense des droits de l'homme) was distinct from both: it focused on human rights problems in its own country and had managed to bring together most of the various ideological and political groups under its umbrella.

The LTDH was formally created in May 1977 when it received its official authorization from the Ministry of Interior. Just a year earlier fifteen individuals, either independents or members of opposition currents, had requested the ministry authorization necessary to form a human rights association. Four months later, several members of the governmental party, the PSD (Destourian Socialist party), and close followers of the party made a similar request to the ministry. As one high-ranking LTDH member told me, the Tunisian government wanted to put a human rights association into operation at that time to respond to US President Carter's 'human rights offensive'. After considerable discussion, a compromise was proposed by the Minister of Interior and agreed to by the various groups: the authorization would be granted and the first executive committee would comprise seven members of the PSD and fifteen independents. The League was to be financed fully by private contributions from its members as well as from fund-raising activities.

The agreement over the composition of the executive committee was to set the structure of the League over the ensuing decade – membership of its executive committee (its most important decision-making body) would consist of an agreed number of representatives from each of the main political forces in Tunisian society (these numbers changed slightly at each successive national congress). This structure led to much criticism from outside the League. Some people argued that a human rights organization selecting people according to political party affiliation violated the basic premise of human rights that human beings are to be seen as individuals, not as representatives of social categories; others accused the League of mirroring Tunisia's political party structure and therefore of being less an institution of civil society than an institution of political society and the state.

Whatever criticisms may be made of the League on this abstract level, the allocation of seats on the executive committee did much to keep the League intact and afloat. However, it certainly didn't solve all the League's problems, some of which it faced from the very outset.

The trade union unrest of January 1978, a series of political trials throughout 1978 and 1979 in which prison sentences were meted out to members of the UGTT and its leadership, and the uprising in Gafsa in 1980, put great pressure on the League during its first few years, at times putting its existence in the balance. PSD members of the executive committee found themselves in increasingly awkward positions and many either resigned or no longer played an active role. Also, the PSD attempted to infiltrate and dominate one of the League's local sections and another section faced a similar offensive from groups on the left.

By 1982 the League had nonetheless gained a sounder footing with more than a thousand members in twenty-four different local sections, and it was able to hold its first national congress that February. At this congress, only two PSD members were kept on the fifteen member executive committee. By then, the League had already become an affiliate of the International Human Rights Federation (FIDH – Fédération internationale des droits de l'homme) despite reservations about the FIDH's strong support for Israel, it had ties with the International Commission of Jurists in Geneva, and its representatives had attended several international meetings.

By March 1985 when the League held its second national congress it had expanded even more, to 3,000 members grouped in thirty-three sections (with requests pending for nineteen more), and it had become an important force on the national scene. By its third congress in 1989 it had almost forty sections and more than 4,000 members.

How had the development of the League occurred, how had it achieved its successes in spite of serious problems, and what were the problems that it now faced? There was no one in a better position to talk about these issues than Khemais Chamari, secretary-general of the LTDH during the mid-1980s, and a man with wide experience in the international human rights community (he is a vice-president of the FIDH).

Khemais is now a man in his late forties and had himself spent time in prison as a result of his activities in leftist movements in the late 1960s and early 1970s. (In early 1987, he was again arrested and charged with disseminating false information and offending the prime minister. He was provisionally released a month later, on grounds of ill health. His trial was postponed repeatedly and when it finally took place, in January 1988, Khemais was acquitted.) He is a leading figure in the Socialist Democrat Movement (MDS – le Mouvement des démocrates socialistes), an opposition political party with social democrat leanings, and currently works as an administrator in a banking school.

Khemais began,

The League was founded in 1977, but for the whole period from 1977 to 1980 it wasn't able to free itself from the idea that human rights meant the rights of particular groups of political prisoners in specific situations. Of course, that left it open to the accusation that it was politically motivated, that it would defend only prisoners with the 'correct' political position.

But since about 1980, a couple of very important ideas began to make inroads: first, that not only political prisoners have rights but also the notion of rights can be applied to all citizens in their daily lives; and second, that rights are universal – this is the problematic of 1789 and the French revolution – they apply not only to my friends but also to my enemies.

These wider ideas began to take hold because the League had made a great effort to change its profile: it made a conscious effort not to be too

closely identified with any particular political group, to diversify its recruit-
ment and take on people from many different socio-economic classes,
and to have important members who hadn't broken with the establishment.

Now, having reached the point where we are today, we see our work as
taking place in the following domains: (1) the daily relationships between
citizens and the authorities; (2) social and economic rights, such as
health care, education, and labor unions; (3) rights of women and
children; (4) environmental rights and the quality of life; (5) the struggle
for tolerance and against ethnic and racial discrimination.

Khemais went on to mention some specific campaigns that the League had waged in the previous months: it had urged investigation into an incident where a policeman had refused medical care to a diabetic prisoner and into another where a policeman had allegedly tortured a suspect; it had campaigned for a national commission of enquiry into an incident where negligence in the handling of fuel oil had led to 46 deaths and 253 injuries; and it had initiated judicial proceedings against a popular newspaper for having published anti-Jewish remarks.

Nonetheless, the LTDH was not without its problems. Speaking generally, Khemais pointed to three fundamental kinds of problems an organization such as the League had to face: how to structure the relationship between the intellectuals and professionals who made up so much of the League's membership and who were most likely to assume leadership roles, and the masses, both within and outside the organization, who would frequently have a different understanding of the human rights struggle; how to resolve the tension between a human rights perspective that necessarily implied certain clear political choices – for pluralism, democracy, and liberalism – and the need to remain open to groups and people who had different political views; how to resolve the tension between universal values, such as those expressed in the various international human rights instruments, and national specificity, identity, and traditions.

More specifically and immediately, however, Khemais pointed frankly to some difficulties that recalled the problems paralyzing the Moroccan Human Rights Association.

The most serious problem from my point of view is how to ensure that
subgroups within the League, reflecting groups in the society at large, do
not take over and manipulate the League for their own ends. You know,
there is now a tremendous demand for membership in the League, yet a
solid tradition of impartial human rights activity is not really present here
in Tunisia. So there is always the danger that we will expand too rapidly
and lose control over our activity. We now have nineteen requests to form
new sections that we haven't yet accepted because of just this problem.

As Khemais and other leaders of the League saw it, the risk of being undermined and manipulated by various groups was a serious one and the League needed to find a way to ensure its coherence and to protect itself from the charge that it was politically motivated.

This problem agitated the League for some time, and its leadership finally decided that the answer might lie in the elaboration of a charter containing the basic principles of the organization, principles that every member would have to openly subscribe to. But in the summer of 1985 this proposed solution was to lead to problems of its own – a broad attack on specific propositions in the charter as well as on the organization as a whole – that came to threaten the League's central role in Tunisian society.

Muhammad Charfi was elected president of the LTDH in March 1989, and shortly after that was named Minister of Education. Now in his early fifties, he was by profession a professor at the Law Faculty of the University of Tunis. As a member of the executive committee of the LTDH in 1985, he was closely involved from the very beginning in drafting the League's charter, and then in defending it against attack.

When I first went to see him in May 1985 he was, as a member of the LTDH's executive committee, caught up in negotiations over a hunger strike then occurring in the southern town of Gabès. Workers there had originally gone on strike to protest being paid less than the minimum wage (then approximately 100 dinars or $120 per month) and being made to work twelve hours a day. As soon as the workers began their strike they were fired, and they then retaliated by occupying the local offices of the UGTT and beginning a hunger strike. The League was being asked to intervene on behalf of the hunger strikers and my conversation with Muhammad Charfi was interrupted a number of times by telephone calls from other members of the League as they attempted to work out their response to this appeal.

In spite of these interruptions Muhammad Charfi, who speaks softly and measures his words carefully, was able to describe clearly the ideas behind the charter, some of the problems it was meant to solve, and those that he expected it to generate.

> *The idea of the charter arose from two events. First of all, there was the challenge to the Jewish candidate for the executive committee. This convinced many of us that something had to be done to ensure that members all adhered to the same basic principles.*
>
> *The second event? Let me give you a little background. In the last few years the League has acquired – and this is a fact – strong credibility in Tunisia, a certain status on the political, social, and cultural chessboard. One of the reasons for this was the extraordinary week the League*

organized last year to campaign against the death penalty at a time when ten people, all demonstrators during the famous 'bread riots' of 3 January 1984, were facing execution. The campaign was fantastic on the national and the international level, it was something that we really worked out quite well. This culminated in a presidential commutation of all the death sentences to life imprisonment. This was a tremendous event, a great success, because the President only very rarely commutes death sentences and usually follows the rulings of the courts.

So now, everyone wants to belong to the League. And this is now our big organizational problem: everyone wants to become a member. This includes, for example, people who are known to believe in a one-party system, people who are rigid Marxists, people who behave on the university campus like little Pol Pots, and Islamists who believe in amputating the hands of thieves. All these people want to become members of the League, because the League has obtained this kind of credibility and because, for some of them, the League is a prize worth winning, because it is an open space that has to be occupied.

So, with all this success and with all these people wanting to join us, we began to ask ourselves the question, 'Are we really among people here who believe in human rights, or are a lot of people just using us to promote political goals?' Up until that point all we asked was that prospective members believe in human rights and in the Universal Declaration of Human Rights (UDHR). But that is pretty loose. So we thought, 'Perhaps we should elaborate a charter, a Tunisian charter. Let's put the dots on the i's with regard to the Tunisian situation and Tunisian problems.' You know, it isn't that we wanted to carry out a police inquiry into someone's beliefs! But whoever signed our charter would have accepted all of it, article by article. That way, at least things would be clear. You can be an Islamist, you can be a Communist, you can be anything you want to call yourself: if you accept our charter's principles, well, you're welcome to the League.

We decided that a commission within the executive committee would draft the charter and then send it to all the local sections. Each section would meet in a general assembly – that is a meeting of all of its members – to discuss the draft and to send us their criticisms and suggestions. Afterwards, we would revise the draft and submit a final proposed charter to the national council which includes the executive committee and the president of each of the sections. The national council would meet at the end of July.

The League was obviously moving very quickly on this matter – it was now May, the draft had already been sent to the sections, comments were due within the next two weeks and by the end of July the final version was to be voted on.

Muhammad Charfi had been on the charter commission – in fact, a number of people I spoke to named him as the person most responsible for actually drafting the charter – and it was important for me to understand what kinds of discussion had taken place there. After all, the charter was meant to settle a number of vexing issues: not only would it outline the League's domain of activity and define its work within that domain, but also the charter would have to reconcile various groups whose ideas were often strongly at odds with one another. It was not immediately obvious, for example, how it might reconcile the views of Islamists who wanted to relate human rights to the Islamic 'patrimony', with the views of committed secularists who held that human rights was an achievement independent of any cultural or religious system.

Muhammad Charfi explained the commission's approach:

The commission charged with elaborating the draft charter decided, after some discussion, that we could start with the model of the UDHR without sacrificing any of our basic principles. We would have to make some stylistic changes because the UDHR is a document that commits states to protect certain rights whereas the League wants individuals to be committed to those rights; but we also had the obvious problem of clarifying our charter on matters that are of particular concern to Muslims. After all, the UDHR was, basically, a compromise between the Americans and the Soviets on the issue of 'real' versus 'formal' democracy. In this compromise, the concerns of the Third World and of Muslims were not taken into account.

So, we took the UDHR as our starting point, and then made some changes to 'Tunisify' the text. For example, where the UDHR says, 'punishments should not be inhuman' we added, 'corporal punishments are to be condemned as are all inhuman punishments and treatment of the detainee'. Where the UDHR says, 'freedom of association and organization', we added 'which excludes a one-party regime'. You see, these may seem like small changes but each change makes the article explicitly relevant to the Tunisian situation. On the other hand, we eliminated a number of things from the UDHR which were not relevant for us, like the provisions about slavery. All in all, in our draft, we had to deal with the problems as they are posed in Islamic societies.

Yet with all this, we wanted a short text of a page or a page and a half, a text that could be printed with the subscription request – not one that would be as long as a novel!

Within the drafting committee had any issues generated particularly heated discussion?

There were three main areas of disagreement. First of all, on the question of corporal punishment there was no fundamental disagreement. The disagreements were on the right to change one's religion, the right of a

*Muslim woman to marry a non-Muslim man, and the rights of illegitimate
children.*

These three aspects touched very sensitive chords in Tunisia since
support of these rights might be seen as an attack on the integrity of the
Tunisian Muslim community and on the integrity of the family.[2] Because
of the sensitive nature of these issues, I asked Muhammad Charfi if he
would describe the discussions in more detail.

*We decided that our draft should retain the UDHR's words, that both
partners have equal marriage rights.[3] On the right to change religion we
would be more explicit than the UDHR and state clearly the individual's
right to change religion.[4] On the rights of illegitimate children we would
be somewhat less explicit than the UDHR.[5]*

At the time of this conversation the draft was being discussed in the
sections and Muhammad Charfi was under no illusions that its passage
would be smooth. 'Let's face it,' he said,

*The paragraph on the right to change your religion – well, that seems to
go against the principles of Islamic law. In Islamic law, it is specifically
forbidden for a Muslim to abandon his religion. But in our drafting
commission, those who argued against this paragraph didn't disagree
with the principle behind it, but said, 'This is going to shock a lot of
religious people, a lot of people.' As for me, well, I'm sorry about that, but
there is a certain basic minimum to human rights and if we're going to
shock we're going to shock. You know, I'm quite willing to play a little
politics and take into consideration people's sensitivities, but still there is
a minimum. Of course, it all comes down to what this minimum is.*

*I'm also expecting some sections to want to go farther than we did in
the draft. For example, we didn't affirm the principle that illegitimate
children should have the same rights as legitimate children. But, first of
all, this is not a problem of primary importance. After all, how many
illegitimate children are there here? Perhaps fifty among the 7 millions of
Tunisians. So, should we have a real battle so that these fifty kids have
inheritance rights? It is true that the unmarried mother is socially
completely unaccepted here. As soon as her stomach starts to swell a bit,
she has to leave her house and go to a woman friend or to a relative; the
day of birth she goes to the hospital and then after giving birth she runs
away, abandoning the child who is put in an orphanage and who may later
be adopted by a couple unable to have their own children.*

I didn't find this reasoning convincing – Muhammad Charfi seemed to be
underestimating the problem, at least as I had heard it described by a
number of Tunisian women. But he insisted,

It is not a crucial problem. You must remember that here in Tunisia the protection of the family appears imperative, essential. To protect the family implies that the status of illegitimate children not be absolutely equal to legitimate ones, or else we would be encouraging free love. On the other hand, society must take illegitimate children in charge so that they have access to society's material advantages. We don't want the illegitimate child to suffer materially from the circumstances of its birth – society must provide for its needs. But that doesn't mean the illegitimate child should be integrated into the family – that would be to harm the legitimate family.

Well, those are the problems that I'm expecting, at the moment. But who knows?

Muhammad Charfi was not only well informed but also sensitive to the mood of the League, for many of his expectations were borne out in the charter discussion over the next few months. But he could not have known that over those months Tunisian national life was to suffer serious shocks and disturbances. In August 1985 Libya expelled some 30,000 Tunisians working there, and Prime Minister Mzali claimed that the resulting economic crisis was so severe that the UGTT should suspend its salary demands – not to do so, he claimed, was tantamount to siding with Qadhdhafi and bordered on treason. The UGTT refused to do Mzali's bidding and the union and its leader, Habib Achour, faced increasingly angry government threats and harassment (there were also nasty verbal exchanges between the Prime Minister and the UGTT leader). As this crisis grew more pronounced, Tunisia was shocked in early October when Israeli planes bombed the PLO headquarters outside Tunis, killing some seventy people. Demonstrations, marches, and special meetings of the national assembly all made the crisis even more acute.

With their unsettling effects on Tunisian society at large, these events shook the LTDH as well; but the League had its own internal problems too, as it was just then deeply engaged in debate over the charter. Some of these larger national events and the charter discussion became linked when, in much of the press, a fierce attack was launched on the League over the summer months, accusing it of being anti-Islam, anti-Tunisian, and neo-colonialist. In addition a leader of the MTI had asked for a public referendum on the Personal Status Code, calling into question provisions that many Tunisian human rights activists considered to be among Tunisia's most important achievements since independence.

I returned to Tunisia in the fall of 1985. Before I went to talk to Muhammad Charfi again, I spent some time with an acquaintance of mine, a member of the MTI. He was very critical of the League, although he had himself been defended by it when he faced arrest and imprisonment and had earlier been one of its supporters. But now, talking

about the League's charter, he accused the League of having sold out to
the West and having gone against the Islamic patrimony. At the other
extreme, a woman I knew, a strong secularist, harshly criticized the
League, saying, 'They caved in like cowards to the Islamists!' She pointed
to the charter's new preamble, added in response to the public campaign
against the League, that referred to the 'liberating principles in our Arab
Muslim civilization'. She said angrily, 'Why should I have to bow to Islam
before I can assert my own rights as a human being?'

What had happened in the few months of my absence that led to so
much controversy about the charter? Muhammad Charfi gave me many
of the details.

*All the sections submitted their comments as they were supposed to do,
and the charter was to be approved in a meeting of the national council
on 28 July. I had returned from abroad just before this, on the 25th.*

*But when I returned from abroad, I found that over the previous two
weeks, the press had mounted a major campaign against the charter. This
seems to have been provoked by the Islamists who were using the charter
and its supposedly non-Islamic character to mobilize opinion against the
League. The charter was said to have been 'imported', to neglect the
special character of Islamic society and the contribution of Islam to the
notion of human rights. Specifically article 8 on the right of either sex to
marry non-Muslims and article 9 on the freedom of religion were attacked
on these grounds.*

*The executive committee met before the national council did and we
had a very heated debate. We decided to take note of the press
discussion and to slightly modify the wording of the draft. We agreed with
the first point, that the charter was too universal, that it didn't take enough
account of Tunisian particularities, and that the Islamic contribution to
human rights should be recognized. We therefore proposed a preamble
to the charter that would say that the charter was inspired by the positive
contribution of Arab Muslim civilization – not that all of it was, but that there
was indeed such a contribution.*

*We also decided to keep article 8, on equality in marriage, as we had
it, but to change article 9 slightly, moving from 'right to change one's
religion' to 'right to choose one's religion'. But on these matters there
really was a great debate.*

*So, for the meeting of the national council on 28 July, we had proposed
the new preamble, to keep article 8 as it was, and to slightly modify article
9. The controversy in the press had already started, but it then began to
increase day by day to reach heights I would never have dreamed
possible. In addition, there was a petition circulating among the Islamists
in the League, saying, 'Careful, this charter is going to violate people's
feelings and violate the cultural identity of Tunisians.'*

So, as the national council meetings began – there were about fifty of us – there were already divergent attitudes. 'What, are we going to bow to pressure? All we have to do is stand fast.' Or, 'Look, this is only the beginning of the campaign against us, and we'd better try to cut our losses as best we can'.

Muhammad Charfi had been right at the center of the debates and was able to give almost a blow-by-blow account.

Among the fifty of us, there was about one-tenth on the extreme left who were adamant against any changes, and were even against the new preamble; about a tenth were Islamists who supported the preamble but wanted to make it stronger, and who were also for a radical reformulation of articles 8 and 9; and then the remaining eight-tenths were people who I believe are really true partisans of human rights, who believe sincerely in the principles of the UDHR. But even in this group views were divided. Some were saying, 'We should go into battle, because even if there is a battle, we will win it'; and others were saying, 'No, this does too much offense to the feelings of the people, all we have to do is change the formulation a bit and it will get through'. So, although in this group they all may have agreed on the principles, they disagreed on how to get these principles accepted in our society.

How had the discussion gone on each of these matters?

As far as the preamble went, there wasn't too much dispute. I defended the new preamble. There were some people on the left who argued, in effect, 'Why do we need this? It's not even true, and it serves no purpose'. But for my part, I sincerely believe that no one owns the notion of human rights. You know, when you support human rights, there is a certain nationalism that comes forward: for an American human rights are the invention of Jefferson, for a Frenchman it is 1789, for an Englishman something else. Well, in these circumstances, I can also cite Omar Ibn al-Khattab, who said 'How can you enslave people when their mothers brought them into the world free?'[6]

So, if each human community is going to search in its own history for an origin to human rights, it will always come up with something. Let's just say that our civilization also made its contribution. You know, I'm not trying to affirm, absolutely not, the superiority of Arab Muslim civilization over others, but I'm also against any attitude that tries to make Arab Muslim civilization out to be inferior to others. I am for a complete and total equality between civilizations.

Now that doesn't mean that today all civilizations are perfectly equal in every respect. Obviously, each civilization has its own character, and at one moment or another in its history it accomplished something that we ought to try to preserve. But to start to say, this one was first, that one was last, well, that's absurd.

So, perhaps we were wrong not to have said something about the Arab

Muslim contribution at the very beginning of our discussion of the charter, but in any case I had nothing against including these ideas, so we added this preamble.

But on articles 8 and 9 we had a very difficult time. The moderate center wanted to soften a bit the so-called 'provocative' character of articles 8 and 9. In article 8, on equality in marriage, they wanted to change equality 'without discrimination on the basis of race, color, or religion' to 'without any discrimination whatsoever'. Retaining the essential, you see, but trying not to rub salt in the wound. Well, this proposal was defeated by a vote of 24 to 23, and we kept the stronger phrase, 'without discrimination on the basis of race, color, or religion'.

As for article 9, the proposal was to modify 'freedom to change one's religion' to 'freedom to choose one's religion', because a number of people thought the wording 'change one's religion' would be too provocative for Muslims. And here the weaker wording, 'choose one's religion' won, again by a very close vote, 25 to 22.

I asked Muhammad Charfi why what might seem a mere quibble over words was in fact such an important issue.

Well, as far as I am concerned there is an absolutely crucial distinction between 'the right to change one's religion', which is the formulation I preferred and that lost, and 'the right to choose one's religion'. Maybe there doesn't seem to be much difference, but since discussion of religion takes place against the background of the punishment for apostasy, it is absolutely essential to guarantee the right to reflect on and change your view of your own religion.

Let me give you an example. You know, here in Tunisia, we are very attached to the notion of interpretation or ijtihad.[7] We have introduced important new ijtihads here in Tunisia as when, for example, we abolished polygamy. And logically, in order to guarantee the freedom of ijtihad, you have to, in effect, suppress punishment for apostasy. Why? Because if you suggest an ijtihad that goes against establishment thinking, and if your right to express and argue for your ijtihad isn't guaranteed, you may be accused of apostasy, of no longer following Islam. No one of course will challenge your right to reflect on your religion, but they will say, 'under the pretext of reflecting on your religion, you have in fact changed your religion, what you're saying is no longer Islam'. So, we have to guarantee the freedom to understand and practice your religion in your own way, and this means taking away the threat of punishment for apostasy.

I mentioned the case of the Sudanese reformer, Mahmoud Muhammad Taha, who had been executed in January 1985 by President Numeiri of the Sudan for just this reason. Muhammad Charfi responded,

Exactly. In fact Taha's case was the focus of this debate, I used his case to make the argument. So for us article 9 isn't so much a question of

allowing a Muslim to convert to Christianity or to Judaism. In fact, I've never heard of such cases in Tunisia – I mean it is technically possible, but such cases don't exist. By the way, I just ought to say that it is very hypocritical for Muslims to rejoice when a former Christian, a former Marxist like the Frenchman Roger Garaudy, becomes a Muslim, and then not allow a certain Muhammad or an Ali to convert when he becomes enchanted with Christianity or Judaism. But this is a purely theoretical problem, it's speculation. What I really want to avoid is that we have a case in Tunisia like what happened to Taha in the Sudan.

Well, as things turned out, in the national council vote at the end of July my position lost, 25 to 22, mostly because people were saying '"Choice" allows for changing religion, but it won't vex, it won't provoke', and because the Islamists among us also were for 'choice'. My argument, on the other hand, was, 'If you have a problem, you have to get right to the bottom of it and solve it'.

It was immediately after the national council voting that the hostile campaign in the press against the League reached its climax. Deep divisions were claimed to be tearing the League apart, the League was said to be split down the middle, with half the people in it for Tunisia and Islam and the other half promoting Western interests and culture. As Muhammad Charfi explained it, at this point the Islamists within the League began to adopt harder positions.

They didn't want to be left on the outside, and they began to call for changes in articles 8 and 9, changes to make them more 'Islamic'. On the question of religious freedom, the Islamists take the orthodox view – freedom of religion means the freedom for each person to practice his own religion – not to interpret it, but to practice it. When one talks of freedom of religion in Islam, the point of reference is the context of the conquering Islamic armies that crossed Egypt and Africa starting in the seventh century and that, contrary to the behavior of other invading armies and conquering civilizations, did not destroy churches and synagogues but allowed Christians and Jews to continue to practice their religions. That's the Islamic meaning of religious freedom: we, the Muslim rulers, allow the Jew or the Christian to freely practice his religion. You know, of course, that at the time of the Reconquista in Spain the Christian rulers prevented Muslims from practicing their religion.[8]

The Islamist position comes from this. Within the League, they wanted to affirm religious freedom in only a very general way. They argued, for example, against the freedom of interpretation, saying, 'Careful, in Islamic law, interpretation obeys certain rules, there isn't total freedom. One has to be a Muslim, one has to be learned, one has to be pious; and one cannot question the foundations of the religion. Not just anyone can interpret.' So, if we followed their argument, it's quite likely that if you put forward an interpretation that challenged something they were sensitive about, they'd attack you by saying, 'You're not pious, we didn't see you every Friday at the mosque', or 'You're attacking one of the foundations of religion, and these foundations aren't open to interpretation'. You know, that is the sort of thing that bothers them the most, because it takes away their monopoly on interpretation.

As Muhammad Charfi explained it, the closeness of the voting had less to do with deep divisions within the League than with the awkward way proposals were phrased and voted upon, and he was quite critical, and indeed self-critical, of the League's careless handling of the voting procedure. He went on to say, 'The press campaign mentioned none of these difficulties and, instead, made every effort to convince the public that the League was divided right down the middle'.

It was clear, from what Muhammad Charfi and others involved in the charter discussions told me, that the League as a whole had found this a very difficult experience. Not only had the public campaign in the press put the League on the defensive, but also the disputes within the League had left many with a bad aftertaste. The League decided to hold a second national council meeting, on 22 September, to reconsider a number of questions raised in the campaign, as well as to recover the initiative.

Muhammad Charfi described what happened:

By the time of the second national council meeting, the League had recovered its unity. All we did at that second meeting was find a new formulation for article 8, which now states that 'Men and women, upon reaching legal majority, have the right to freely choose their spouse and to begin a family on the basis of their own personal convictions and consciences'. It also specifically states that the Tunisian Personal Status Code constitutes an important advance as regards the rights of women and the protection of the family.

We also replied to the argument that the UDHR had a Western spirit by saying that the UDHR didn't represent only Western views but expressed at one and the same time the views of the capitalist world, the communist world, Africa and Asia. The UDHR, therefore, was a compromise between the great world civilizations. And furthermore, contrary to what some people were arguing, the League stated its view that the UDHR was not an ideal that we should gradually approach, but constituted the minimum universal human values that one had to accept if one called oneself 'a man of liberty'.

Of course, we recognize that the UDHR is something that itself will have to be modified, and maybe some day when we have more weight on the international level we'll be able to make some contribution to that. But for now, the attitude of the League, as we developed it in the national council, is that the UDHR constitutes a minimum and that it is not a Western document, but was elaborated by communists, capitalists, Africans, Asians, etc.

Did he think, I wondered, that the controversy over the charter would now subside?

> *Well, we closed the door to further discussion of the charter by passing a resolution at our September meeting saying that this was to be the last modification until the next congress in a few years' time.[9] So, at that point there was no real hope for our opponents. And also, by the end of the summer the campaign against us had already subsided because our opponents saw they could not break up the League from inside.*

But perhaps even more important in blunting the attack against the League were, as Muhammad Charfi admitted, the very charged larger political events of the late summer and early fall: the expulsion of Tunisian workers from Libya in August, the increasingly bitter disputes between the UGTT and the government and, finally, the Israeli bombing of the PLO headquarters outside Tunis in early October.

I asked Muhammad Charfi to look back over the charter episode: was this a battle that had been worth fighting?

> *Well, without being too optimistic, I really think the charter was a big achievement. I don't think there are too many Arab countries where such a charter could have been adopted. Even if the earlier version of article 8 was better, and if I preferred the defeated wording of article 9, having both of these in Tunisia today is a solid achievement.*
>
> *One of our major accomplishments in the course of all the discussion over the charter was to affirm the distinction between law and religion. Let's say a Muslim woman wants to marry a non-Muslim man. And here, on one side, is a great theologian who says that Islam prohibits such marriages. But on the other side is Fatima or Leila, daughter of Muhammad, who indeed wants to marry a particular non-Muslim man. Well, I believe the great theologian has every right to say that such an act is a sin, he has every right to go and preach to young women and advise against these marriages. But he has no right to prohibit these marriages; the tribunal and civil officials must accept her choice, not the voice of the theologian. This is the proper distinction between religion and law. We at the League never wanted to change Islam, but we wanted to affirm that the rule of law coexists with religion, side by side with religion, not against religion. Each norm must be given its proper sphere of application.*
>
> *Or say that someone wants to convert from Islam to another religion: this too may be seen by established Islamic thinking to be against Islam. But the League must defend the legal right of any given individual to marry whomever he or she pleases, and to choose whatever religion he or she pleases; the League doesn't have to say whether this particular act is Islamic or not. I think this is the proper position, to defend the distinction between religion and law.*
>
> *But, at the same time that we were willing not to get involved in religious*

law – sort of giving the Islamists a gift that didn't cost us anything, because it is outside of our interests – we also wanted something in return, and we got it in the charter: the recognition that our Personal Status Code, the law that contains the abolition of polygamy and of divorce by repudiation, is an absolute minimum and that the League would oppose any retraction of the rights contained in that law.

So, I don't think I'm being too optimistic. Although we had to react under the pressure of a very heated public debate – we had two very difficult months, and I can tell you that the pressures during this period were exceedingly intense – we still found a way to formulate our position that both solved the problems and put an end to the debate.

And how would he assess the League's role and significance as an organization in Tunisian society, now?

You know, the League in Tunisia isn't at all the equivalent of a human rights league in France or in the United States or in England. In those democratic countries, political parties fill the political stage, and the human rights organizations are marginal – they busy themselves with the particular cases of individuals whose rights have been violated. Here, because our freedoms are so weak, our political parties are weak too. They don't fill the political stage, so the League is called onto this stage too. Now, when the UGTT is attacked everyone turns to the League and wants to know what the League's position is. So, the League is pushed into a role that is much more important than what its fundamental role should be.

Why shouldn't the League play a more political role? After all, in a situation where no political party was effectively addressing the daily problems of poverty, unemployment, crime, inadequate health care, over-crowded and ineffective educational facilities, why shouldn't the League do it? Muhammad Charfi answered,

But that would be very dangerous, then we'd be turning into a political party. Of course, we can't avoid acting politically, but we don't want to act in the narrow sense of the word 'political'.

In any case, what I think is important, and what is one of the possible explanations for the League's importance, is that the governmental party doesn't want competitors, so it refuses to allow opposition political parties to operate. We, on the other hand, just put forward ideas. We aren't competitors for power, and they let us operate. That's our strength. If we become competitors for power we'll lose both our identity and our field of free action.

After the struggle over the charter and the campaign in the press, did he think the League had lost some of its support, that it had perhaps become more distant from the mass of Tunisians?

On this, I can't be so optimistic. You know, we often hear the argument about priorities: 'First we have to fight for public freedoms – for freedom of the press, for freedom of assembly and association. Those other issues – changing religion, marriage between Muslims and non-Muslims, and so on – they concern only marginal people.' After all, maybe once a year a Tunisian Muslim woman decides to marry a non-Muslim foreigner – I could look that up to find out exactly how many there are. But every day there are demonstrators who aren't allowed to demonstrate, newspapers and magazines are prohibited, people are forbidden to create political parties. There are attacks on the basic human freedoms of millions of Tunisians every day. So why should the League knock itself out for the one Tunisian woman when there are so many other problems? This is perhaps the weightiest criticism we face, and if you take into account our political context perhaps this argument is valid. But on the question of principle it isn't.

Even so, the charter discussion was very useful because now, even if many people don't share our ideas, at least we are accepted for what we are, without too many misunderstandings. Before, you know, there was a lot of misunderstanding, a kind of confusion, and that's why the charter was necessary. Now things are clear: we are not anti-Islam, we are not against Islamic civilization, we are not pro-West. We may have a way of looking at things that is not the way of the majority, I don't know. But in spite of that, we're willing to cooperate with everyone, and we're accepted with our differences.

In any case, for the role we play, that is plenty.

And then he added, with a laugh, 'After all, we're not asking to govern the country.'

11 Organizing women

The attempt to launch the women's magazine *Nissa* was one recent example of Tunisian women's efforts, going back more than a half century, to organize and promote women's rights and other social concerns. Moroccan and Egyptian women, too, had been engaged in similar efforts (although in Morocco's case independent women's organizations came into being only more recently). Looking more closely into these initiatives would mean opening a vast subject concerning not only the construction of civil society in the Middle East, but also the position and prospects of women in the Arab world.

I knew it would not be possible for me, in the context of my current work, to treat these questions with the thoroughness they demanded, but I did hope to shed some light on them by examining in detail *Nissa*'s development and by glancing at similar efforts by Moroccan and Egyptian women.

'THE CULTURAL REVOLUTION IS HAPPENING RIGHT NOW, RIGHT BEFORE OUR EYES' (MOROCCO)

Among the Moroccans I spoke to about these issues was Fatima Mernissi, a sociologist in her late forties. (Shortly after I spoke to Fatima she was to become, at the end of 1988, one of the founders of the new Moroccan Human Rights Organization.) She began our conversation by pointing out what was behind the rapid change in the position of women in Morocco.

Perhaps two phenomena go a long way to explain these changes: first of all, the importance of youth – about two-thirds of Morocco's population are under 25; second, the massive schooling of men and women – this is something whose importance I was late in recognizing. I used to think we should be talking mostly about poor women, about illiterate women. Now I think that the educated woman, the educated elite woman is a very, very important subject. It's these women, the teachers and others belonging to the petite bourgeoisie, *who are in the process of changing the world around them, because their situation as it is is untenable. There are too many archaic aspects in marriage, in the relations between the sexes, in the work situation. These educated women were nourished with a desire for independence, they have an image of themselves that isn't like my generation who grew up in secluded, private space. These women grew up in an independent Morocco.*

Where did she think that the central problem for women now lay?

As I see it, the central problem for women now is sex. This is the domain that is still taboo – we can't even talk about it – and the domain where women suffer the most: the foreman where she works wants to sleep with her, the cashier who is supposed to collect her money tries to sleep with her, the store owner where she shops tries to get sexual with her, in the street she can't walk alone without being accosted. Even the man she loves, the man with whom she'll begin to have a sexual relationship, will start to exploit her sexually. She'll have to have abortions or curettage because of him, and then he'll leave her and marry a girl who is supposed to be a virgin. Or maybe he'll marry her, and then he'll totally regress. Once he's her husband he'll regress and treat her as though there was no notion on earth of human rights.

There are similar attitudes within the political parties. Because we women are a small minority in public spaces, and because we're still often uncomfortable there, we are manipulated. Even by the left. I went to some labor union meetings for a time in the 1970s, but for me it was like a mosque. I still have a lot of respect for many of these people, but things were always being manipulated.

I asked her whether women in Morocco nowadays would let themselves be manipulated in this way.

Well, with the new generation of women things are changing. First of all some of these younger women are now so well schooled in political activity that men can't run circles around them as they did before. For me, writing was a revolutionary activity; for them it is politics. And now we're finding not only women who want to engage in politics to change things, but also women who go into politics just for the money, just like the men.

Can you imagine what an immense change this is? It's completely new: women who want to enter parliament, who want to win elections, who feel more comfortable in the masculine circuits of power than I could ever feel. So do you see how traditional I really am? [Fatima said with a laugh] And some of these women, they even know how to manipulate, they like to manipulate, they want to manipulate.

You know it is only recently that men here, and men on the left, began to realize that women are progressive and willing to challenge authority even more than the men are. So now the left, for its own survival, has begun to come in our direction, although the big parties of the left have never even had a regular page in their newspapers concerned with women's problems. But women won't wait for them any longer: there's a group of women here who have just started up a weekly newspaper, 8 Mars, and it's working out very well. That's a phenomenon, that's an extraordinary change.

To some other Moroccan women I spoke to *8 Mars*, although an important step forward, had serious failings and they preferred *Nissa* to it. As some said, *8 Mars* was too closely tied to one small new political party; and one woman said, '*8 Mars* is too theoretical – even I can't understand a lot of it, and I'm a teacher. It doesn't speak enough to the large majority of women and to their problems.'

But as Fatima had mentioned, changes were taking place rapidly. Among other developments, the USFP was forming a women's section, and a new, more popular, less theoretical journal called *Kalima*, oriented towards women's problems, began publication in early 1986. Perhaps Fatima was right when she said to me one afternoon, 'You see, in Morocco the cultural revolution is happening right now, right before our eyes'.[1]

'IT IS NOT ENOUGH TO BE AWARE OF OUR RIGHTS, WE HAVE TO HAVE POWER' (EGYPT)

Egypt is usually seen by other Arabs, as well as by Egyptians, as having made substantial advances on the question of women's freedoms. In 1985 a broadly based Arab Women's Solidarity Union (AWSU) was formed, headed by the well-known Egyptian writer Nawal Saadawi, in part to protect and improve Egypt's Family Law (as its personal status code is commonly known), in part to articulate women's other problems.[2]

Before I went to talk with Nawal Saadawi and her colleagues I spent some time with Hoda Lutfi, an Egyptian woman historian in her mid- or late thirties. She put the formation of the AWSU and the struggle over the Family Law in a historical context.

Historically, when I think of the development of the women's movement in Egypt I think of the nationalist movement, because I think the two go together. You see, at the beginning the woman's question was mostly raised by men, the main question being how to improve women's situation, women's education, so that women would make better mothers. The woman's movement that emerged at the turn of the century was primarily constituted by men's intellectual demand for women to produce better men.

By the Nasser period, the needs of society had changed radically. At that time, the need was to build national industry and this required the active participation of both men and women. The state deliberately wanted to give equal opportunity in education and in work to men and women, and a number of women became architects, doctors, and so on. But again, this pressure was not the result of the activity of women's organizations, which mainly did charity work of one sort or another, but of deliberate government policy. Of course, women never approached equal proportions with men in high-level occupations and the main preoccupation of women, and of men about women, remained building families. But in some areas, such as the mass media, women did come to play a very important role as producers and directors. Even today, both the head of the Radio and the head of the Television are women.

But Nasser's failure was that he didn't try to change consciousness. In education, there were no real changes of content. But at least he did say, 'Equal pay for equal work'. And there were many social measures instituted for the benefit of working women, such as obligatory kindergartens for the children of employees in large enterprises.

How had things changed in the Sadat period?

Shortly after Sadat came to power, he introduced the 'open-door' policy, oriented toward entrepreneurship and the accumulation of individual wealth. This meant that the ideology of building the national economy was deemphasized and government interest turned away from the public sector. Women were regarded by private enterprise as more of a risk and not as productive as men. So, in that period there were setbacks. The new businesses that grew up then in the service, tourist, and import–export sectors, were dominated by men; women were relegated to secondary, lower paying roles. And discrimination against women began to become a serious problem.

Then Hoda summarized these historical developments by pointing to women's changing use of the veil and the recent controversy over the Family Law.

If you look at what happened with the veil you can see symptoms of these changes. Around the turn of the century women began taking off the veil – of course here I'm referring to the urban middle and upper classes, because in the lower classes and in the rural areas the situation with regard to the veil is very different. During the Nasser period, shedding the veil became even more common. But now, on the contrary, there is a strong call for women to return to the home, to once again keep their bodies fully covered and their faces veiled. Of course part of this has strict economic causes – the general economic crisis, the increasing competition for jobs caused by the population increase and the return of Egyptians who had worked in the Gulf.

But this has also been reflected, most recently, in the problem of the Family Law. From 1929 to 1979 this law hadn't been amended at all; then in 1979 it was changed. Although these changes were for the most part positive, they were changes imposed from above – another symptom of the regression of women's status. But the new law that was just passed in 1985, although almost the same as that of 1979, constitutes a step backwards as regards the rights of a woman to obtain a divorce if her husband takes a second wife, and also gives a woman somewhat less of a right to the family home after the divorce.

In fact, as the debate over the proposed Family Law had developed and grown more heated, many Egyptian women had begun to fear that the legal advances achieved under the 1979 amendments were at risk. Members of several women's organizations began to meet to see if common action could be agreed. Among them was Nawal Saadawi, a prominent author and novelist who had served several prison terms for her leftist views and activities. Nawal is the author of *The Hidden Face of Eve* (1980), a book that is one of the touchstones of the worldwide women's movement. Nawal had traveled widely too: she had visited Morocco and knew Fatima Mernissi well, and she had made an important presentation in Tunisia several years earlier that Tunisian women still referred to.

Nawal, probably in her early to mid-fifties, cuts an impressive figure: she is tall, with striking gray hair, a very animated face, and winning manner. She received me in her home in central Cairo and she began to tell me of the AWSU's history and her view of the struggle for women's rights.

Nawal's views are often phrased in broad ideological terms, but she also had specific ideas about the AWSU's purposes, and frequently referred to her own personal predicament as a controversial author as well. As she began to respond to my questions about the AWSU, she managed to address each of these levels in her first few sentences.

First of all I would like to tell you that I look at women's problems as problems of the whole society, in all its aspects – economic, political, religious, social. We are half the society, and in some countries we are more than half. So, we are the majority and we should have a say in everything. That is how I see women's problems. And that means that the major problems for us as women in Egypt and in the Arab world in general are the problems of economics and democracy. I can tell you that up until now, I don't think we have democracy in any Arab country, or any real freedom of the word. I am still censored in Egypt, I am blacklisted from the television and from the radio, and this means that I can't directly answer people who write or speak against me. So what kind of democracy is that?

And when I say 'democracy', I mean a deep democracy where people, not the government, have the authority. Democracy isn't what Sadat understood it to be: you allow a few people to organize political parties, and then you issue a law that doesn't allow the majority of people to form political parties. That is against democracy. So women, more than half of society, couldn't organize their own political party. If I have 1,000 women who want to organize a party we should be allowed to do so. This is how the AWSU came about, but I'll tell you about that a little later.

Now, what is democracy? The real distinction isn't between Western democracy and Eastern democracy. The real distinction is between capitalist democracy and socialist democracy. You cannot have real freedom in a capitalist society, it is impossible. And you cannot have real freedom for women in a capitalist society. The problem in capitalism is that you are supposed to have freedom in the economic sphere, but what you actually have is domination by the people who have money. And this is tied to the domination by men in the family, and these two kinds of domination reinforce one another.

Only women are willing to discuss this problem, the relationship between the class problem and the patriarchal problem, the relationship between the family and the state. But because women have no political power in either the East or the West no one listens to them.

Nawal then went on to talk about how the situation had deteriorated since Nasser's time.

Under Nasser, women were trying to become more independent. But it was more or less a false independence because we didn't have real freedom and because the class system was not disappearing in actual practice, only in theory. Nasser started well and he tried, but he was overcome by the people and the forces around him.

But under Sadat and the 'open-door' policy, things got progressively worse, because you cannot have real freedom in a society that is dependent economically on other countries. How can I be free if I am taking my food from my enemies, for instance? If I criticize the United States and criticize Zionism and criticize capitalism, and at the same time depend economically, take my wheat and bread from the United States, how can I say I am independent? It's a paradox, but people avoid looking at it: the newspapers won't touch these issues.

This led Nawal directly to the need for women to organize, to make their potential political effect actual.

You know, in the Arab countries and Egypt we, as women, have been thinking for a long time of the need to unite to gain political power. Because we've understood from our experience that it is not enough to be aware of our rights, we have to have power. And there are two main arenas of power in the world, political power or military power. We're outside the military, so we have to use political power by bringing women together politically.

Yet we're prevented from forming political parties because of our laws, and also because we are women, because of traditional attitudes. And also, men think we will have a racist [sic] attitude, they think that if women form a political party, it means it will be against men. Even among Marxists and on the left, when we say we need a political party they say, 'Oh, this is racism, this is against men'. But this isn't true. A political party of women is another power on the left, because women will also be fighting class and patriarchy. But they don't understand this. In any case, the more experience we get, the more convinced we are that we need to have political power and we need to organize.

Well, when I was in jail under Sadat I was thinking about this: I know that writing is a kind of power, and I had been writing since the 1950s. But an individual who writes can be killed easily, can be put in jail easily. An organization can't be silenced as easily.

When I got out of jail, I wanted to start such an organization and so, in 1982, we started the Arab Women's Solidarity Union. At the start there were four of us at the core – all of us had been in jail together under Sadat. We were about fifty women – university women, women from the left. But the group wasn't pure left, it was composed of women who really were very enthusiastic and understood the problem of women. And I was elected president.

How had they begun their activities, and how had they handled the problem of meeting the legal requirements to form an association?

We started having meetings, had articles in the media, in the newspapers, and journalists came and interviewed us. We then tried to register with the government, because without this we would be considered an illegal association and we'd probably all be put in jail. But the government rejected us – I suppose the authorities thought this was dangerous, a group headed by Nawal Saadawi and having some members who were in jail under Sadat. They thought we would be a new force against the 'open-door' policy, against the Sadat legacy, against capitalism and the US, and so on. So we were being rejected for political reasons. They sent our names to the police and to the security forces, and we started to get harassed.

But then we started to create hell for them – we wrote articles, we got some well-known political people and journalists to write about us, asking why we were being prevented from forming an association of women. It's not a political party, it's not against the law; the law permits any group of women or men to form an association.

We fought very hard on this, with campaigns and publicity. And then we went to a well-known lawyer who studied our case and said, 'Try to register again. If you're rejected, I'll fight your case.' The authorities may have heard about that. We presented our papers again and this time they were accepted. That was in January 1985.

But even after we received recognition it wasn't clear sailing. The authorities are very intelligent – they give you a licence on paper but they fight you economically and from underneath. They take the carpet out from under you so you cannot do anything. First they wanted to know where our funds came from, then they wanted to know who all our members were, then they required all sorts of formalities – including talking to the security police – for the conference we want to hold next year. What they were trying to do was to limit our activities. And then we've had problems trying to get a headquarters. But we're fighting, we're challenging, and we're going to succeed.

Now that the AWSU had been accepted, officially, as an association, what kinds of activities did it plan to engage in?

Well, our basic aim is to organize ourselves and gain some political power, because as individuals your effect is very limited. We're trying to bring together women from different classes, from different places, from both cities and villages. Perhaps it seems far-fetched, but it is also very near – bringing women together. And we've had to fight for this, to fight the government; and we've had to fight against our own usages, because women are not used to working together. So, just the aim of building a women's organization that has some political power, that isn't just a charity, is a basic element in our strategy.

One of our main activities has been to mobilize people on the issue of the Family Law. We were holding meetings and speaking out on the Family Law even before the association was registered. Once we were registered, we expanded our meetings, invited women from many different political parties, tried to get some unity between women from the various political parties.

We also started to confront fundamentalist religious groups, the groups that were trying to change the Family Law. At that time, the Family Law of 1979 was still in effect, but we knew that there was a lot of pressure to have it changed in a direction that would satisfy some of the demands of the religious groups. So we began to fight what we call a prophylactic battle, so that the law wouldn't be changed. But here we failed, and the Constitutional Court repealed the 1979 law. So we accentuated our activities, and held a big meeting to which hundreds of women came. We were about to begin a big demonstration outside when they sent the police and forbade our demonstration.

But in any case, as a result of these meetings our pressure was being felt, even though we were not really successful and the 1979 law was repealed. And the new law that was passed in June 1985, although it wasn't as bad as it might have been, still was a step backward from the 1979 law. I'll give you one example of how: in the 1979 law, polygamy as

*such was considered harmful to the first wife, and the first wife had the
right to an automatic divorce if she sought it. In the law of 1985, the first
wife has to prove that she is harmed by the polygamy, and the judge may
decide not to accept her claim. So this makes things more difficult for the
first wife. There were other steps backward, but this was the major thing.*

*But even the 1979 law did not touch the real slave position of women in
the family, because in the 1979 law divorce was still the absolute right of
the man – he could divorce his wife without having to give any reasons.
Polygamy too was his absolute right. So all these laws are just touching
the surface: the real unequal relationship between the husband and wife
is still there, and has not changed in the almost sixty years since the 1929
law.*

*We've also become involved on an international level and on the Arab
level. We've gained the status of a non-governmental organization at the
UN, something even the Arab Human Rights Organization hasn't gotten
yet because their papers weren't complete.[3] And we're planning to hold
a conference here next year, bringing together many women from all over
the Arab world. And we sent a delegation of sixteen women to the UN
conference in Nairobi. Luckily we received some money for this from
Sweden; otherwise we couldn't have gone because our own government
gave us nothing, gave us no help at all.*

One of the aspects of the AWSU that Nawal hadn't referred to while
discussing its problems was the matter of internal tensions and disputes.
Yet I knew for a fact that there had been significant divisions within the
AWSU over, among other issues, whether it should adopt a confront-
ational approach or a more conciliatory one in putting forward its
position. This had come to a head over the Family Law and had led
several important women to withdraw from the AWSU and to start
another group.

I had already been to see another woman involved with the AWSU
since its early days, and she was one of those unhappy with the con-
frontational approach Nawal advocated. She told me,

*Although Nawal was the one who originally had the idea to start the AWSU,
her early public efforts, writing many newspaper articles in support of it,
probably did more harm than good, because her position was very
anti-governmental. And at the outset the meetings were very personal, full
of gossip, with no constructive work, no readings.*

She continued,

*All the difficulties came to a head over the Family Law. A number of
women, myself included, were opposed to public action on this, because
I think the main aim of the AWSU should be cultural and that it should not
confront the authorities on political issues. After all, the AWSU operates*

under ministry rules to that effect: it should think and propose, but not confront. This is even more so because the AWSU position on the Family Law is basically the same as the government's, and our opponents are elsewhere.

I then asked her to what she attributed the problems within the AWSU.

Well, I think it has to do mostly with the general situation of the Arab Third World countries – there is so much backwardness, especially for women. All you hear are slogans, such as 'Everything for the Arab homeland'. But where is this Arab homeland? And don't forget that we're experiencing profound civilizational disintegration at this very moment. So religious fundamentalism is on the upswing – for the religious groups women are a big issue and basically they are against women's rights, and they talk a lot about returning to the past, reinstituting the veil, and so on.

Even in the recent history of Islamic thought, figures like Al-Afghani and Muhammad Abduh were all arguing for Islamic law and authenticity, which work against women.[4] There have been just a few minor attempts to argue for women's liberation but reactions to these attempts were always very strong. So our movement first of all requires solid thought, consistency, not just individuals who act spontaneously and then regret their actions. It is hard for me to have respect for so many of these women – they argue for liberation but at the same time go around bedecked with expensive jewelry and covered with make-up. And even on feminism we can get no agreement, because many women are now arguing that Western feminism is imperialist and divisive.

I have to say that I am very pessimistic about the whole situation. For Arab women today, everything is still seen as purely personal, even though the big task is to relate what is going on here to what is going on in the rest of the world and in the West.

I wanted to raise some of these issues with Nawal Saadawi, and I phrased them in the context of problems the Tunisian women's journal *Nissa* was having and those that the Moroccan and Tunisian human rights associations were facing as well. I told Nawal that I wasn't interested in what might be termed personality clashes, but rather in what her assessment was of the fundamental reasons behind the AWSU's difficulties. 'I think the internal problems are superficial,' Nawal began.

The real problem is that we are facing pressure from the outside and this creates pressures inside. Let me give you an example.

When the government attacked us and it didn't look as though we would be allowed to register, and the police began to harass us, one of our original group, a woman who was in prison with me, left us. But part of the reason was also that for her women's problems are not the priority, she is looking primarily at other political issues.

Another problem is that one of the main parties on the left has its own women's section. Now, because I'm considered a socialist all the party members say, 'Why doesn't Nawal come to us, why does she want to start her own organization?' Well, I told them, 'Look, I can't join your group because your party doesn't give priority to women. If you begin to look at the relations between class and patriarchy and adopt our ideology, I'll come to you. But why should I join you if I don't approve of your ideology?'

But they don't understand. Like most of the Marxist and leftist groups in any country, they're traditional, orthodox. You should see some of the men on the left – within their own families they are oppressing their wives and daughters. It's classic. And they think I am against men. I don't divide men from women. We have lots of men in our organization, lots of young men. Men aren't our enemy at all.

But, you know, the problem isn't only with the men – women themselves are sometimes completely unaware of what the problems are, because they haven't studied them. Some women think that simply because they are women they know about women's problems. I tell them that women's problems are like medicine. It is a subject, it is a science. You have to study it. You have to read history. You have to know what class is, what slavery is, what the relationship between class and male domination is, what the relationship between the family and the state is. It is a science. I studied medicine for many years, but I studied women more, I gave years of my life to women. But some women think that because they are women, they know about women. And they want to lead us around with their incomplete knowledge. That's when I have to say, 'No, sorry'.

Nawal was obviously a controversial figure in Egypt, and certainly some of the mixed reactions she generated affected the atmosphere within the AWSU. Nonetheless, under her presidency the AWSU had continued to grow in size and in the scope of its activities, although it still remained prey to internal dissension. The AWSU successfully held the conference it had planned for September 1986 and the conference stimulated great enthusiasm and debate. By early 1989, the AWSU was well established and had published the first issue of a quarterly magazine, called *Nun*.[5]

TUNISIAN VOICES (2): 'WE WANTED A DIFFERENT KIND OF ORDER ... BUT WE JUST DIDN'T HAVE THE CONSCIOUSNESS IT REQUIRED'

In the period from the 1930s to Tunisian independence in 1956, Tunisian women succeeded in founding a number of major organizations, including the Muslim Women's Union of Tunisia (of a reformist, modernist Islamic orientation), the Union of Tunisian Women (socialist-communist) and the Group of Destourian Women (affiliated with

Bourguiba's Destourian movement). Other women's groups were influenced by or affiliated to the Egyptian Muslim Brothers and the Scout movement; still others were involved in running the School for the Young Muslim Girl, kindergartens, and other educational and social institutions.

Their activities spanned both the national and international arenas and the women's organizations encouraged advances in women's education, carried out welfare works among the poor, raised the political consciousness of women in the nationalist struggle, organized assistance and care for those wounded fighting the colonial occupation, supported Algerian independence by providing aid for fighters as well as for Algerian women and children, wrote in newspapers, printed tracts (sometimes clandestinely), fought to improve the status of women within Muslim society and campaigned for the right to have abortions and contraception.

At independence in 1956, Bourguiba sought to dominate the women's movements, just as he sought to dominate other aspects of Tunisian national life. Those movements that upon independence tried to gain formal recognition as legal associations found their applications systematically rejected, and when Bourguiba promulgated the Personal Status Code, he awarded no recognition to the women's movement nor to its leadership, both of which had been powerful elements in the nationalist struggle.

In addition, he exercised his control over the one official women's organization he did permit to exist, the National Union of Tunisian Women (UNFT – l'Union national des femmes tunisiennes) by appointing to its presidency in 1958 a newcomer to the women's movement.[6] As a result, the women's movement was unable to regain its pre-independence *élan* and the UNFT languished throughout the 1970s under the leadership of Fethia Mzali (wife of the future prime minister Mohammed Mzali).

But in the late 1970s and early 1980s women again began to struggle to assert themselves in the public arena, and the effort to launch *Nissa* in 1985 was the product of several years' prior activity.

Among the women I met who were involved with *Nissa* were Nadia Hakimi and ᶜazza Ghanmi. Both are in their mid- to late thirties; Nadia now works in publishing design after having earned a geography diploma in France; ᶜazza studied medicine in Tunis and now teaches in secondary schools where she helps train paramedicals. Both women had signed the letter of 'disillusion' that appeared in *Nissa*'s fourth issue and had withdrawn from the magazine. Before we began to talk about *Nissa*, ᶜazza and Nadia looked back over the rebirth of the women's movement in Tunisia in the late 1970s.

During our conversation ᶜazza did most of the talking but Nadia came in wherever she thought amplification or correction was needed. They began by mentioning how difficult it was in the late 1970s for women to come together and discuss their own problems freely. ᶜazza started,

> We began to meet as women in 1979, forming a women's club within the Tahar al-Haddad Cultural Center, in Tunis.[7] This was the only cultural center in all of Tunisia run by a woman. Around this time Nawal Saadawi of Egypt came here to give some lectures, and that generated a lot of discussion and interest. We were very politicized at the outset, not in Nawal's direction which is close to that of the Communist party, but we were sympathetic to the extreme left – this was, after all, the dominant current among the student intellectuals of the time.
>
> Within the women's club, our first big debate was whether or not to have a political platform – this was a debate taking place throughout Tunisia at that time, in all cultural arenas. I remember that the club's platform at that time said that the women's struggle was tied to the struggle against imperialism, to the Arab world's and the Third World's struggle for liberation. At that time you couldn't get into a cultural club of any sort without agreeing to the platform.

Why were platforms such a necessary part of activity?

> You have to understand that with all the repression that existed then – the lack of freedom of expression, the lack of freedom of the press – the left could not speak publicly in Tunisia. So naturally, politicized groups on the extreme left tried to work instead in the cultural arena. As a result, you couldn't really be in a cultural club unless you were politicized. Of course, the problem with a platform is that it stifles originality.
>
> At the same time, as women, we were already having some problems with our local and national authorities. In the summer of 1979, there was an international colloquium on family planning run by the Summer University of Tabarka – you may remember the slogan 'at Tabarka, you don't get sunburned like a fool'. The Tunisian government sent only one Tunisian woman delegate – and she actually was an Algerian lawyer, married to a Tunisian and living here. Other Tunisian women – feminists who had studied in France – weren't allowed to participate because they were prepared to say, in effect, 'The problem of family planning isn't simply a question of state programs but is a problem of how women are treated, whether women have choice in their lives.'
>
> During this colloquium the local authorities started to accuse some of the Tunisian women of being whores! They wanted to bring charges against the women for having talked to a Frenchman on the beach or for having had a drink in a café with a foreigner. And they'd plaster the name of the girl all over the newspapers. All this had the effect of motivating many more Tunisian women to pursue these issues.
>
> As a result, in the fall, many more women joined the Tahar al-Haddad club and the debates became much more lively. We'd have eighty or

ninety women there sometimes and not enough chairs to go around. You know, everyone was there because it was almost the only place where there was a real debate, where there was a real stake, and every group wanted to get a piece of the cake. So the extreme leftist groups were there, the Communists were there, the independents were there.

Out of all these debates, some fundamental issues emerged that are still with us today: do we as women take a position on all political issues, or should we limit ourselves to women's questions? What is the nature of cultural activity – is it also political? What is the role of ideology? What is a women's movement? Does the women's struggle come first, or must we subordinate it to the struggle for national liberation? What is our relationship to the West?

And what, in fact, was feminism? You know, I remember saying to myself at that time, 'Me, I'm not a feminist, at least not a Western-style feminist'. But in fact, I'd never read even one feminist text, I had no idea what feminism had become after 1968 in Europe. It was kind of a defense mechanism: 'We're feminists, but we haven't sold out to the West'.

Finally, after months of talking and talking, we were all sick and tired of it, and what we really wanted was to get down to work. We adopted an identity card for the club, one that simply said that we were a women's club, that only women could join, we would hold public debates to which men could be invited, we were a club for reflection and study of the condition of women in Tunisia. And we would do all this democratically.

In fact, everything turned on the notion of democracy: the question of what language to use was based on our idea of democracy, our rules of order were based on democracy, the fact that we rejected all kinds of hierarchy was based on democracy.[8] You know, given the domination by the PSD over public institutions and the domination by the extreme left in other arenas, the women's club Tahar al-Haddad was really the only democratic place in all of Tunisia, the only place where people could actually get up and express different ideas, and still meet the following week to continue the discussion. It was something truly exceptional in this country.

How did they actually proceed internally if they rejected all kinds of hierarchy?

Our procedure was quite original, at least as far as we knew in Tunisia: when an essay or position paper was ready, we would present it to the full membership signed by its authors. This meant that if there were two or three different positions, each would be signed by its authors. Unlike every other institution in Tunisian society, we weren't looking for unanimity: for what seemed like the first time in Tunisia, we were respecting the right to be different. In fact, it became a kind of standing joke among some men, who'd say, 'Oh, feminism, you mean the right to be different'.

ᶜazza returned to the chronology:

After those four or five months of intense debating in 1979–80, we wanted to begin to do real work, to study the condition of women. We divided up into commissions. Of course, then we needed a coordinating group to oversee this work; but at the same time we didn't want any hierarchy. Well, we set up a coordinating group but because of this dilemma, they were unable to function effectively.

But behind this was also another question that plagued us from the beginning and plagues us even now: what is our relationship to the public at large? Over this issue – whether we should confront or be soft with the public – a number of women left the club.

cazza went on to say that this was a particularly bad time for the Tahar al-Haddad women's club. In addition to the above problems,

The attitude in the public at large began to get more hostile – the public began to develop a sort of Tahar al-Haddad-itis, you know, a kind of disease. Among the men in the cafés, the club became a big item of conversation. Every Saturday the club would meet for three, four, or five hours, and then we'd all break up and go to the café at the Hotel International. And as we'd get there, the men would start to say, 'OK, are they already over, your women's meetings? Are you finished already?' And then some of the men, even men of the left, supposedly enlightened men, began to forbid their wives to go to the meetings.

And, of course, some of the women gave in to this pressure. Some would come to the meetings but then refuse to come to the café with us, refuse to be seen in public with us. Some of them would start to gossip about others, 'Oh, you know who I saw with so-and-so the other day?' They'd say these things to their husbands, or among their circle of friends. You know, these women were perhaps feeling guilty about their own desire for autonomy and were compensating by accusing other women.

Also, you have to understand that many of the men on the left saw the Tahar al-Haddad club as a sign of their own personal failure. First of all, divorces among us were falling like raindrops. Also, this was a period when the left was at sea ideologically, when it seemed unable to respond ideologically to society's problems. The left was beginning to lean towards populism, trying to identify with the masses and afraid of appearing alienated from them. As a result, they began to argue more and more that certain questions, like women's questions, shouldn't be raised because that would upset and disturb the population. Again, this big question of our relationship to the population, and of the intellectual's relationship to the population, was behind much of the debate.

You know, you can call that first period, up to 1981, a period of methodology. This second period was when we tried to apply feminist practice, when we tried to pose and answer fundamental problems. And that is when the real conflicts, the real breakdown started to occur.

I asked ^cazza how they began to pose these fundamental problems and what kinds of difficulties this led to.

First we started putting ourselves into small study groups. I was in 'Women and the Family' and right away the question of sexuality was raised. One of us who was a bit more up on feminism than the rest said, 'Sexuality isn't only heterosexuality, it may also be homosexuality'. 'Ah, yes, that's true,' we said, nodding our heads, and we began to talk about that. But we knew nothing at all about these things. It was really a revolution for us to start thinking about these things.

Up until then we'd been thinking that homosexuality was something physiologically abnormal, socially abnormal. But now, we weren't supposed to allow ourselves to think in that way. On the other hand, we couldn't say that homosexuality was normal either. So the whole question was suspended. And then, what about procreation, what role did it play for women? It was really disorienting us, making us crazy. You know, we'd end up saying, 'What am I anyway? Did I choose to be what I am, or am I here where other people decided to put me?' These really became existential problems for us.

At this point, a couple of women began to say, 'We should really start from our own daily experience if we're going to look at the woman's condition'. Already this was a big step forward: the 'woman' now wasn't the 'other' – the peasant woman, the working woman, the woman in the household, the woman in the shanty town. The 'woman' was also 'me', and my particular experience became just as important as anyone else's, and could give just as good an insight into the woman's condition.

^cazza explained that throughout this period, well into 1982, the women continued to work in small groups, exploring various themes in the respective committees, and coming together in a full group every three or four weeks. She continued,

The question of feminism kept coming up again and again. Whatever we'd be discussing, the same questions would come up: what is feminism after all? What is the difference between emancipation and liberation? What is the relationship between liberation and feminism? Is feminism a new approach, free of the old ideologies? And so on. Whenever the question of the relationship of women to culture was raised, or any such kind of question, it was always, 'Are we looking at this from a feminist perspective?' At that time, there were some women who already called themselves feminists, others who'd say, 'I don't know what feminism is, I don't know whether I'm a feminist or not'.

You have to understand that, at that time, the word 'feminist' was an insult, it was the main insult. Now of course things are different – it's amazing how in a few months words that were so charged can become so banal. But then it was really an insult, the word 'feminist' meant you'd sold out to the West, and it also meant that you might believe anything at all about sexuality, and that you had no morals.

Anyway, within the club at that time, there emerged a group with similar sensibilities, the group that Nadia and I were in, that was perhaps a bit more marginal than the others. We continued to raise these questions: what is sexuality? What is homosexuality, heterosexuality? We believed that the crux of the problem was, in fact, the woman's body, the vagina, the uterus. We raised questions like, what is marriage? What is it to live with a man without marrying him? What is it to be a feminist writer? I know that over those two years, I experienced unbelievable upheaval on the level of my own self. From the moment you began to raise these questions you didn't know who you were anymore. These questions that people had always refused to raise – well when you raise them about yourself and your own life, it is very destabilizing, very unbalancing.

But there were also some aspects that helped us through this period. First of all, there was some comfort in knowing that at least we were willing to raise these questions, however difficult they might be. Also this group – 'the single women' as we sometimes called ourselves – ran fewer risks in a way: we didn't have husbands and children who'd be there to remind us every minute, 'Careful, you're forgetting your duties.' There were a few married women with us, too, women who, perhaps because of their strong personalities or their somewhat different upbringing, had somehow succeeded in their married lives and were able to share these questions with their husbands. All in all, we were five or six in this group. The others called us 'the marginals', or 'the sexuals'.

But tensions within the club as a whole were becoming more acute. Nadia explained,

We just weren't able to agree on how to approach the whole feminism question, and a number of women had left the club just because of this. So, we thought maybe the best thing would be to do a questionnaire and try to take stock. Also, this was a time when a lot of aggressive things, nasty stories, were circulating about us in the cafés, from house to house, from dinner to dinner. It all poisoned the air. So we really had to take stock. With the questionnaire we were hoping to figure things out in a less excitable, less impassioned way. But it really led to nothing, it didn't help at all.

The women of the club then tried to reach out, to organize colloquia to which they invited Moroccan and Algerian women. ᶜazza took up the story:

We planned three colloquia. The first, in 1983, was to be on 'Sexuality, contraception: choice or constraint'. In 1984 it was to be 'Women and power' and in 1985 'Women and feminism'. In the course of these colloquia things began to explode.

In fact, the first one worked out very well, the first day was really extraordinary, it was like a dream. There was even one moment that was so good it was frightening. I started to notice that there were a couple of women who seemed about to lose control of themselves: they were beginning to break down in tears. There was one who was crying – she never spoke during the whole session, but just cried. On the other hand, there were some women who were stiff as boards, and others who would laugh and joke at their own problems. That discussion went very deep, and I'm sure I wasn't the only one who was a bit afraid that some of the women wouldn't recover from it easily.

The remaining discussions were much less successful and tensions among the women in the club were increasing all the time. Relations became even more strained when a number of women became incensed at the work of one newspaper cartoonist. ᶜazza explained,

I can't remember any cartoons off-hand now, but they were of the type: two women are standing in a bus, and one of them gets pinched by a man standing behind her. She says to her friend, 'Tell me if the guy is good-looking. If he is, I won't say anything.' Wait, I do remember one – it practically encouraged men to attack women. A guy is sleeping and dreams of killing his wife for some reason or other; and then he wakes up smiling, saying, 'Night brings good advice'.

Well, week after week of this – some of us just got sick of it. We decided to launch a campaign to get the newspaper to stop publishing the cartoon. We didn't even realize that there was a big debate in France just then over a Ministry of Women proposal to introduce an anti-sexist law that would prohibit expression that defamed women.

We called upon the LTDH to support us. Most of them were on our side, but there were a number who said, 'Careful, don't pull the cord too hard on this issue or it will break'. We told them that we couldn't break the cord because, as far as we were concerned, there was no cord. What we were concerned with was our fundamental right to walk unmolested in the streets. The LTDH did give us its support, and we mounted quite a campaign. But we were attacked a lot for this and a number of club members were against the campaign. Everyone was saying to us, 'Why are you taking this so seriously? These are only jokes, only cartoons.' But we couldn't let these kinds of pictures, these debasing words about women, go on circulating.

The controversy went on for a long time and it was only about a year later that Prime Minister Mzali's wife went before the National Assembly and said that such things in the national press were unacceptable. After that, finally, the paper stopped publishing the cartoons.

The club had by then lost much of its momentum – ᶜazza and Nadia, for example, had both stopped going to meetings for several months. But a number of women had begun working in other arenas to draw attention to women's issues. It was at this time that a women's section was created within the research office of the UGTT, something women had been trying to obtain for years.

ᶜazza continued, 'So, after a while, there were two main, overlapping groups of women – the Tahar al-Haddad club, and the one within the UGTT.' Nadia interjected, 'But a real need for joint activity arose after the Israeli invasion of the Lebanon, in June 1982. In fact, it was this that led, eventually, to the founding of *Nissa*'. ᶜazza went on,

> After the Israeli invasion there were a lot of women who were looking for some way to express their outrage. All the other demonstrations were so mild, it was a joke: it was towards the end of summer, the students were still away, and the opposition groups were so divided that they couldn't mount a big demonstration. Well, about fifty to sixty women managed to get together for a demonstration in front of the Arab League. We would have had more people there but for many of us it was a bit of a problem to stand there shouting, 'Arab Palestine, Arab Palestine', at a time when the wave of Arab nationalism and their reactionary position on women was becoming a problem in itself.

Nadia added, 'You know for me, there was another problem. I was uncomfortable demonstrating with women, only with women, on an issue where we could be demonstrating as a mixed group. That whole idea bothered me.'

ᶜazza continued,

> In any case, our women's demonstration was quickly dispersed. But we felt the need to take stock of this initiative as well as whatever else we were involved in. And also, there were a number of women involved in the demonstration who had never been in a group of women like this, and who had never been in the Tahar al-Haddad club. We wanted to do something but we didn't know what.
>
> Then came the Sabra and Chatila massacre of Palestinians in Lebanon and we mounted another demonstration, this time in front of the UN offices. Again this demonstration was dispersed, but with a little more violence this time. By now we had been meeting for some time, asking ourselves, 'What should we do now?' We couldn't really go back to the Tahar al-Haddad club, because that had become purely cultural.
>
> Meanwhile, we were working on the issue of the Israeli invasion. After Sabra and Chatila, we wanted to put out a signed text, but we didn't know what to call ourselves. So we decided on 'The Democratic Women' – 'democratic' you know, to distinguish ourselves from the National Union of Tunisian Women, which is one of the organs of the PSD. And this was when all our discussion started about whether we should form a women's

group, whether a women's group should take a position on all matters in public life or only on what you might narrowly call 'women's questions'. Already, there were marked differences in our points of view.

So we started to say that with all these differences, maybe we should look for something minimal that would bring us together, but would also allow those women who wanted to do more to do it within the framework of this new association. We didn't meet regularly and these discussions dragged on for a year or more. This now had nothing any longer to do with the Tahar al-Haddad club, although many of our women were also members of the club. There were about thirty of us, thirty women, in all.

So here we were, thinking of forming some kind of association, but we couldn't really agree on what to do. This was a time when there was a sort of liberalization of the political system in the air. We figured we should take advantage of that and try to form the association as soon as possible. So, as we began to draft our by-laws and in order to make the formal application, we had to ask two important questions: 'What distinguishes us from other similar organizations?' and 'How do we avoid being infiltrated and undermined by groups with other interests?'

For example to protect ourselves from the Islamists we wanted to put the idea of secularism in our statute. But some women said, 'No. We agree with the principle but it is no good to say it explicitly because for most people secularism means atheism.' And then some others began to say, 'Why do we have to go through this whole debate again? We know that for women the question of secularism is crucial, because we have to have separation of the state and religion, and we have to have statutory law in order to protect and promote women's rights.'

How did they manage to resolve these differences?

Well, we never did, really. We were completely blocked on these kinds of questions. And then, all of a sudden, we hit on the idea of the journal. For a while we had parallel meetings, one group pursuing the idea of the journal, the other concerned with forming the association.

But the journal moved forward much more quickly than the association, which lost momentum. For the journal, we had some discussion over who the directrice would be – to fulfill the legal requirements you have to have a directrice – and we wanted someone who wasn't too identified with one tendency or another within our group. We finally agreed on Emna bel-Hajj Yahya and we all agreed that we would each have an equal say in producing the journal. This was towards the end of 1984. We had put in our application during the month of Ramadan that year, in July, and we were accepted in November.

It was as we began to produce Nissa *that the problems really started.*

We had now reached the moment when the history of *Nissa* proper could be said to begin. Some of the problems *Nissa* faced were certainly related to the general problem of launching any publication in Tunisia and I recalled that Abdelaziz Krichen had had to abandon hope of continuing beyond the fourth issue of his promising journal, *Mensuel*. But some of *Nissa*'s difficulties were related directly to the fact that this was a magazine run by and for women, within a society in which women faced particular problems.

As ᶜazza and Nadia began to discuss the problems that arose during the first three issues of *Nissa*, leading to the letter of 'disillusion' that they both and two other women had signed in the fourth issue, it became clear that these problems still touched them deeply. Their anger and pain, as well as the passion that they had already displayed in their account of the recent history of the women's movement in Tunisia, were apparent in their tone of voice and their facial expressions.

I asked them what they thought were the central problems and how these were handled. ᶜazza responded,

> The problems began right in our first issue, on the Personal Status Code. First of all, how would we decide what kind of article would be acceptable? The Personal Status Code was then being attacked by the Islamists, but at the same time it was strongly defended by the government. There was no question, of course, of allying ourselves with the Islamists, but we didn't want to sound like a mouthpiece for the government either. Yet, if we argued too strongly for progressive changes in the PSC, the journal might be confiscated by the authorities and the directrice could be held legally responsible in any judicial procedures brought against us.
>
> So we wanted the directrice to take a stand, to say what she would be willing to assume responsibility for. But she wouldn't do that, she said she'd judge each specific text on its merits.

I thought the directrice's position was defensible, given the legal problems she might face and given the difficulties in elaborating an abstract position independent of specific articles. I asked ᶜazza and Nadia what position they thought the directrice should take. Nadia answered,

> Someone who is an activist – and she was chosen directrice because this was to be her role – has to be a person who, along with the rest of us, is willing to take upon herself the difficulties of confronting authority. She has to be willing to stand up to those in power, with all the risks involved.

Nadia hadn't really answered my question, but ᶜazza broke in,

> Another problem in the first issue was also symptomatic of a larger problem. One article generated a lot of disagreement and some people wanted it not to be published. But we said, 'Wait a minute, remember "democracy". Don't tamper with the texts. If it might get the journal

prohibited, we can discuss that. But we can't suppress an article just because we don't agree with it.' The text finally did appear, but only after quite a fight.

And then there was another argument over an article Nadia wrote criticizing government statements that women should be elected to a certain quota of municipal positions in the approaching municipal elections. Under the title 'Equal competence', Nadia argued that women were just as competent as men for these positions and ought to be elected in appropriate numbers. She wrote something like, 'The question isn't whether a man or woman should be elected, it is a question of competence: we have to demand that competence, not incompetence, rules.' After a lot of argument it was finally not published because the coordinating committee never met to discuss it!

ᶜazza went on to talk about the second issue.

So, none of these problems were resolved in the first issue and, what was worse, a lot of mistrust was created. For the second issue, problems again arose over the subjects – we had decided to treat racism, abandoned children, and the story of a Lebanese girl martyred when she was killed planting explosives.

Nadia explained, 'Most conflict arose over the question of abandoned children. First of all, again we heard, "But why raise this question now, people aren't ready to read about this"'. ᶜazza interrupted,

That was the main battle – the question of abandoned children who have no patronymic and who are therefore without papers and who suffer many disadvantages under our civil law. The battle to give them the right to a patronymic had been going on for years, but the government was running scared before the Islamists who argued that to give these rights to abandoned children would be an assault on the integrity of the family. But these children are really in a terrible situation: they are housed separately from other children and many of them become autistic, schizophrenic, and grow up totally isolated from society with hardly any rights whatever. And we also had some controversy over how to deal with racism because of the Serge Adda incident at the LTDH.[9] It was a real struggle, day and night, to get the articles on racism and abandoned children approved, and we had to fight over every word – putting out the second issue was a disastrous experience.

Beyond these disputes over subject matter and content, I wondered how successful the women had been in their effort to avoid the usual hierarchical structures. ᶜazza answered,

Actually, through all this the main argument was over how the journal should be run: what responsibilities the directrice would assume, whether

*we would publish articles we didn't agree with, and how we should reach
decisions on these matters.*

*The third issue can only be called a 'crisis' issue: we were unable to
come up with any solutions on how to settle our differences. This issue
came out during the summer, when a lot of us weren't around to follow
things through. Then, after we came back to spend a month working on
the production side, the journal was thrown back in our faces with the
words, 'This is a load of crap'. But it was full of their articles! Through all
this, Nadia was being exploited shamelessly, and was working day and
night to try and get all the production and publicity aspects worked out.*

^cazza's voice had risen during her last few sentences, and anyone could
have heard her anger and resentment, even her rancor. Obviously many
of the people at *Nissa*, at the time, were feeling terribly disappointed and
frustrated, although certainly not all for the same reasons. ^cazza went on,

*Finally, at the end of the summer, we all realized that things couldn't go
on like that. We decided we'd all go to a hotel for two days, pay for the
accommodation, and hash things out. The first day we'd discuss the
orientation of the journal, and the second day how it would function.*

*Some of us had already come to the conclusion that, as much as this
went against our original objectives and our aim to keep an egalitarian and
democratic structure, some sort of centralization was necessary – at the
very least we needed an editorial committee. You know, someone,
somewhere had to be able to decide things.*

*Well, to cut a very long story short, although we arrived very relaxed and
prepared to discuss everything, it soon became apparent that things had
been manipulated beforehand. All of a sudden, just at the end of the
meeting, a vote was called for – and we never used to handle things by
voting. Well, some of us refused to vote. But we were outnumbered and
the votes were pushed through. The whole thing was rigged from the
outset. I was really crushed by it all, and was on the verge of tears. One
of them saw me in that state and said, 'Ok, get the psychodrama out of
here'. They were really pushing things to the limit.*

*It was after all this that we decided to quit the journal. A couple of
women came to us later saying, 'You can't leave, you've got no right to
leave, this is a collective project, you've got to stick it out'. Well, we went
to a couple of meetings more, to see if things could be sorted out. But we
kept facing accusations like, 'You're trying to marginalize us', and 'We
don't need an avant-garde', and so on.*

*Finally, one of the women said, 'As for me, I don't want to hear another
word about feminism, we're not a feminist group here'. I answered, 'Look,
this journal was started by a group of feminist women, not by just anybody.
But when women who weren't feminists wanted to come and work with
us, we said, "Fine". And we didn't say it had to be a feminist journal, we*

all just agreed that we wanted to start a journal. But you can't start now and say that anything that has to do with feminism is off limits!'

They came back with, 'No, what we need are more academic studies'. And, 'We want to reconsider the question of mixed participation, we think we should have both men and women on the journal'. And finally the directrice said, 'In fact, I don't even see why we did a women's journal in the first place, or why we should restrict it to a women's journal now.'

As ᶜazza and Nadia saw things, this was now a betrayal of *Nissa*'s original purpose. I had already been once to see the directrice, Emna bel-Hajj Yahya, before *Nissa*'s fourth issue and the 'disillusion' article had been published but after the disputing between *Nissa*'s various factions had already taken a serious turn. On that occasion, sitting with Emna in her office at the National Library, I sensed that she too felt pain at the dissension within the *Nissa* group and that she would be reluctant to talk about it. Rather than discuss the dispute directly I had asked her to describe *Nissa*'s aims, whether she thought the journal was primarily a cultural or a political one, and what its relationship to feminism was. She responded,

> The aims of Nissa, as I see them, are to focus on the situation of women, to study it, analyze it, transform it for the better, in the direction of emancipating women. As far as feminism goes, we have a serious debate on this, and there are many different opinions within the team running the journal. I guess you have to say that the journal is political in the sense that it seeks to change the situation of women, but I see it as a cultural journal, because 'cultural' is a more encompassing term.

When I went to see Emna a second time, after the fourth issue of *Nissa* and the letter of 'disillusion' had been published, I asked her for her view of the dispute. Understandably she was reluctant to talk about personalities, and that wasn't my particular interest either. But she did say,

> The women who wrote the letter of disillusion think that they are the more radical ones, and that the rest are timid. But in fact that's not true, and that's not the issue at all. Whether there is hierarchy or not there is always some form of domination – it is just that some people and groups dominate better when the mechanisms are formal ones, others dominate better through informal structures. Those who resigned did so really because their perspective wasn't the dominant one, and they couldn't accept the fact that their point of view didn't dominate.

Emna then turned to what she saw as the larger issues.

> In any case, I think the roots go deeper than that. The problems running through Nissa are very complicated. First of all, there are financial

problems, and on this level alone our future is very problematic. We just haven't been able to sell enough copies. And then, we've never benefited from the normal financial assistance that the Ministry of Cultural Affairs routinely provides: they offered to buy only ten subscriptions whereas they usually buy a thousand from other cultural journals; and we didn't benefit from the government subsidy for paper, although this may have been our own fault. And then, those of us running the magazine, we all also have to work for a living, and most of us also have to run a household. We just don't have enough time for all these things.

Did she believe there were other problems related to the fact that they were women? 'Well,' she went on,

this is hard to say. Perhaps we had expectations that we could get more fulfillment from this kind of situation, perhaps our expectations were higher than a man's would be in similar situations because it is so difficult for us to feel normally in society. Perhaps some of us expected that our relationships with one another would be good, and always good. But that's not possible. In groups there are always difficulties, whether they are composed of men or of women.

Finally, I asked her whether the journal had met official hostility because it expressed political views that were opposed to the government. 'Well,' she said,

in my view it isn't the job of the journal to raise the question of democracy or other political questions. Its only job is to raise women's questions. And I think the regime as it now is believes that in the woman's domain it is all right to allow free expression. But if we decide to discuss political issues, they may begin to think otherwise and they might then close us down.

I spoke to Emna again towards the end of 1986 when the seventh issue had appeared (dated April 1986) but not the eighth. She seemed discouraged by the persisting difficulties at the journal: deep divisions within the staff continued, as did the serious financial problems. Emna was not sure that the next issue would ever see the light of day.

As it turned out, an eighth issue did finally appear, but in a less attractive, less expensive format, and almost a year had elapsed since the seventh. It was to be *Nissa*'s final issue.

When I returned to Tunisia in the early summer of 1989, more than two years had elapsed since *Nissa*'s last issue. None of the women I spoke to at that time, including Emna, had any intention of trying to bring *Nissa* back to life. But, at the same time, several remarked that many of the women involved with *Nissa* were still very active in organizing women in public life, some had become significant journalists on the Tunisian scene, and women's issues were in general thought to be better treated in the popular press than they had been a few years earlier. But one could also hear in their voices the hurt, frustration, and disappointment that continued to color their memories of this experience.

One woman who had been closely involved with *Nissa* but had managed to stay somewhat distant from the clashes between its various factions summed up her feelings for me.

> We were, throughout the whole experience of Nissa, unable to resolve our different points of view about the relationship between the political and the cultural, about our distinct political perspectives, about the relationship between women's issues and broader issues. We also had unresolved differences between women who saw themselves as radical feminists, who insisted on directly attacking taboo subjects like sexuality, the body, religion, and who wanted to focus on their own experience and not worry what other people thought, and more moderate feminists who sought to look at all women in Tunisia rather than just at one's self, who sought deliberately to shorten the distance between ourselves – a female elite – and the mass of Tunisian women.
>
> The problem, in fact, wasn't so much that we couldn't resolve these difficulties, because in fact such differences probably can't be resolved, but that we couldn't work with these differences to create a pluralistic magazine. We, and I speak about all of us, just didn't have the minimum tolerance necessary for other points of view. We just couldn't carry this effort off. And don't get me wrong – all this isn't at all because women are less tolerant than men, but basically because we live in an intolerant society.
>
> Much of our inability to work together had its corresponding organizational correlate in our inability to solve the problem of hierarchy, a problem that haunted us from beginning to end. We wanted a different kind of order, we expected to be able to create one, but we just didn't have the consciousness it required, nor were we aware of the kinds of changes and discipline in personal behavior that such a new order would require.

At the end of our talk I asked her to sum up what she thought of the contribution of *Nissa* and the Tahar al-Haddad club. 'Well,' she said,

> if I had to sum up the contribution of both, I think I would say that, above and beyond the work of the Tunisian women's movement of the 1930s, 1940s, and 1950s, their merit was their feminist perspective, their focus on patriarchal power, and their arguing that all this constituted a block inside us, inside women. This made it clear to us that the war was not with men but with ourselves, with the way in which we allowed this patriarchal power to block our own expansion as people.
>
> This awareness has given tremendous energy to women in all areas – in the labor movement, in the teaching profession, in journalism, in all kinds of creative areas. All of this has enabled women to confront much more successfully the external violence they experience every day in their lives.

Part IV

Conclusion: 'Dispute and struggle'

12 'Dispute and struggle'

MISUNDERSTANDINGS

Once, entering a Cairo restaurant with several Moroccan lawyers who had been attending a meeting of the Arab Lawyers Union, I noticed one of the lawyers having what seemed to be a misunderstanding with the head waiter about a table. I hadn't heard the lawyer's words but as I eavesdropped, the Egyptian head waiter said to him, 'Perhaps you had better speak in French'.

Was this, then, just a language problem, with the Moroccan lawyer and Egyptian head waiter speaking different varieties of Arabic? Perhaps the Egyptian heard the Moroccan's language as a recognizable but largely unintelligible Maghrebin dialect (Tunisian and particularly Algerian and Moroccan dialects strongly resemble one another but all three are very different from Egyptian); or perhaps the lawyer had ill-advisedly tried to 'Egyptianize' his Moroccan Arabic with terms he had picked up from Egyptian films and television programs widely available in his own country?

Or perhaps the lawyer, who had been speaking all that day with his colleagues from other Arab countries in modern standard Arabic, understood by educated Arabs throughout the Middle East, had simply continued in this vein in the restaurant; but the Egyptian may have heard this as a belabored and unsuccessful effort to speak classical Arabic.

In his retort was the Egyptian suggesting, somewhat sharply, that the Moroccan was not fully Arab, that he might be more comfortable speaking in the tongue of the former colonial power? Or was the Egyptian more concerned with establishing his own credentials and saying, in effect, that he too had international competence and should not be talked down to in colloquial Arabic and treated simply as a 'local'?

Unfortunately the Moroccan lawyer was not disposed to discuss this incident – when I raised it with him he avoided my questions with a dismissive wave of the hand.

Misunderstandings, language differences, distinct national histories, international relationships – all against the background of a deep common heritage: these may seem to be the causes or signs of insuperable difficulties in communicating and understanding throughout the Arab Middle East. However, as intractable as these difficulties may sometimes seem to be, they are inseparable from life in the modern world and, in one form or another, characterize most areas of the globe. (For example the West too is built on a common heritage but language differences within Europe are if anything greater than those in the Arab world and 'misunderstandings' – to say nothing of wars – abound; the same, too, can be said for the United States.) One could easily argue that these 'misunderstandings', played out against a common heritage, are as likely to lead to the flowering of a rich, productive, creative culture, as they are to barriers, hurdles, and insurmountable difficulties.

The incident at the restaurant certainly tells us little about the mixture of misunderstanding and creative culture that we find in today's Middle East, but it does provide us with a timely reminder of the kinds of problems we have been facing throughout this book, as we have tried to see how ideas, vocabulary, understanding, and communication move over a wide and diverse region. And the incident should remind us, as well, how difficult it sometimes is to probe sensitive matters directly.

I have tried to keep the variety and complexity of the Middle East in the forefront throughout this book, rather than simplify, flatten, or dissolve them. The approach I have taken (although I didn't plan it this way at the outset) has little in common with a one-way journey from start to finish, and resembles more a tour along the circumference of a wheel, with periodic forays along the spokes towards the hub, only then to step back and visit a different point on the perimeter.

This approach may seem unnecessarily indirect and some readers may have found us circling around the subject rather than addressing it directly. But for me this approach has had certain advantages. For one thing, it reflects one of my deeper aims in this book, which has been less to solve problems than to portray and, in some sense, encompass them. For another, while we have consistently had our sights focused on the center, on the key concepts we have been trying to explore, we have also come to appreciate why this center is so very hard to reach – as we would expect it to be when the 'wheel' of social life is spinning very rapidly.

This approach has also helped me to show how empty I think such simplifying phrases as 'the Arab mind', or 'the Islamic world view' are; and I can only hope that by now the reader shares my view.

STAKES

In the guise of a conclusion let me try to avoid such simplifications and merely try to look at all the material in this book from a slightly different vantage point.

Over the course of this book (and roughly in the order of their appearance) we have heard people talking about everyday events, economic and social development, creativity, local, national, regional, and international historical developments and comparisons, sports, national character, religious doctrine and varieties of interpretation, political power struggles, personal growth, proverbs, social history and the history of ideas, political thought, organizational problems, ideological disputes, women's rights. (This list might easily be extended; also, there are certainly many other areas that could have been profitably addressed: literature, poetry, theatre, film, music, schooling – to name just a few.)

These were the domains of social experience people drew upon to discuss the central ideas in this book, ideas about the 'individual', 'liberty', 'democracy', 'civil society', 'history', 'crisis', 'religion', 'identity', 'human rights'. The variety of domains shows us to what extent these ideas have penetrated social life – indeed, one would be hard put to find a significant area that is not touched by the concepts we have been focusing on here.

Yet not only do these notions touch all (or most) domains of social life, but also they have themselves emerged in their own right as crucial categories of thought, and have to some degree come to constitute their own domain – elements in visions of society.

I have tried, throughout this book, to allow speakers to bring forward and discuss the crucial categories of their own thought, to elaborate their own visions of society. In doing this, we have come to appreciate the significance concepts such as 'human rights', 'democracy', and so on, have gained as cultural symbols. For example this was the crux of Laroui's historical argument about 'liberty' as Jamal Zyadi presented it – to show how 'liberty' emerged from an implicit aspect of social behavior to an explicit idea in its own right.

But a similar problematic is relevant to the other key ideas that have been addressed in the course of this book. Of course, it is only when a concept has emerged as an explicit symbol, competing with other strong symbols as magnets for people's loyalty, that serious disputes over the symbol's meaning can begin to occur, and that serious social and political contests arise to seize control of the symbol and to invest it with meaning. In this way, significant cultural symbols become stakes over which people contend, fight, and sometimes even risk their lives.

It should be clear from the speakers we have heard that the key concepts in this book have now emerged as major cultural stakes throughout the Middle East. This emergence is a civilizational 'event' of primary significance, although its implications are not yet clear. Of course, this 'event' is somewhat deeper and more hidden than the topical and spectacular events packaged and presented to us daily in our news media, but there is every chance that such hidden developments in the Middle East, these changes of attitude and transformations of culture, will in the long run have more profound effects, both within and outside the region, than the more 'newsworthy' items to which our attention is inexorably drawn.

What are some of the positions on these issues that are currently being staked out?

Speakers have consistently drawn our attention to two notions to set the context within which their discussions were to be placed: 'history' and 'crisis'. The pre-colonial Arab experience, the colonial period, the expectations and disappointments of the independence period, the critical problems of today's everyday life, all have been in the forefront of discussion.

But many voices also convey a warning, to themselves and to their compatriots: this context must not be taken to be an implacable force, a 'monster', that controls destiny, but should be seen instead as the stuff of life from which the present and future must be fashioned.

Now, who are the people who will fashion this future, how do they see themselves? This brings us face-to-face with the notion of social and cultural identity.

Identity was tied tightly to religion by a number of speakers, but many also tied it to other notions. In the 1950s, identity tended to be articulated in terms of the struggle to be free of colonialism and to establish (or reestablish) the nation; in the 1960s and 1970s people sought national identities in terms of capitalist or socialist options; from the mid-1970s on, the religious dimension has become increasingly significant. But it would certainly be a mistake to assume that this is the final twist in the quest for identity.

(It should be noted, as well, that the search for identity is not an exclusive concern of the Arab Middle East: European national populations are raising similar questions as they begin to confront their own minority cultures and their own racist attitudes, and as they contemplate the implications of European integration; in the US similar questions are being posed as a result of changes in the nation's global role; in eastern Europe, these questions arise with the disintegration of the Soviet empire.)

However, because this last quarter of the twentieth century happens to be our own historical moment, and because religion has assumed a leading role during this period, it is perhaps worth saying a few more words on this subject.

First of all, it should be said that to talk of 'an Islamic revival' or of a 'civilizational confrontation between the Islamic world and the West' begs more questions than it answers. The importance of Islam in today's Middle East, and the complex feelings many Muslims have towards the West, are not mere extensions of a historical opposition between Muslims and Christians, between Islam and Christianity; nor is the nature and essence of their religion a matter about which Muslims show much more agreement than Christians do about theirs.

In any event, much of the movement towards religious visions of society in the Middle East is a response to urgent contemporary problems – housing shortages, unemployment, poor educational facilities, and so on – as well as to the current residue of historical problems: neo-colonial structures and international dependency. The search for religious visions reflects, as well, the desire to construct societies free from the ills of 'modern' Western society: its materialism, lack of social cohesion, lack of common purpose, absence of a sense of community.

How these tensions may be satisfied within an 'Islamic' vision, whether they can or will be satisfied within such a framework is an open question. Let me risk stating the supremely obvious: in Islam, as in all world religions, the nature and practice of belief are not fixed once and for all, nor are they identical from place to place or from group to group. When we hear people refer to an 'Islamic' vision, at the very least we must wonder whether our attention should turn to one nation or to another, or to the views articulated by a state-supported class of religious scholars or by popular preachers, by reflective thinkers or by bands of activists, by rationalists or spiritualists, by urban or rural dwellers. This only hints at the complications because, of course, these social categories themselves are not unitary.

But is there not, as some Muslims will argue, an agreement on the 'basics', even if there is disagreement on the 'details'? Wouldn't it be possible to build societal visions on these foundations?

Before turning to the 'basics', let's look briefly at one of the 'details' – the matter of temporal power and the authority of the state. Some Muslims will argue today as others have argued in the past, that the ruler is God's representative on earth, that revolt against the ruler is tant-amount to revolt against God, that obedience and order are paramount. But we have also heard in the course of these pages other, opposing views: man, ordinary man, is God's representative on earth, and freedom and justice are Islam's central values.

Here is one religious thinker talking to me about the role of the state in Islamic doctrine:

> *As man is the representative of God on earth, there is an equality between the governed and the governor – Islam gives no more weight to the views of the governor than to those of the governed. This is of great importance and has three correlates. First, Islam does not provide a foundation for the state. Of course there is a tie in Islam between religion and politics, but our basic texts do not call for the state. That is why I believe that Islamic society must be basically a non-state society, where civil society must attain real power in order not to be absorbed by the state. Second, whatever state we have, it must not be very strong, it must only be strong in essential but limited domains. What these domains might be will of course be the subject of much dispute and struggle. Third, human freedom is absolutely central to Islam, because only with such freedom will dispute and struggle possibly lead us to the best answers.*

Certainly if such issues are 'details', it is difficult to see how concrete social visions can avoid them, and how such visions can find an ultimate warrant in religious doctrine.

However, even the 'basics' may not be beyond discussion and dispute. What is more fundamental to Islam than the nature of prophecy and the sacred character of the Qur'an? But, as one person phrased it to me,

> *We are only now beginning to ask the very hard questions. For example, why were there more than 300 prophets before Muhammad and since Muhammad there have been none? Why does God have to send further messages to correct deformations? If deformations and such difficulties are a problem, why did God not send 1,000,000 prophets?*
>
> *Also, is the Qur'an unequalled and unable to be equalled? What if we took a good literary text and made people read it for centuries, and raised them in an environment where they were told by everyone that the text was un- equalled – wouldn't they also come to believe that that text was unequalled?*

Some Muslims are also raising the most radical questions possible within a system of religious belief, questioning religious thinking itself. For example I have heard people pose questions such as: are there aspects of Islam itself and, more generally, of religious thinking that lead to backwardness in the modern world? Does the domination of public life by religious structures necessarily lead to authoritarian systems that so stifle individual freedom and creativity that progress (or movement towards the 'Truth') no longer becomes possible?

It often took some time before people were willing to be heard raising such questions, and they are not yet being raised publicly (it is often hard to draw the line showing where official censorship ends and self-censorship begins), but they are in the air.

This brings us to another theme that has been central to this book: the question of the individual, and notions of freedom or liberty.

Clear distinctions were drawn by many speakers between social visions based on 'rights' and those based on 'duties', between visions where the rights of the individual would be paramount and those where community rights would dominate. We were frequently asked to see this historically, to recognize that societies under external threat need to mobilize themselves collectively and consequently to muffle the individual's voice. Many Middle Easterners today still strongly feel such threats (less perhaps from invading armies than from an international system that deprives them of much decision-making power in their own societies), and arguments encouraging collective mobilization (whether phrased by state officials defending 'national security' or by political, religious, and cultural movements defending 'values') feed on and grow stronger from these threats.

In the discussions about the individual and human freedom, there have been few references to the personal, the emotional, and the psychological. Most of these references were made by women, struggling against the hold of a male-dominated public world. For many women the struggle for greater freedom is not only public, not only on the level of civil society, but is a battle taking place in their own inner world too, a battle against 'the block inside us', as one woman said. Perhaps symptomatic of this double battle was the broad meaning many women gave to the notion of 'democracy', as they used it to refer not only to political expression but also to interpersonal relationships.

The notion of 'democracy' has been a touchstone for many speakers. We have heard a wide range of views: from a 'traditional' but highly elaborate proverbial picture that awards little, if any, space to consensual political behavior, to a search for egalitarian structures with minimal hierarchy, to arguments for a strong leader, a benevolent despot, to a more or less taken-for-granted support of one-person, one-vote democracy. We have also heard of the importance of organizing civil society and speculation about how civil society might be reflected in societal decision-making.

And, finally, there has been the complicated notion of 'human rights' itself – a notion transparently betraying its Western origins, and just as transparently manipulated by opportunistic local and international political powers. Yet few Middle Easterners I spoke to seem ready to dismiss the idea from their cultural repertoire: they may challenge its foundations, or its provenance, or the content given to it by specific groups, but the concept itself has come to constitute a symbol of great power.

I have refrained, throughout this book, from providing a definition for 'human rights', nor have I even suggested one. This may seem surprising from someone like myself, who worked for a considerable time for an organization that put forward a very strict working definition. But my task here has been different, and to carry it out I have preferred to see the idea of 'human rights' not as a collection or list, but as conveying visions of how various units in society – the individual, the family, the tribe, the community, ethnic groups, associative groups and professional organizations, the state and its various institutions – relate to one another. When people asked me about the subject of my research I would sometimes answer along these lines, describing it as 'Ideas about person, community, and society in the Islamic Middle East'.

These visions may be very different, conflicting, or even contradictory. Taken together they can perhaps best be seen as constituents in a complex cultural 'cocktail' (in the sense of Muhammad Guessous' use of this word), constituents that may occasion disputes but that nonetheless provide a framework for discourse which, at the very least, allows basic communication about the nature of society to be carried on.

I cannot begin to predict how these visions will play themselves out, what the flavor of the cultural cocktail will be in a few years time. To borrow and modify (to my own taste) the words of Abdelqadr Zghal, it is impossible to be a prophet in any part of the world. All the countries we have looked at have the superficial similarity of being politically dominated by monolithic state systems and dependently situated in the international arena. The forces at play in each society may even be similarly labeled – political parties, state administrative structures, Islamist militancy, labor unrest, student discontent, ethnic tensions, civil society associations, simmering unemployment ... the list can probably be made as long as one wishes.

But however one labels these forces, in each of these countries they have their own particular nature. How these forces will interact, how the context within which these interactions occur will change, are questions I shall leave to others who can drink their cultural cocktails more deeply than I can and still remain sure of their footing.

CHALLENGES

I have been posing questions throughout this book; I have only hinted at or suggested the questions that were raised to me. But in the course of my interviews with intellectuals from many different walks of life and of various ideological and political persuasions, I was asked direct questions again and again. We have already seen a sample of these in the preface.

But there were other questions, and some sharp comments as well. For example one well-traveled Egyptian lawyer said to me, 'Why are you dealing only with Morocco, Tunisia, and Egypt? If you're talking about these issues, Jordan and Kuwait would show you very interesting things. And then there is Algeria, and Syria, too.' He then went on to explain in some detail why examining these other countries might throw fresh light on certain aspects of my study.

Also, in answer to my ready-to-hand description of my project as focusing on intellectuals and their ideas of person, community, and society in the Islamic Middle East, I heard in return, 'But in the Islamic world, there is no real concept of society'. And, 'Here there is no idea of the person, of the individual as a distinct entity conscious of his or her singularity and uniqueness'. And finally,

> But you're wasting your time on the ideas of intellectuals. Our societies are undergoing pervasive crises. The ideas that are being formed, that are going to be the guiding ideas of our societies, are not being formed by intellectuals – intellectuals are increasingly marginalized – but are being formed on the streets, outside the domain of intellectual discussion and discourse.

Other people questioned my use of their words. As one person said, 'Look, if you are going to use my testimony, I want to see the text of my words before you publish them' (which, of course, I have done). Another thanked me heartily for sending him the transcripts of our interviews and announced in a matter-of-fact manner, 'I think we are going to publish them here' and 'someone in the States is also asking me if he can publish some sections'.

The people I was talking to clearly had their own ideas about what I was doing and were not afraid to voice them. Taken together (and keeping in mind the religious scholar's questions in the preface), these questions, comments, and criticisms, although specifically directed at me and my work, also amount to a deep challenge to our own 'traditional' view of research, a view that usually takes the research to be the sole creation of the researcher, of the book's 'author'.

These challenges question the role, function, and even the competence of the researcher, who is forced to present and to justify not only his project but also often his own personal beliefs, his politics, his professional record; they question the substance and direction of his current project; and they question the researcher's assumed exclusive control over the research product. And finally, the speakers we have heard may, if they are so inclined, push this challenge further and question the researcher's text on the basis of their own lived experience that goes far deeper into this book's subject matter than the author can ever hope to go.

Many of these challenges influenced my work as I carried it out. How successful I have been in responding to them in this book is for the reader to judge. I can only hope that among the readers there will indeed be some whose voices appear in this book and who, finding what I hope they will feel to be a reasonably faithful rendition of their thoughts, may be moved to push their thinking further, and to further challenge my own. Perhaps, in taking this book as a whole, they will gain a better sense of why our discussions proceeded as they did, and why this book has taken the shape it has.

Perhaps, too, they will see how one Westerner, a New Yorker who has spent most of his life on two 'Western' continents and the rest of it studying a third, has approached the problem of communication and understanding across cultural, even civilizational, boundaries. Taken in this way, this book may be seen as portraying the West as much as it portrays the Middle East. If this is so, then the work of the researcher will come full circle and become, at the same time, the work of an informant.

Appendix
Statistical profile

	Morocco	Tunisia	Egypt
Area (sq. k.)	447,000	164,000	1,002,000
Population (millions) *			
1989	24.2	8.1	52.5
Average annual percentage rate of growth of population			
1980–7	2.7	2.6	2.7
1987–2000	2.4	2.1	2.3
Future population estimates (millions)			
2000	32	10	67
2025	47	14	99
Percentage of married women of childbearing age using contraception			
1970	1	10	—
1985	36	41	32
Life expectancy at birth			
both sexes 1987	61	65	61
females 1965	51	51	50
1987	63	66	62
males 1965	48	50	47
1987	59	65	59
Education: percentage of age group enrolled in education			
Primary education [a]			
total 1965	57	91	75
1986	79	118	87
male 1965	78	116	90
1986	96	127	96
female 1965	35	65	60
1986	62	108	77

		Morocco	*Tunisia*	*Egypt*
Secondary education				
total	1965	11	16	26
	1986	34	39	66
male	1965	16	23	37
	1986	39	45	77
female	1965	5	9	15
	1986	27	33	54
Tertiary education				
total	1965	1	2	7
	1986	9	6	21
Number of females in education per 100 males				
primary	1965	42	52	64
	1986	62	80	77
secondary	1965	40	44	45
	1986	67	71	—
Urban population as percentage of total population				
	1965	32	40	41
	1987	47	54	48
Average annual growth rate (percent) of urban population				
	1965–80	4.3	4.0	2.9
	1980–7	4.5	2.9	3.7
Percentage of urban population in largest city				
	1960	16	40	38
	1980	26	30	39
Percentage of urban population in cities over 500,000				
	1960	16	40	53
	1980	50	30	53
Economic statistics				
GNP per capita (US$)				
	1987	610	1,180	680
GNP per capita, average annual growth rate (percent)				
	1965–87	1.8	3.6	3.5
GDP (millions of US$)				
	1965	2,950	880	4,550
	1987	16,750	8,450	34,470
GDP average annual growth rate (percent)				
	1965–80	5.4	6.6	6.8
	1980–7	3.2	3.6	6.3
GDP distribution according to sector (percent) [b]				
Agriculture				
	1965	23	22	29
	1987	19	18	21

		Morocco	*Tunisia*	*Egypt*
Industry				
	1965	28	24	27
	1987	31	32	25
Manufacturing				
	1965	16	9	—
	1987	18	15	14
Services				
	1965	49	54	45
	1987	50	50	54
Cereal imports (000 metric tons)				
	1974	891	307	3,877
	1987	2,251	1,170	9,326
Food aid in cereals (000 metric tons)				
	1974/75	75	59	610
	1986/87	611	396	1,977
Average index of food production per capita (1977–81 = 100)				
	1985–7	109	114	106
Energy consumption per capita (kg of oil equivalent)				
	1965	124	170	313
	1987	242	496	588
Consumer price index (1985 = 100) *				
	1989	120	128	207
Consumer price inflation (percent) *				
	1989	5.5	7.8	17.6
Trade deficit (millions of US$) *				
	1988	1,165	1,295	4,300
Total long-term debt as percentage of GNP				
	1970	18.6	—	—
	1987	117.9	69.7	108.7
Total long-term debt service as percentage of GNP				
	1970	1.7	—	—
	1987	8.2	10.8	5.3
Total long-term debt service as percentage of exports of goods and services				
	1970	9.2	—	—
	1987	30.8	29.4	21.5

Source: All figures are from World Bank (1989) except those with an asterisk (*), which are from EIU Morocco (1990), EIU Tunisia (1990), and EIU Egypt (1990) respectively.

Notes: (a) Percentages may be more than 100 because some pupils attending primary school are younger or older than the country's standard primary school age.
(b) Percentages add to more than 100 because manufacturing production is included in industry production.

Notes

PREFACE

1 Were the research beginning now, Algeria would have to be added to this list (and perhaps Kuwait excluded).

  By listing these countries I do not mean to suggest that they are free, or even relatively free, from human rights violations. Perusal of recent Amnesty International reports would refute such a suggestion.

2 Morocco and Tunisia had been part of the French colonial empire until the mid-1950s and following independence continued to retain strong ties to France, Western Europe, and the US. Egypt, well integrated into the British Empire throughout the nineteenth and into the twentieth century, turned away from Europe somewhat during the Nasser years (1954–70) but again opened itself to Europe and the US during the Sadat period (1971–81), an openness that continues up to the present. Egypt currently receives the second largest amount of US foreign aid (after Israel).

3 For an interesting discussion of some of these issues (although not with particular reference to the Middle East) see Edward Said (1986).

4 Where people I talked to referred to a written article or book, I often read it so that I could return with more germane questions the next time; and I would sometimes read a recent writing to prepare for a discussion with a particular individual.

5 Before this research project I had previously written a book, *Moroccan Dialogues*, based largely on my anthropological interviews with Moroccan villagers (Dwyer 1982). In that book I translated and reproduced conversations word-for-word. In the interviews in this book, held variously in French, English, and Arabic, I have edited the spoken word more actively, trying to blend the advantages of the spoken word – its spontaneity and sensitivity to human interaction – with those of the written word – coherence of presentation and stylistic control. A long argument would be necessary to support these different procedures and this is not the place for them (see Dwyer, in press).

6 At one point, several people referred to a poll of French opinion in the mid-1980s showing that more than half of those polled thought Islam was a force for war, many more than thought the same of Judaism, Protestantism, or Christianity. A more recent poll showed more than two out of three French having a very negative view of Islam (Solé and Tincq 1989).

7 Their criticisms of the faults of Western scholarship were on the whole similar to those put forward by Maxime Rodinson (1980: first published in 1968) and by Edward Said (1978), faults I had tried to avoid in my book, *Moroccan Dialogues*.

8 The Arab Maghreb Union (AMU) (grouping Mauritania, Morocco, Algeria, Tunisia, and Libya) was formed in February 1989, with the aim of building regional cooperation and economic integration. The Arab Cooperation Council (ACC), also formed in February 1989, was part of Iraq's effort to assume a leading role in the area by reinforcing economic cooperation between Egypt, Iraq, Jordan, and North Yemen. (Unlike the other members of the ACC, Egypt has continued to keep its political positions distinct from those of Iraq.)

Earlier, in 1981, Saudi Arabia, Kuwait, Oman, Qatar, Bahrain, and the United Arab Emirates had joined to form the Gulf Cooperation Council (GCC), again with the overt aim of increasing economic cooperation, but also with the clear (if unstated) objectives of trying to counter the regional ambitions of Iraq and Iran and to avoid the intervention of the superpowers in the area.

The fragility of these structures was brought into high relief following the invasion and annexation of Kuwait by Iraq in August 1990. At the Arab League summit called to discuss Iraq's action only the GCC was united in its response; the five countries of the AMU adopted five different positions and the ACC was, to all intents and purposes, rendered inert.

Even before the Iraqi invasion of Kuwait concrete cooperation in these associations had been moving forward slowly. (As some observers noted, although in 1989 you were able to drive from Morocco to Iraq, inter-Arab trade still represented less than 10 percent of the region's total trade: Rodenbeck and Mallet 1989.)

9 I remember having joked with Muhammad right after he said this, 'Well, if I want to sell a lot of copies of this book, maybe I should try a title like *God, Sex, and Money in the Middle East.*'

1 INTRODUCTION

1 Personal interview. Unless otherwise indicated, all quotations given here come from my interviews with the individuals cited. Some preferred not to have their names mentioned and of course I have followed their wishes. In all cases, I have made every effort to preserve the integrity of the speaker's remarks, and to reflect some sense of their chronology and sequence as well.

When I refer to the speakers, I sometimes use first or last names, indicating that my relationship with them is somewhat informal. Where I use their full name, the relationship is more formal.

2 For statistical profiles of each country see the Appendix.

3 A fuller discussion of each country's current situation will be found in subsequent chapters.

4 See Khelil 1985.

5 Nor are Western Europe and the United States immune to such sentiments: the stock market 'crash' in October 1987 brought similar feelings out into the open, but deeper questions about the ability of the United States and

Western Europe to compete in the world economy, and about ecology, global warming, population growth, and nuclear proliferation, have been encouraging 'crisis' thinking in the West for some time now. Recent developments in Eastern Europe and the Soviet Union may have displaced these crises somewhat, but they have not made them go away.

6 This argument is made by Clifford Geertz (1968).

7 See Umberto Eco (1986) for this view.

8 Nor do I think these suggestions are of much use to any of us for whom 'crisis' has become a major theme and a prevailing mood, coloring our vision of the current world situation and of our lives within it. This stance has been very clearly summarized in a lapidary phrase by the anthropologist, Stanley Diamond, 'Anthropology ... is the study of men in crisis by men in crisis' (1974: 93). Diamond's thinking continues: 'Anthropologists and their objects, the studied, despite opposing positions in the 'scientific' equation, have this much in common: if not equally, still they are each objects of contemporary imperial civilization. The anthropologist who treats the indigene as an object may define himself as relatively free, but that is an illusion. For in order to objectify the other, one is, at the same time, compelled to objectify the self.'

2   UNIVERSAL VISIONS, LOCAL VISIONS

1 I witnessed such a scene in a small southern Moroccan village.

2 The first stage of this period goes from the establishment of the Islamic community in 622 to the death of the Prophet in 632; the second continues through the rule of the next four leaders of the community, known as the rightly guided (*rashidun*) caliphs, and ends with the assassination of the Caliph Ali in 661.

3 The Qur'an (the word of God communicated to the Prophet Muhammad through the angel Gabriel), and the *Sunna* (the life of the Prophet, known through the various sayings and traditions (*hadith*) attributed to him by his followers), are the primary sources of Islamic law (*shari^{c}a*). Also taken as sources of law are the consensus of the community (*ijma^c*) and conclusions reached by analogical reasoning (*qiyas*) based on the primary sources. The body of Islamic law, then, consists of these sources and the commentaries and interpretations developed by reputable, established Islamic thinkers.

It should be clear from this that, given the vast historical and geographical sweep of Islam, believing Muslims may draw many different, discordant, even contradictory lessons from the Islamic patrimony.

4 I use the term 'Islamist' to refer to groups that explicitly aim to strengthen the role of Islam in public life. These groups vary widely in their objectives, in their tactics, and in their visions of Islam; where appropriate I prefix an adjective like 'moderate', 'militant', or 'extremist'. I prefer the term 'Islamist' to 'fundamentalist' because of what has become the latter's pejorative connotation. When speakers have used the term 'fundamentalist' I have kept their usage.

5 The Baha'i religion originated in nineteenth-century Iran and holds that God is at the origin of all religions and all must be revered as steps in a progressive

revelation. Baha'is revere their own prophet Baha'ullah, and so are seen as heretics by Muslims. Baha'ullah was exiled from Iran to Acre, so the headquarters of the faith are on Mt Carmel, in what is now Israel.

6 The Arab Nationalist movement had its roots in the pre-World War I Arab reaction to Ottoman control over Arab lands. It took many forms in the inter-war period but emerged with renewed force in the 1940s in Syria, emphasizing the liberation of the Arab homeland from colonial domination and the building of a broad Arab nation going beyond existing national boundaries. The Arab 'spirit', Arab culture, and the Arab heritage were to be the unifying forces behind the new Arab nation.

7 In general, Christian and Jewish minorities (known as *ahl al-kitab* – peoples of the book) were accorded a 'protected' status (and thus were also known as *ahl al-dhimma* or *dhimmi* – protected peoples): they were allowed to retain their religious practices, their places of worship, and the autonomy of their own internal law, but were also required to pay a special tax, the *jizya*. They were not treated as the equals of Muslims: for example, a *dhimmi* man could not marry a Muslim woman nor keep a Muslim slave, whereas a Muslim man was permitted to marry a *dhimmi* woman and keep a *dhimmi* slave.

Historically there was constantly a tension between more restrictive and more lenient interpretations of the rights of *dhimmi*s in Islamic lands. With the colonial period, and the privileged relationships the colonial power often forged with the *dhimmi*s, Muslim attitudes towards them tended to harden.

8 The effort of the Tunisian Human Rights League to elaborate a charter is treated in detail in Part III.

9 This Tunisian law established, among other provisions enhancing women's rights, a woman's right to obtain a divorce and legalized adoption. For more detail see Part III.

10 There are today about 3,500 Jews in Tunisia, down from approximately 120,000 in 1948.

3 EGYPT SINCE THE JULY REVOLUTION

1 The Muslim Brothers (or the Society of Muslim Brothers – *Ikhwan al-Muslimin*), founded in Egypt by Hassan al-Banna in 1928, spread from there to many other Islamic countries. By 1948, there were 2,000 branches of the Muslim Brothers in Egypt alone. The Society first approved the July revolution, but tension between the Society, then representing the largest organized political force in the country, and the government was not long in appearing. This culminated in an assassination attempt on Nasser's life by a Muslim Brother in October 1954. Nasser reacted immediately, arresting thousands and executing six of the Brothers' leaders in December. His attempt to eliminate the Muslim Brothers from Egypt was never fully successful and they remained a constant source of opposition throughout his rule. The Society remains strong today in Egypt and in a number of other Arab societies, including Jordan and Syria.

2 The union was to last only three years, but it was one of a number of efforts Nasser made to provide Egyptian support for like-minded movements – his ill-fated support for Yemen from 1962 to 1967 and his active support for the Algerian Revolution and then later for its leader Ben Bella after 1962 are

only two examples. Libya's leader since 1969, Muʿammar Qadhdhafi, taking direct inspiration from Nasser, was to pursue the aim of union between Arab states and managed to form a brief union between Libya, Egypt, and Syria in 1971, shortly after Nasser's death, and another with Morocco from 1984 to 1986, among numerous other failed efforts.

3 For this period of Nasser's rule, I have found John Waterbury's book (1983) to be the most useful. In particular, for some of the points I have made in these paragraphs, see Waterbury 1983: 57–85, 314. I have also found Vatikiotis (1976) and Hopwood (1985) helpful for some general historical information I have adduced in this section.

4 In comparing the relative merits of Nasser's and Sadat's economic policies, John Waterbury's judgement may provide the soundest assessment: that whatever the economic advances during Sadat's period may have been, they came not as a result of *infitah* policies but were, aside from foreign remittances from emigrant workers, the delayed effects of Nasser's initiatives in petroleum, canal revenues, and tourism. The benefits of Nasser's policies were either postponed or never realized because of his foreign policy failures, particularly the 1967 war with Israel. Had Nasser survived several more years, and had he had at his disposal the revenues from foreign remittances that grew during the 1970s, his economic policies might have had substantial success. For more details of this argument, see Waterbury 1983: 204.

5 As examples, a constitutional amendment in May 1980 allowed him unlimited terms as president, and peace with Israel was ratified in 1979 by referendum, thus bypassing parliament.

6 Sura 42, verse 38 of the Qur'an enjoins Muslims to conduct their affairs through *shura* (usually translated by 'mutual consultation'). Commentators see *shura* as the central notion in this sura, which has the word as its title.

7 In May 1990 the Supreme Constitutional Court declared the 1987 elections invalid because independent candidates had been unfairly discriminated against. The laws the 1987 Parliament had already enacted were declared valid but no new legislation was to be allowed. New elections were likely but as of this writing had not yet been scheduled.

4 EGYPTIAN VOICES

1 His paper was titled 'Search for a new identity for the social sciences in the Arab world'.

2 The French, under Bonaparte, began a short-lived occupation of Egypt in 1798 but had to withdraw their troops in 1801 after attack by Turkish and British forces. From that time on Egypt was a province of the Ottoman Empire, although ruled from Cairo in an effectively independent manner. In 1882, through a combination of colonialist machinations by the British and mismanagement by Egypt's rulers, the British gained control over the Egyptian political and economic system, relinquishing this formally in 1922. However, British influence and control continued well after this and can be said to have definitively ended only with the July revolution in 1952 and then with the Egyptian takeover of the Suez Canal in 1956.

3 See Farah 1986. The Copts are members of the Christian Church of Egypt, founded according to Christian tradition by St Mark, one of Christ's early

followers and author of one of the gospels. Consequent to doctrinal disputes, the Coptic Church became somewhat isolated from the rest of Christendom from the fifth century on.

4 The Arab Socialist movement blended some of the notions of the Arab Nationalist movement (see Chapter 2, note 6) – namely the idea of a broadly based Arab homeland erasing existing national boundaries – with socialist ideals. Under the leadership of Michel Aflaq and Sala<u>h</u> al-Din al-Baytar, both Syrians (the first from a Christian Orthodox family, the second from a Muslim family), and embodied in the *Ba°ath* (Resurrection) movement founded in Syria in 1932, this blend led to the formation of like-minded branches in Jordan, Iraq, Lebanon, Egypt, and North Africa. The movement was socialist in the sense that it wished to achieve the dignity of man through liberation from economic exploitation, poverty, disease, and ignorance; however, it challenged Marxist materialist notions and ideas of class struggle, putting forward views of the Arab 'spirit' and cooperation and justice among peoples. It recognized Islam as the central element in Arab unity, but argued for a separation of religion and the state.

The Syrian *Ba°ath* party (made a legal political party in 1946 and of which Aflaq was the head) strongly supported the drive for unity with Egypt in 1958. However, relations were tense between the *Ba°ath* and Nasser, who was more a pragmatist than an ideologue; the *Ba°ath* supported Syria's withdrawal from the union in 1961.

Nasser continued to put forward a variety of Arab socialism that, less rigid than the *Ba°ath* version and benefiting from his own charisma, became the official ideology of Nasser's Egypt.

Different wings of the *Ba°ath* party (having become more militaristic and narrowly nationalist) gained power in Syria and Iraq in the 1960s and remain in power today, implacably hostile to one another. Aflaq himself was forced to leave Syria (in 1971 he was condemned to death in absentia) and lived thereafter in Baghdad where he remained head of the Iraqi *Ba°ath* party until his death in 1989.

5 Nadia may have been thinking of groups such as the Young Egypt movement which, beginning in the 1930s, combined a xenophobic Egyptian nationalism with religious extremism and a martial spirit. Young Egypt provided the basis for a number of subsequent political parties, and its spirit is still a significant force in Egypt today. It achieved recognition as a legal political party in April 1990.

6 See Chapter 2, note 7.

7 See, for example, Kepel 1985, Munson 1988, and Etienne 1987.

8 The conflation by many Westerners of all strands of Islam with some of its more extreme manifestations is very annoying to many Muslims. This annoyance was transparent one evening when I sat down to talk with an Egyptian journalist. When I explained to him that I was interested in discussing the ideas of one particular set of Islamic thinkers, he seemed to breathe a sigh of relief and said, 'You know, just a week ago I had an American journalist sit down in that very same chair you are in and ask me if I could take him to see "some real fundamentalists, the kind who wear beards, or wear veils, and who don't drink". That guy had no idea of what Muslims are, to say nothing of extremist Muslims.'

9 There has been, since the first centuries of Islam, a long history of Islamic

discussion treating such basic issues as the notion of justice, the relationship between the individual and the community, between innovation and tradition, between reason and revelation, between the rights of God and the rights of man. This discussion gained new life towards the end of the nineteenth century in the work of leading thinkers of the so-called 'reformist' *(salafiyya)* movement, such as Jamal ad-Din al-Afghani and Muhammad Abduh. This led to an extremely rich flowering of discussion through the early decades of the twentieth century, discussions that are prolonged in revised form in much of the present-day debate.

There are many scholarly studies of these and related issues in the early centuries of Islam. See, for example, Rosenthal 1960 and Khadduri 1984. The classic study of Arabic thought over the last two centuries, from the roots of the reform movement to its flowering in the early twentieth century, is Hourani 1962.

10 These accusations, by the way, are familiar coming from those on the left towards former 'comrades' who have come to use an Islamic vocabulary and who are said to suffer from the 'fear of being left out' or to be 'nostalgic for involvement with the masses'. Such comments can be heard not only in Egypt, but in Morocco and Tunisia as well.

11 The Muʿtazila started as a political movement in the first century of Islam and then developed into an important theological school. Its political origins lay in the dispute over the succession of the Prophet's cousin and son-in-law Ali to the caliphate (the head of the Islamic community) in 656. In this dispute, which is the fundamental discord in Islamic history and led to the divergence between the Shiʿa (which supported Ali's claim and through him that of his son Hussein and his followers) and the various Sunni groups (which rejected Ali's claim), the Muʿtazila emerged adopting a neutral stance, neither supporting nor rejecting Ali's claim to the caliphate. This stance led to the development of theological doctrines such as 'the mean between the two extremes' (known as *iʿtizal*, hence the derived name of the group), and to a highly developed scholastic and rationalist theology. Among other major elements of their doctrine were the notion of free will and human responsibility, the view that human justice could be established through the exercise of human reason, and that justice was often to be found in 'the mean between the two extremes', in 'moderation'.

12 For a short discussion of *shura* see Chapter 3, note 6.

13 An 'extremist' Islamist group in Egypt that was responsible for the assassination of Sadat.

14 See Chapter 3, note 6.

15 Ibn Taymiyya (b. 1263/661, d. 1328/728) was a Muslim religious thinker who emphasized the importance of reason and discussion on social and political matters not governed explicitly by revelation. He also took the position that many other Muslim thinkers have supported, that the general interest *(meslaha)* is the ultimate aim *(maqasid)* of Islamic law.

5 CULTURAL OBSTACLES?

1 I do not necessarily share the sociologist's assessment, but when I made some counterarguments he dismissed the common Moroccan terms for 'person' –

<u>*khelq*</u>, *ben 'adam* – as meaning 'a generic human being', not 'an individual'. In any case, it is not the accuracy of the sociologist's analysis that is in question; more relevant is his general attitude toward the notion of 'the individual' in Moroccan culture.

2 The term 'project' or 'social project'ʼ– in Arabic *meshruᶜa* – has great currency in political discourse throughout the Middle East and is an element often cited to distinguish movements that have (or seek) a coherent vision of the nature of society from those that seem to adopt a purely pragmatic, step-by-step, case-by-case approach.

3 In its classical formulation, Marxist/Communist ideology might be said to provide such a 'purposeful' vision, and this vision certainly attracted much support in the Middle East throughout the 1950s, 1960s, and 1970s. Today such visions require radical reformulation, and much of this is now being done within a religious framework. 'Purposeful' visions, conveying ideas of social justice, economic development, community strength and/or religious renewal, are understandably particularly attractive where societies believe themselves to be in crisis.

4 Muhammad Iqbal (1875–1938), an Indian Muslim, was a seminal figure in the Islamic reform movement. He was, as well, a supporter of the idea of a separate Muslim state within India.

5 For an explanation of *Sunna* see Chapter 2, note 3.

6 Ibn Khaldun was a fourteenth-century analyst of Arab society and history, born in Tunis. His writings show him analyzing human behavior (rather than divine reasons, or the imperatives of nature) in order to understand the laws of human society. This style of thought situates him as one of the precursors of modern sociology and history.

7 Islamic brotherhoods are religious orders that follow the practices of a founding individual who is believed to have developed a particularly pious path and found special favor with God.

8 These are treated in detail in Part III.

6 INDEPENDENT MOROCCO

1 To the author's credit, he does not argue that the 'fundamental' Moroccan traits are immutable, but rather that they are socially conditioned and that it is within the power of people to change themselves. Indeed, he both leads into his book and closes it with lines from the Qur'an that say, 'Never will God change the condition of a people until they change it themselves' (Sura XIII, verse 11).

2 Recent figures on numbers of Berber speakers are hard to come by, as the Moroccan government does not include language in its census data, but in the early 1970s an estimated 30 to 40 percent of Morocco's population were thought to be native Berber speakers. Most Berber speakers also speak Arabic, and the universalization of Arabic is increasing with the spread of education to the countryside and the emigration from mountain areas to the cities. The distinction between Berbers and Arabs is primarily a linguistic one and although there are also some significant cultural differences between Berber and Arabic speakers, there are considerable cultural differences between Berber-speaking communities, and between Arabic-speaking

communities, as well. In any case the cultural differences in no way diminish the degree to which the different populations identify themselves as Moroccans or as Muslims; the French colonial power seriously misread this situation and, in promulgating legislation during the colonial period designed to divide Berbers and Arabs, only succeeded in drawing them closer together.

Morocco historically also had significant Jewish populations, some arriving after having been expelled from Spain during the Inquisition, and others having been in place since before the advent of Islam in Morocco. After the birth of the Israeli state in 1948 and then following Morocco's independence from France in 1956, much of the Jewish population emigrated, either to France or to Israel (in 1945, between 2 and 3 percent of the Moroccan population were Jews, and this had fallen to 0.2 percent by 1974). Christian populations in Morocco reached significant levels only during the protectorate period and declined rapidly after it ended: in 1945, 5.8 percent of the Moroccan population was classed as 'foreign', with almost all of these being Christian; by 1974, this had fallen to 0.7 percent (Ibrahim 1980: 6a).

3 The opposition between areas under central control *(bled el-makhzen* – the land of central rule) and areas escaping central control *(bled es-siba* – the land of dissidence or 'anarchy') is a theme that runs throughout Moroccan history. The terms *Makhzen* and *siba* are still used by Moroccans today and are applied, respectively, to central authority and disorder or chaos. In particular, the term *Makhzen* (originally meaning 'treasury, strongbox' and by extension referring to the government as a whole) is frequently used by Moroccans as a label for the country's political system, as a shorthand for a set of characteristics that includes a strong central authority with political and religious legitimacy, dependent local and regional administration, a deeply embedded patronage system, and highly elaborate techniques of divide and rule.

4 See World Bank (1989: 154, 208–9) for these figures.

5 Muhammad V had been chosen Sultan with French approval in 1927, but he began to take on an increasingly important role in opposing French rule, particularly after the end of World War II. The French deposed and exiled him in 1953 but, when nationalist activity continued unabated, they were forced to reinstate him and return him to Morocco in November 1955 as a prelude to independence.

6 In the border dispute, a treaty signed in 1972 was ratified by Algeria but not by Morocco. In March 1989, following a thaw in Moroccan–Algerian relations and the creation of the Arab Maghreb Union, King Hassan announced plans to ratify the treaty formally.

7 A French court eventually sentenced two French officials to prison terms and Moroccan Minister of the Interior Muhammad Oufkir to life imprisonment in absentia for his involvement in the affair. Colonel Dlimi, one of Oufkir's aides, was also implicated in this affair. Oufkir was later to be behind the 1972 coup attempt (as it failed, he either committed suicide or was killed – reports differ – and King Hassan has kept his wife and children in prison or under house arrest since that time); Dlimi, later promoted to General and Commander of the Armed Forces, also died in mysterious circumstances in a roadside accident in 1983, amid allegations of discontent within the military over Hassan's rule.

8 The sources for the economic data in the preceding paragraphs are: state

ownership of companies (EIU Morocco 1989a: 12); unemployment (EIU Morocco 1988: 13); trading partners (EIU Morocco 1989d: appendices); debt (EIU Morocco 1989c: 24).

Some further figures may be useful to supplement the statements made in these paragraphs on Morocco's economic situation:

- Rapid urbanization: 32 percent of the population lived in urban areas in 1965, 47 percent in 1987 (World Bank 1989: 224).
- Cereal imports: their volume rose from 891,000 metric tons in 1974 to 2,251,000 in 1987 (World Bank 1989: 170).
- Unemployment was estimated in 1988 to stand at well over one million with more than 45,000 of these being university graduates and persons with professional qualifications (EIU Morocco 1989a: 11).
- Trading partners: France contributes 38 percent of foreign investment and Spain 9 percent (EIU Morocco 1989b: 16–17); the EC takes 61.3 percent of Moroccan exports and provides 52.5 percent of Morocco's imports (EIU Morocco 1989a: 20–1). Morocco has recently been increasing its share of EC–Maghreb trade. EC exports to Morocco remained relatively stable in 1986–7, declining 0.6 percent, while exports to Tunisia were down 9.9 percent and to Algeria down 18.3 percent. Morocco and Tunisia increased exports to the EC in 1987 (Morocco up 4.5 percent and Tunisia up 10.1 percent), with Algeria down by 21.4 percent (EIU Morocco 1989a: 20–1).
- Worker remittances: they fell about 22 percent in 1988 from a total of $1.6 bn in 1987 (EIU Morocco 1988: 12; EIU Morocco 1989a: 14).
- Tourism: income from tourism seems to be on the increase, with revenues increasing 22 percent in 1987 over 1986, and numbers of visitors showing a 26 percent increase in 1988 over 1987. In the first quarter of 1989 tourism was up by 50 percent over the corresponding period in the previous year, an increase accounted for largely by visitors from the Maghreb (up from 5,583 to 82,160 in April alone), and particularly from Algeria, in response to the founding of the AMU (EIU Morocco 1989c: 21). However, in terms of infrastructure Morocco lags behind some of its main competitors, having only 65,000 hotel class beds, compared to Tunisia's 105,000 and 350,000 in the neighboring Canaries (EIU Morocco 1989b: 22).
- Trade gap: in the first half of 1989 it rose 65 percent over the same period in 1988 (EIU Morocco 1989d: 18).

9 On the recent economic situation described in this paragraph see EIU Morocco (1989a: 13) and de la Guérivière (1990).

10 Tempering this positive picture somewhat has been the recent closure, for a combination of political and economic reasons, of two important journals, *Lamalif* and *Kalima*.

11 King Hassan was sufficiently concerned about relations with France to intervene directly to encourage two Moroccan girls studying in France to discard 'Islamic' dress when this matter threatened to cause difficulties for the French government as well as a heightening of the already tense relations between North African immigrants and racist elements in France.

In September 1989 Hassan made his first official visit to Spain since his rule began in 1961.

12 Peres' visit led Syria to break off diplomatic relations with Morocco, but these were resumed in 1989.

7 MOROCCAN VOICES

1 See Salmi 1985a and 1985b. Salmi's perspective in his book on human rights is revealed by the quotation from Bertolt Brecht that heads its introduction, 'In democratic societies, you don't see the violent character of the economy; in authoritarian societies, it's the economic character of violence that you don't see' (1985b: 5).

2 See Mernissi 1987. Since then she has published a further study, on the subject of women heads of state in Islamic society (Mernissi 1990).

3 The jellaba is a body-length outer garment with a hood that covers the head but allows the face to be seen.

4 As he said to me, 'You have to understand that when you make statements about proverbs you face a number of problems.

First of all, although you can find general themes there are also many variations, and the meaning of any proverb, or any set of proverbs, is often equivocal. They often do not have one very clear or precise meaning and they can sometimes even have opposite meanings.

Second, most of the proverbs I have collected come from the cities, although there are also some from the countryside, basically from central Morocco. Some comparisons could be made of different shades of meanings here; one could also argue that there are different shades of meanings in proverbs collected in colloquial Arabic and those collected in various dialects of the Berber language, and different shades of meaning in proverbs that are of orthodox Islamic origin and in those that come from "popular" culture. But, in any case, a lot of proverbs have moved back and forth between all these contexts, so it would be very risky to try and draw any hard and fast distinctions.'

5 I remember that a Moroccan villager answered me with this proverb when I told him that I was returning to the US after having lived in the village for more than a year.

6 As my research was nearing its end, Jamal found employment: he was hired by the political party in which he was a sincere if critical militant as an assistant to their parliamentary group.

7 In recent years Laroui found himself in sympathy with official policy on the Western Sahara and was enlisted by the palace on several occasions to carry royal messages to other Arab countries. He was also appointed private tutor to the King's eldest son and heir apparent, Sidi Muhammad.

I tried several times to see Laroui during my visits to Morocco but he had always either been away, or had pleaded that he was too busy.

At the time of my talks with Jamal, Laroui's *The Concept of Liberty* was available only in Arabic. It was later published in a shortened French version in Laroui 1987.

8 The Arabic word, *ḥurriya*, currently used to translate 'liberty' or 'freedom', emerged in this sense in the nineteenth century to translate the 'freedoms' demanded by European ambassadors for their own civil and commercial interests and for their religious minorities. (For a more detailed examination of the Arabic word, see Rosenthal 1960.)

9 Hadiths are sayings and acts attributed to the Prophet in collections established in the centuries following his death. See Chapter 2, note 3.

10 For *shura*, see Chapter 2, note 6.

11 See Chapter 6, note 3.

8 CONSTRUCTING CIVIL SOCIETY

1 Organization on this level is conventionally referred to by intellectuals in Morocco, Tunisia, and Egypt as the organization of 'civil society' – a term used to great effect by Hegel and then taken over by Marx through whom it became part of the vocabulary of today's normal political discourse.

9 INDEPENDENT TUNISIA

1 One indication of the enduring identity between government and party that existed throughout Bourguiba's rule was the comprehensive victory by the party in the last elections to take place under Bourguiba, in November 1986: here, the governmental party won all 125 parliamentary seats.
2 One example of this suppression (we will see others as Tunisian history moves forward) followed Bourguiba's dispute with Salah ben Youssef over the French autonomy proposal in 1955, a proposal that Bourguiba accepted but that Ben Youssef and his supporters opposed, claiming that it fell short of the full independence Tunisia merited. In the few years following independence, Ben Youssef's real or imputed supporters faced a series of trials that removed many of them from political life. Ben Youssef, in exile, was condemned to death in absentia and was assassinated in a West German hotel in 1961 on the orders of a close confidant of Bourguiba, only several months after he had had an unproductive meeting with Bourguiba in Switzerland.
3 Ben Salah remained a strong rallying point for socialist and 'progressive' forces. After his escape from prison in 1973, he went to Europe and founded a political movement, the Popular Unity Movement (MUP – Mouvement d'unité populaire) that throughout the 1970s attracted the sympathy of much of the Tunisian opposition on the left.

 A fate similar to Ben Salah's – trial or threatened trial, and eventual exile – befell a number of members of Tunisia's political elite in ensuing years, several of whom had once occupied important governmental posts (for example, former Minister of the Interior Driss Guiga who took the blame for the brutal suppression of the 1984 food riots, and Muhammad Mzali, prime minister from 1980 to 1986).
4 The ratio of females to all students moved from 33 percent (1958) to 38 percent (1977) in primary schools, from 22 percent (1962) to 28 percent (1977) in the secondary, and from 20 percent (1963) to 25 percent (1977) at the university level (Toumi 1978: 43).

 For the figures in the preceding paragraphs: on population (Toumi 1978: 17); on the GNP and salary increases (Toumi 1978: 22, 33); on student numbers (Toumi 1978: 41–2).
5 For more detail on the MTI see Part I.
6 In particular, applications by the Islamist group MTI to form a political party called 'Al-Nahda' (Rebirth), and by a group of women to form 'The Association of Democratic Women', had both been turned down. The application of the 'Democratic Women' was later accepted in August 1989.

 Relations between the government and the MTI have remained very tense and the MTI request to form a political party has repeatedly been turned down. In early 1990 the MTI received authorization to publish a newspaper but claimed that government pressure on printers made publication impossible during the first few months. Finally, in June 1990, Al-Nahda's weekly *al-Fajr* (Dawn) began to appear regularly. In its first five months two issues were censored and did not reach the newsstands.

7 The economic data in previous paragraphs come from the following sources: on the trade gap (EIU Tunisia 1990: 24); on tourism (EIU Tunisia 1990: 23); on the debt (EIU Tunisia 1989: 19); on the investment campaign (EIU Tunisia 1989: 15); on unemployment (EIU Tunisia 1989: 14).

8 In April 1990 a coalition to participate in the approaching municipal elections was formed by three groups on the left: the MDS (Mouvement des démocrates socialistes) and the Tunisian Communist party (both fully legal), and the Popular Unity Movement of Ahmed Ben Salah (not recognized as a legal party).

9 One person mentioned to me in early summer 1989 that there were some 3,000 applications for associations on the desks of the Ministry of Interior. Action on these applications was being delayed, I was told, because the government feared activity in civil society and had not yet decided what kind of relationship to civil society it desired to have.

10 ORGANIZING FOR HUMAN RIGHTS

1 Abderrahim Jamai was here referring to major outbreaks of popular unrest that led to many deaths and arrests – see Part II for more detail.

2 Opponents of these rights argue that the right to change religion would allow apostasy and would be against the widely accepted tenet of Islam that apostasy is forbidden and is to be punished by death. Awarding illegitimate children rights equal to those of legitimate children would threaten the strength of the family since it would encourage extramarital relationships and upset the orderly rules of inheritance. And allowing Muslim women to marry non-Muslim men would mean that, by the patrilineal reckoning enshrined in Islamic and Tunisian law, children of this marriage would follow the religion of their father and be non-Muslims. (Consistent with this reasoning, marriages between Muslim men and non-Muslim women are permitted in Islamic and Tunisian law.)

3 Article 16, paragraphs 1 and 2 of the UDHR states: 'Men and women of full age, without any limitation due to race, nationality or religion, have the right to marry and to found a family. They are entitled to equal rights as to marriage, during marriage and at its dissolution. Marriage shall be entered into only with the free and full consent of the intending spouses.' The LTDH draft keeps these words.

4 Article 18 of the UDHR states: 'Everyone has the right to freedom of thought, conscience and religion; this right includes freedom to change his religion or belief, and freedom, either alone or in community with others and in public or private, to manifest his religion or belief in teaching, practice, worship and observance.' The LTDH draft reads, 'Everyone has the right to freedom of thought, conscience and religion; this right includes the freedom to change his religion or belief or his interpretation *(ijtihad)* of it, and the freedom to express these by teaching or practice, to publicize and to observe it, either alone or in community with others, upon the condition of respecting the rights of others.'

5 Article 25, paragraph 2 of the UDHR states: 'All children, whether born in or out of wedlock, shall enjoy the same social protection.' The LTDH draft reads: 'All children should benefit equally from care and social protection.'
6 Omar Ibn al-Khattab was the second caliph following the death of the Prophet Muhammad and led the Islamic community from 634 to 644.
7 *Ijtihad*: the use of reasoning to reach judgements and, also, the judgements reached by reasoning. This has the implication, as well, of innovation.
8 In 1492 the Christian King Ferdinand and Queen Isabel succeeded in reconquering Granada, marking an end to almost eight centuries of Muslim rule in Spain.
9 In fact, there was little discussion about the charter in subsequent years, and little at the next congress held in 1989.

11 ORGANIZING WOMEN

1 But the 'cultural revolution' has its 'counter-revolution' too. *Kalima*, after three years of successful publication and having reached a circulation of 10,000, announced in April 1989 that it would cease publication. At least three of its issues in the preceding year had been confiscated by the authorities because of articles on homosexuality, women's rights, and the problems of the Moroccan press. In a statement explaining his decision, the editor of *Kalima* said, 'Our aim was to show, in good faith, the shadowy as well as the well-lighted areas in our society. This was seen as insolent by the authorities. It is for this reason that a number of administrative measures have been applied to penalize our effort.'
2 Amendments to Egypt's Family Law were made in 1979 by a Sadat presidential decree and were strongly supported by Sadat's wife, Jihan. The amendments awarded to married women some additional rights, including: requiring the man to register his divorce and to inform the wife that she had been divorced (rather than permitting divorce by simple public repudiation); increasing alimony payments; prolonging the period of the divorced wife's automatic custody of the children; requiring the husband to provide housing for a divorced wife with custody of children; permitting the woman to obtain a divorce if court mediation failed to reconcile the couple, and to obtain an automatic divorce on the grounds of a husband taking a second wife; permitting women to work without having to secure the husband's approval.
   These amendments – which some opponents derisively referred to as 'Jihan's law' – came under attack, both on procedural and substantive grounds, and were a target for opponents of Sadat's rule. In early 1985 the Constitutional Court overturned the amendments on procedural grounds. In July 1985 after much heated discussion and debate in Egyptian society at large, the Egyptian parliament passed a new Family Law that was almost identical to Sadat's 1979 decree, except in one important respect: the woman's right to divorce after a husband's second marriage was no longer automatic but was made subject to a court decision.
3 The AHRO was awarded this status shortly thereafter.
4 Al-Afghani and Abduh were prominent thinkers early in the Islamic reform movement. See Chapter 4, note 9.
5 *Nun* is the name of the letter in the Arabic alphabet that begins the word *nissa*

(woman). It is also one of the titles of Qur'anic verse LXVII which is also known under the title 'The pen' and which refers to the act of writing. *Nun* managed to appear three times without interruption. After its third issue, however, the authorities suspended its right to publish. The official reason given was that *Nun* did not possess the capital fund required by law; some sources close to *Nun* argue that suspension simply reflects official dissatisfaction with the magazine's content.

6 His appointee, Ra[dh]ia Haddad, showed growing independence from Bourguiba over the years, particularly in the late 1960s when she argued, in the context of Bourguiba's denunciation of Ben Salah, that blame should not be pinned on one man. Bourguiba had her tried and convicted for bad management and diverting funds, a conviction she successfully appealed after Ben Ali deposed Bourguiba.

7 Tahar al-Haddad (1899–1935) was involved early on in the nationalist struggle in Tunisia. With the publication of two books, one on the Tunisian workers' movement and written from a socialist perspective, and particularly a second, *Our Women in Society and Law*, in which he strongly argued against the subordinate position of women in Tunisia, he attracted the hostility of the Tunisian establishment and was attacked from all sides. Today, he remains a key figure in the development of 'progressive' Tunisian thought, particularly on the issue of women's rights.

8 Discussions at the women's club at that time took place in French. I did not directly address the question of why this should be the case in a country where the national language is Arabic but which had also experienced 75 years of French colonial rule and in which the use of French was still favored by a self-styled 'modernizing' intellectual elite. Very probably, the use of French at the club at that time reflected both the colonial legacy as well as the view of many women in the club that they were an avant-garde and were at odds with the 'patriarchal' values of the society around them. Similar discussions taking place today are much more likely to be in Arabic. For example, the 'Democratic Women' now put out their statements and publications primarily in Arabic although they had begun by using French.

9 See p. 143.

Bibliography

Benslimane, Y. (no date – 1985) *Nous, Marocains*, Paris: Publisud.

Dessouki, A.E.H. (1983) 'The transformation of the party system in Egypt, 1952–1977', in A.E.H. Dessouki (ed.) *Democracy in Egypt*, Cairo: American University of Cairo Press.

Diamond, S. (1974) *In Search of the Primitive*, New Jersey: Transaction Books.

Dwyer, K. (1982) *Moroccan Dialogues*, Baltimore, Md: Johns Hopkins University Press.

—— (in press) 'Opposition et composition: réflexions sur la transformation du vécu en texte anthropologique', in R. Bourqia and N. Hopkins (eds) *Mécanismes d'articulation au Maghreb*, Rabat, Morocco: Editions al-Kalam.

Eco, U. (1986) *Voices*, London: BBC Publications.

EIU Egypt (1990) *Egypt Country Report, No. 1, 1990*, London: Economist Intelligence Unit.

EIU Morocco (1988) *Morocco Country Report, No. 4, 1988*, London: Economist Intelligence Unit.

—— (1989a) *Morocco Country Report, No. 1, 1989*, London: Economist Intelligence Unit.

—— (1989b) *Morocco Country Report, No. 2, 1989*, London: Economist Intelligence Unit.

—— (1989c) *Morocco Country Report, No. 3, 1989*, London: Economist Intelligence Unit.

—— (1989d) *Morocco Country Report, No. 4, 1989*, London: Economist Intelligence Unit.

—— (1990) *Morocco Country Report, No. 1, 1990*, London: Economist Intelligence Unit.

EIU Tunisia (1989) *Tunisia Country Report, No. 4, 1989*, London: Economist Intelligence Unit.

—— (1990) *Tunisia Country Report, No. 1, 1990*, London: Economist Intelligence Unit.

Etienne, B. (1987) *L'Islamisme radical*, Paris: Hachette.

Farah, N.R. (1986) *Religious Strife in Egypt: Crisis and Ideological Conflict in the Seventies*, New York: Gordon & Breach.

Geertz, C. (1968) 'Thinking as a moral act: the ethical dimensions of anthropological fieldwork in the new states', *Antioch Review* 28, 2: 139–58.

de la Guérivière, J. (1990) 'Maroc: face aux problèmes socio-economiques', *Le Monde*, 15 March.

240 *Bibliography*

Hopwood, D. (1985) *Egypt: Politics and Society 1945–1984*, London: Allen & Unwin.
Hourani, A. (1962) *Arabic Thought in the Liberal Age: 1798–1939*, London: Oxford University Press.
Hussein, ᶜ. (1985) *Nahwa Fikr ᶜarabi Jadid* (Towards a New Arab Thought), Cairo: Dar al-Mustaqbal.
Ibrahim, S. (1980) *Population and Urbanization in Morocco*, Cairo: American University of Cairo Press.
Kepel, G. (1985) *The Prophet and Pharaoh: Muslim Extremism in Egypt*, London: Al-Saqi Books.
Khadduri, M. (1984) *The Islamic Conception of Justice*, Baltimore, Md: Johns Hopkins University Press.
Khelil, H. (1985) *Journalisme, Cinéphilie et Télévision en Tunisie*, Quebec, Canada: Editions Naaman.
Laroui, A. (1987) *Islam et modernité*, Paris: Editions la Découverte.
Mernissi, F. (1987) *Le Harem politique: le Prophète et les femmes*, Paris: Albin Michel.
—— (1990) *Sultanes oubliées: femmes chefs d'état en Islam*, Paris: Albin Michel.
Munson, H. (1988) *Islam and Revolution in the Middle East*, New Haven, Conn.: Yale University Press.
Rodenbeck, M. and Mallet, V. (1989) 'Arab hopes emerge amid shifting political sands', *Financial Times*, 29 December.
Rodinson, M. (1980) *La Fascination de l'Islam*, Paris: Maspéro.
Rosenthal, F. (1960) *The Muslim Concept of Freedom Prior to the Nineteenth Century*, Leiden: Brill.
Saadawi, N. (1980) *The Hidden Face of Eve*, London: Zed Press.
Said, E. (1978) *Orientalism*, New York: Pantheon.
—— (1986) 'Intellectuals in the post-colonial world', *Salmagundi* 70–1: 44–64.
Salmi, J. (1985a) *Crise de l'enseignement et reproduction sociale au Maroc*, Casablanca: Editions Maghrébines.
—— (1985b) *Les Dividendes de la violence*, Casablanca: Editions Maghrébines.
Solé, R. and Tincq, H. (1989) 'Le rejet de l'Islam et l'attrait de la France', *Le Monde*, 30 November.
Toumi, M. (1978) *La Tunisie: pouvoirs et luttes*, Paris: Le Sycamore.
Vatikiotis, P.J. (1976) *The History of Egypt from Muhammad Ali to Sadat*, London: Weidenfeld & Nicolson.
Waterbury, J. (1983) *The Egypt of Nasser and Sadat*, Princeton, NJ: Princeton University Press.
World Bank (1989) *World Development Report 1989*, London: Oxford University Press.

Index

(The names of persons interviewed in this book are in italics, as are the pages containing their testimony)